Industrial Crisis

Industrial Crisis

A Comparative Study of the State and Industry

edited by

KENNETH DYSON and STEPHEN WILKS

Martin Robertson · Oxford

© Kenneth Dyson and Stephen Wilks, 1983

First published in 1983 by
Martin Robertson & Company Ltd.,
108 Cowley Road, Oxford OX4 1JF.

British Library Cataloguing in Publication Data

Industrial crisis: a comparative study of the state and industry
1. Industry and state — History
I. Dyson, Kenneth H F   II. Wilks, Stephen
338.9'009181'2   HD3611

ISBN 0-85520-543-1

Typeset by Margaret Helps & Associates, Norwich
Printed and bound in Great Britain by
Billing and Sons Ltd., Worcester

Contents

Contributors

Kenneth Dyson, Professor of European Studies,
University of Bradford

Martin Edmonds, Senior Lecturer in Politics,
University of Lancaster

Josef Esser, Professor of Politics, University of Frankfurt

Wolfgang Fach, Professor of Politics, University of Konstanz

Diana Green, Principal Lecturer in Politics,
City of London Polytechnic

Michael Kreile, Professor of Politics, University of Konstanz

Kjell Lundmark, Lecturer in Politics, University of Umea

Stephen Wilks, Lecturer in Politics, University of Liverpool

Preface

If this book had been written 15 years ago, we would have been addressing the question of the state and industrial planning; from 1950 to 1973 the perspective was economic growth. It is indicative of changes both in political economy and in academic fashion that we now find ourselves concerned with the question of the state and 'industrial rescue'; after 1973 the perspective has been 'crisis'.

Essentially, the book comprises a comparison of industrial policies across six major OECD countries in the context of the current concerns of industrial policy-makers about industrial decline and crises. The economies of these countries appeared to have difficulties in coping with severe inflationary shocks followed by severe deflationary shocks, particularly when these shocks were accompanied by the emergence of developing countries as major producing centres (Beenstock, 1982) and by the institutional rigidities that seem to affect stable societies (Olson, 1982). It proved increasingly difficult to sustain the view that capitalist economies were experiencing short-run cyclical crises and that industrial policy could serve as a 'holding operation' or as a mechanism for 'fire-fighting'. The prospect of a long-term structural crisis opened up a range of possibilities, including both a threat of 'a crisis of crisis management' for the state and a new challenge to the development of political strategies for the 'post-industrial society'. Industrial crises began to be accompanied by the threat of financial crises among private banks whose lending to corporate and sovereign borrowers was 'over-extended'. Meanwhile, levels of unemployment in Western Europe and the United States continued to rise, and industrial production fell to levels, and at a rate, that recalled the experience of the 1930s.

The book is concerned with the question of how, if at all, the state or institutions within the capitalist economy use, and perhaps mobilize, resources to help firms and sectors adjust to changes in market conditions when these firms and sectors are faced by crises whose management requires collective responses. We are not, therefore, centrally concerned with industrial relations and the internal politics of the firm. Our argument is that the capacity of the state, or of the capitalist economy itself, to mobilize and use resources for crisis management effectively is conditioned by ideologies and institutions, and (more deeply) by the historical and structural factors that have shaped the development of these ideologies and institutions. Cross-national comparison draws attention to the existence and role of this 'high politics', of different rules of the game and their influence on the process of managing the interplay of sectional interests in situations of industrial crisis.

Clearly, the speed of industrial decline, the scale of industrial crises and uncertainty about the future make such a topical analysis tentative. Contributors have assessed responses to industrial crises in particular countries by reference to long-standing characteristics of economic institutions, market ideology and industrial policy. Analysis of management of industrial crises is located firmly in a discussion of the nature of national political economies, in particular of their institutional structures. We have attempted to offset the formidable pressures towards fragmentation that affect edited collections of country studies by provision of a comparative framework in chapters 1 and 2. The concluding chapter seeks to provide an integration of the issues that are raised in the comparative and country chapters and adds fresh dimensions, including the dangers of financial crises and the risk of examining industrial crises in a traditional framework of assumptions that endorses economic growth and industrial modernization as unambiguously desirable 'goods'. The complex counter-pressures and strategic dilemmas that confront industrial policy-makers seem to threaten 'a crisis of crisis management'. At the same time, such a threat needs to be seen in the context of the remarkable flexibility of capitalist economies, for instance the expansion of the informal 'black economy' and the facility of political imagination.

Particular thanks are due to our contributors, who have tolerated with patience our demands for additional analysis and revisions. We would also like to acknowledge the help of the Faculty of Social and Environmental Studies of the University of Liverpool. Its financial support for a workshop provided a valuable opportunity for contributors to meet and to exchange ideas with other interested academics and observers. We would especially like to thank Martin Edmonds, Josef Esser, Wolfgang Fach, Wyn Grant and Peter Walters.

K.D. and S.W.

REFERENCES

Beenstock, M. (1982), *The World Economy in Transition*, London, George Allen and Unwin.

Olson, M. (1982), *The Rise and Decline of Nations*, New Hartford, Connecticut, Yale University Press.

1

The Character and Economic Context of Industrial Crises

Stephen Wilks and Kenneth Dyson

The headlines that describe large corporate bankruptcies, factory closures and the redundancy of thousands of employees need little dramatization. They portray perhaps the most riveting of economic phenomena, the visible evidence of both the lethal potency of an impersonalized competitive market and the market power of large business units that undertake divestments in the interests of long-term strategic plans. Industrial crises 'demystify' capitalist economies by raising issues of interest and justice that pose ideological dilemmas for governments, who must attempt to reconcile social and economic goals. The headlines about actual or suggested industrial 'rescues' have become more frequent, and the crises they reflect more prolonged, as the 1970s have given way to the 1980s. For the public they convey a sympathy for the communities destroyed, the careers shattered and the social and personal problems of adjustment that are created by capitalist development; also, a surprise at the problems besetting household names (from Laker to AEG Telefunken), resignation in the face of decisions taken by the remote 'visible hands' of government and business corporations, and perhaps a feeling that 'there but for the grace of God . . .'.

Large business failures also pose political and economic problems, which are associated with their impact on social welfare. From the political viewpoint, there will be pressure for government to act to avert or ameliorate such crises, either through defensive intervention or by moderating the effects of capital mobility by retraining, severance payments, longer notification periods and so on. From the economic standpoint, the market, which has precipitated the crisis, must also adjust to its effects, a process not necessarily smooth or calculated to increase social welfare. The simplest and perhaps the most accurate economic conclusion is to reject the waste of resources that is represented by idle plant and unused skills. The most poignant

1

tragedy of corporate failure arises from the way in which perfectly good products, plants and workforces may be sacrificed to strategic rationalization in the face of recession, or to inefficiencies in senior management or in other parts of the company. Furthermore, the costs of adjustment (in the form of unemployment benefits and welfare payments) are all too often borne by government.

This book examines the way in which advanced market societies have reacted to the problems of the decline and collapse of large business corporations, public or private. A comparative perspective on the problems of coping with decline and corporate crisis is developed in chapter 2 and in the conclusion. Broadly speaking, our objective has been to illuminate some of the ways in which advanced market societies have responded to the problems of structural modernization in the face of different cost structures, intensified international competition, recessionary shock and managerial failure. One useful, if admittedly pragmatic, approach is to examine the extraordinary cases where routine processes of market or administered adjustment have failed to function efficiently or to satisfy criteria for social welfare. The scale and intensity of industrial crises is clearly a major indicator of the weakness of an economy. More importantly, however, analysis of measures that are taken by public and private actors in response to these crises gives an insight into processes of industrial policy-making.

It follows from this broad objective that the cases of 'crisis' examined in this book are varied. As examples of actual and potential corporate crises have proliferated, and because we have attempted to identify national patterns of crisis management, the coverage is eclectic without, hopefully, being anarchic. Contributors have examined the cases that have proved the most serious, because they are the largest in terms either of financial aid or employment. They identify also a variety of cases that contributors feel reveal the basic characteristics of crisis management in their countries. While there may be no such thing as a 'typical' industrial crisis, there are typical national reactions to crises. In practise then, the book is concerned with collective action, public or private, that is taken in response to severe financial difficulties of large business corporations. Because the cases examined reflect current problems, they are to a large extent self-selecting. We did not choose deliberately to exclude failure among financial institutions. There were, for instance, in 1974 banking crises in Germany, when the Bundesbank closed the Frankfurt Herstatt bank after fraudulent and irresponsible foreign exchange dealings, and in the UK as a result of the collapse of the 'secondary banking' sector (Sampson, 1981, chapter 9). More recently, of course, there has been increasingly acute concern about the exposure of the international banking system to several over-extended sovereign borrowers (notably Poland and Mexico); this, combined with escalating industrial bad debts, gave rise in the latter half of 1982 to real doubts about the viability of one or two German and several large North American banks. The implications of these incipient financial crises are taken up in the concluding chapter.

The principle of self-selection can be applied also to the service sector. Although cases such as Laker Airways and industries such as tourism seemed possible candidates for study, the majority of 'crises' over the past decade have in fact occurred in the manufacturing sector of Western economies. These cases have been more visible and more controversial, and have received greater attention from governments for whom concern about 'de-industrialization' has meant concern about the contraction of the manufacturing base. Of course, a focus on large business corporations makes no distinction between publicly and privately owned enterprises. Coverage is also broadened, where appropriate, to include 'sectoral' crises. Clearly, some sectors are in serious and visible structural decline: steel, shipbuilding and textiles are notable examples of sectors that have suffered from intensified international competition from new, low-cost producers. Others have fallen victim to the prolonged recession: basic chemicals, aluminium smelting, airline operations and motor vehicles (especially trucks and tractors) are examples. The various chapters therefore examine to some extent sectoral crises in order to provide a contextual appreciation of corporate crises and of the options for managing them.

The term 'crisis' has been used throughout the collection rather than more neutral terms such as intervention or adjustment. We would claim colloquial accuracy in that the events described are portrayed by the media as crises and are discussed in terms of urgency, finality and threat. In three other ways the term 'crisis' is appropriate. For the corporation involved, its financial difficulties necessitate a rapid and qualitative change that suggests a fundamentally different basis for the concern: new ownership, new management, re-capitalization or, if events go badly, receivership. For public agencies, 'crisis' denotes a requirement for immediate governmental action. A commercial failure acts as a catalyst that affects the way a long-standing problem is visualized and obliges government to make a decision.

Second, 'crisis' is an appropriate term because it carries descriptive implications about the way in which decisions are taken. Various studies have examined the combined impact of speed and importance on organizational decision-making. While such studies offer useful insights, they do not suggest a substantial consensus about crisis and decision-making among social scientists. On the one hand, Downs (1964, pp. 175–90) argues that crisis produces a restriction of options and of participants. Crisis appears to narrow the process of decision. On the other hand, Wilensky (1967) suggests that crises overcome the distortions of organizational intelligence that are generated by centralization, hierarchy, specialization and respect for doctrine. Communication goes 'out of channels', involves new participants and ideas, and thereby helps to improve the quality of decisions. Some generalizations appear possible. Simon's classic distinction between 'programmed' and 'non-programmed' decisions (Simon, 1976, chapter 6) underlines the unstructured character of decisions at times of crisis and the importance that intuitive judgement plays at such times. Crisis has an ambiguous character. It suggests threat (Edelman, 1977, pp. 43–9), creates anxiety, and thereby impedes standard processes of communication and consensus-building. At the same time, it offers opportunities for new people and new ideas. Crisis can break the forces of political and administrative inertia. In other words, crisis is unpredictable because of the very openness that it creates. This book is not, however, concerned to test the propositions of organization theory. The focus is on the relationship between state and society, how that relationship is defined and re-defined in response to industrial policy issues, and on what industrial crises reveal about the character of both state and society.

Third, the term 'crisis' summarizes the analytical approach of this book. Corporate crises provide an opportunity to investigate the 'revealed preferences' of policy-makers. Such crises and the way they are handled by government constitute a microcosm of the government–industry relationship and highlight the basic orientation of industrial policy. Like a microscopic slide, crises can be studied to reveal the details of political will, institutional action and policy assumptions. In other words, crises separate the flamboyant rhetoric that is so characteristic of the industrial policy field from the substance of policy. This approach is, of course, always open to the criticism that the case studies are atypical. However, provided unwarranted generalizations are not made, the exceptional character of industrial crises does in fact enhance the value of the approach. Crises are important as *de facto* sources of policy redefinition and articulation. Whether or not governments learn constructively from their mistakes, they certainly learn to make policy seem consistent with actions. Thus, as the chapters on Britain and France testify, party priorities and policy goals are often redefined and articulated in response to the experience of crisis.

The term 'crisis' is used below in a specific manner to denote cases where failure of business corporations has given rise to serious collective discussion of exceptional action to circumvent the market. Clearly, not all business failures are crises in this sense. Only the most far-reaching failures reach the policy agendas of governments and banks. This book is concerned with this type of business failure, and the approach adopted is, therefore, political/institutional rather than economic/managerial. Economic and managerial theories clearly contribute valuable insights into the problems that result from the failure of large business corporations. The main premise of neoclassical economics in this context is, of course, that support for lame ducks is the route to disaster. Economies must build on their future strengths by identification of new opportunities; only free capital mobility will ensure an optimum use of society's resources. However, such insights are pitched at a high level of abstraction. In general, prescriptive economic analysis at the micro-level tends to be too dismissive of 'subsidy'. Crisis interventions not infrequently involve an element of subsidy which can be justified by at least three coherent lines of economic argument. First, there is undoubtedly a short-term case for subsidy in an underemployed economy where resources would not be reallocated. This argument is given great practical credibility for governments when the subsidy would be less than the exchequer cost of closure (Mottershead, 1978, p. 479). A second classic argument would hold that the market is short-sighted and that this constitutes an important market failure. Investments with long lead times, or the development of capacity to meet future demands, are hence further arguments for subsidy. Finally, subsidy can be justified where a competitor industry abroad is being subsidized. Subsidy 'transparency' is highly partial. Energy costs, for instance, can provide a powerful hidden subsidy such as the 'suspiciously cheap brown coal' (*The Economist*, 7 February 1981, p. 16) provided to German steel-makers.

Although arguments for subsidy exist they are regarded as exceptional, and neoclassical economists find particular and understandable difficulty in establishing general principles that explain in practice patterns of government assistance to industry. One such attempt is Corden's principle of 'sectional income maintenance', which suggests that aid through protection can be explained by a desire to 'prevent severe falls in incomes of any significant section of the community'

(Corden, 1976, p. 216). Alternatively, one can look to explanations offered by Marxist economists, such as Aaronovitch and Smith (1981), or to the 'economics of politics' arguments of writers such as Brittan (1977) or Peacock (1979). But both the Marxist and the public choice arguments have a strong normative and deterministic bias, tending to downplay political processes and to ignore the structured mediation of institutions. Similarly, the microeconomic theories of business behaviour or the highly abstract prescriptions of welfare economics tend to attach little importance to the impact of government intervention on industrial adjustment. The analysis of industrial policy and politics in this book should, therefore, serve to supplement an economic analysis by throwing light on factors that are conventionally held constant in formal economic theory.

The examination of individual cases of industrial crisis forms an important but not a dominant part of each chapter. Each country study incorporates an interpretation of recent industrial policy and an analysis of the key institutions relevant to crisis management. Such institutions are not of course confined to the public sector. Response to industrial crises depends on the structure and disposition of the banking sector (whether, for instance, there is a tradition of investment banking), the ability of large business undertakings to internalize crisis management by reallocation of labour or by merger, and to a more limited extent, on the character of the trade union movement. The chapters adopt, therefore, a broadly similar approach and are organized around empirical examination of important cases. They constitute also important assessments of the changing character of the relations between state and economy in individual countries. The chapter headings indicate the broad national context of each argument.

INCIDENCE OF CORPORATE CRISES

The conditions for a corporate crisis are the threat of liquidation of a large corporation, of extensive retrenchment or of the closure of a factory, a division or an overseas subsidiary. The decision about whether such events are regarded as a crisis, signifying an unacceptable change and necessitating collective remedial action, depends on the viewpoints of the interested parties. Judgements about 'market failure' and crisis are in part qualitative and subjective; they depend on the ideological context. The question, 'whose crisis?' has been resolved largely by adopting the viewpoint of government, and to a lesser degree — to the extent that they operate as self-conscious vehicles of adjustment — the viewpoint of the banks. In other words, by concentrating on cases where government has acted, directly or indirectly, we have been selecting cases where corporate crisis has also become a governmental crisis and has prompted a 'crisis intervention'. Alternative viewpoints, which may be subsumed within government's definition of a crisis, would stress the interests of the workforce, the consumer, the local or regional community or the trading partners of the corporation.

This preliminary definition of crisis raises two further points which should be stressed. First, the various chapters, especially the chapter on the United States, reveal clearly that states are fragmented in their dealings with industry. Crisis definition depends, therefore, on the interplay between finance and spending departments, between political parties, between levels of government and between executive and legislature. Definition of crisis and a decision to act is, therefore, a complex and unpredictable political process, although, as we also emphasize, political ideology may establish some coherence through a shared definition of problems.

The second point concerns crisis thresholds. As recession deepens, pressures for structural adjustment intensify and more potential crises develop, one would expect either that the strength of precedent and claims for equal treatment would prompt more crisis interventions, or that shortage of resources and economic arguments for greater competitiveness would reduce the inclination of government to intervene. The former response appears true not just of Italy but also of Sweden in the 1970s, as repeated rescues by nationalization took place. The latter response is certainly true of Britain, where massive programmes of redundancies and factory closures by such firms as BL, Imperial Chemical Industries and British Steel have been tolerated and even encouraged by government in a manner that would have appeared intolerable prior to 1979. The international attempts by the Organization for Economic Cooperation and Development (OECD) and the European Economic Community (EEC) to raise the threshold of crisis intervention by the doctrine of 'positive adjustment' are examined below.

In any market economy thousands of companies are formed and liquidated every year. In Britain, for instance, in 1973, the 'best' year of the 1970s, 0.5 per cent of companies on the register (about 2600 companies) went into liquidation. In 1981 the comparable figure was 1.2 per cent (8600 companies) (*Midland Bank Review*, Spring 1982, p. 2). Only a very small proportion of such liquidations will cause public concern, and comparative quantitative measures have little meaning. Impressionistically, however, the number of potential crises is proliferating in all countries, and the likelihood of a crisis being defined (that is, of extraordinary action being taken) will increase or decrease in line with four variables. The incidence of crisis reflects the structure of industry, the health of the national and international economy, the policy goals of the government in power, and the expectations of the public.

As far as *the structure of industry* is concerned, concentration, diversification and internationalization have an impact on the incidence of crisis. Concentration is probably the most important factor. The tendency for an increasing proportion of manufacturing output to be controlled by a decreasing proportion of giant corporations has considerable implications for business behaviour and for policy (Hannah, 1976). A financial crisis in a large corporation has a greater impact in terms of sheer size and speed of the ill effects, and because its dominant position in relation to an industrial sector may well make the corporation indispensible. Rationalization of competition through strategic merger and the creation of 'national champions' has its own logic, particularly with reference to the construction of viable business enterprises in the international economy. Understandably, however, such firms become so important that their possible closure becomes a self-defining crisis. On the other hand, product and geographical diversification should reduce the likelihood of crisis in that 'conglomerate' corporations can cross-subsidize and rationalize among sectors and products. Internationalization might also be thought to bring stability to the extent that foreign profits can be used to weather domestic recession. But the foreign-owned sector is a potent source of crisis for the host country of transnational corporations. Overseas subsidiaries tend to be vulnerable to abrupt closure arising both from their peripheral commercial importance for the company involved and from the utilitarian economic calculus that the parent company tends to apply to their operations. Hence a distinctive problem of divestment has grown up in the 1970s and reached serious proportions for developed as well as developing countries (Hood and Young, 1982; Grunberg, 1981). For the host government, the resulting crisis can prove unusually difficult to manage: witness the 1975 Chrysler crisis in Britain. Lack of information and lack of influence for a host country typify a policy process that involves, effectively, diplomatic negotiations with the parent company.

The contemporary form of industrial crises reflects the fact that many firms are now subsidiaries and operate in two environments: in the first place, in an external environment in which they compete in the market for sales and revenue and depend on the government's success in controlling inflation and cost structures; in the second place, in a complex internal environment that is provided by the overall corporate plan and budget to which they are subordinated. The great discretionary powers of top 'parent company' management draw attention to the 'internal political economy' of the firm, to the importance of such factors as organizational loyalty and bargaining power. Parent companies may decide not to respond promptly to market signals that indicate losses by a subsidiary (a factor in the case of Chrysler UK); or they may decide to axe a subsidiary because of long-term strategic goals rather than because of direct market signals (as in the case of British Leyland's divestments of its Italian and Belgian subsidiaries). 'The visible hand' of management is not a new phenomenon, as Chandler shows for the United States before 1918 (Chandler, 1977). Industrial decision-making has become internalized within firms as administrative controls replace or at least supplement the market. Indeed, the success of transnational corporations in controlling their 'internal markets' is increasingly advanced as an explanation for their continued survival and expansion (Buckley and Casson, 1976, pp. 33 and 113). Firms seek self-protection by strategies of product and geographical diversification and by attempts to control their political and economic environments.

A theory that came to dominate policy-making towards industrial crises from the mid-1970s, particularly in the USA, was based on an analogy with the human body. All industries were supposed to go through an inexorable 'life-cycle' of maturity and decay. Consequently, whole sectors like automobiles, steel and textiles could be consigned to a dustbin category of 'sunset industries'. The only industries worth support were the new 'sunrise industries' such as electronics, information technology and bio-technology. However, in 1983 the notion that sectors and firms in 'mature' sectors were not worth the management of their decline was challenged by reference to signs of industrial renaissance within the traditional sectors of American industry (Abernathy, Clark and Kantrow, 1983). Sectors like automobiles, steel and textiles could experience 'dematurity'; the 'life-cycle' could be reversed. They were able to exploit new market segments that were in no sense 'mature' (for example, the growth of the very small car market) and to adopt a diversity of new technical solutions (for example, the impact of air jet looms in the textile industry). Management of crises in traditional sectors, nevertheless, depends on a willingness to shake the production system to its foundations and to stress quality of production process as well as of product.

Trading conditions within *the national and international economy* are, of course, the primary determinant of the incidence of industrial crises. The dominant economic feature of the past decade has been the two 'oil shocks' of 1973–4 and 1979–80. The rise in oil prices that resulted from Arab use of the 'oil weapon' and the embargo that accompanied the Yom Kippur war produced in 1974–75 an international liquidity squeeze and a recession of unprecedented depth in the OECD economies. In most of the member countries real GNP fell, and the sharp and unexpected fall in demand and output precipitated acute financial difficulties for many large concerns. In 1974, for instance, every European volume producer of cars made a loss (Central Policy Review Staff, 1975, p. 52). A healthy recovery took place in 1976, as the growth figures in table 1.1 indicate. However, the second oil shock of 1979–80 produced a further period of acute recession with all the prerequisites for a high incidence of corporate failure. Oil prices rose more gradually (between December 1978 and December 1980 by 170 per cent, from $13 to $36 a barrel) as a result of the Iranian revolution, a harsh winter and continuing high demand for oil. The transfer of purchasing power to the oil producers, and the deflationary effect on the international economy before unspent 'petro-dollars' were 'recycled', caused a deterioration in company liquidity that was exacerbated by historically high interest rates, especially in the United States, and by restrictive monetary policies. Indeed, Shonfield interpreted the first response of governments to the 1979 oil shock, as expressed at the Tokyo Summit in July 1979, as markedly more defeatist than that of 1974,

Table 1.1   Growth in output in six OECD countries, 1966–81

| | Annual percentage changes | | | | |
	1966–70	1971–75	1976–80	1980	1981
Germany	4.5	2.2	3.6	2.1	– 0.3
France	5.4	4.0	3.3	2.0	0.3
Italy	6.2	2.5	3.8	3.8	– 0.2
Britain	2.5	2.1	1.3	– 3.0	– 2.2
USA	3.2	2.7	3.7	– 0.1	2.0
Sweden	4.1	2.7	1.2	1.4	– 0.9

Sources: European Commission (1981, p. 58); OECD (1982b, pp. 14 and 142)

writing that 'the leaders of the mixed economies of the West agreed
. . . that there should be no attempt whatsoever to cushion the shock
to their economies of the rise in the cost of energy. . . . unemployment, already high by post-war standards, would have to rise further'
(Shonfield, 1980, p. 3). Some economies nevertheless proved more
resilient than others. The varying performance of the countries that
are the subject of this collection is illustrated by table 1.1, which
shows fluctuations in the growth of output. Within the EEC the most
dynamic economy of the four that are studied here was Italy, which
achieved a growth rate of 4 per cent across the main economic cycle
of the 1970s (measuring from the peak in 1973-74 to the subsequent
major peak in 1978-80), followed by France with 2.9 per cent,
Germany with 2.7 per cent and Britain with 1.2 per cent (European
Commission, 1981, p. 59).

The third variable explaining the incidence of crises is the refine-
ment of relevant *policy goals* by governments. The traditional policy
goals of safeguarding employment, promoting competition, encouraging regional balance, stimulating exports and protecting strategic
defence industries have been supplemented by more sophisticated
goals. Governments have become increasingly concerned with the
competitive strength of industry and, therefore, with productivity,
innovation and strategic 'growth' sectors; or with specific problems such as energy conservation, small urban enterprises or public
purchasing. The general point is that, the more responsibility government takes for industrial success, and the more specific policies it
develops in the process, so the more likely it will be that corporate
failure will threaten a policy goal and be defined as a crisis suitable
for public action.

The fourth variable concerns the *expectations of the public* and
the wider societal response to corporate collapse. To some degree
crises are defined and action is taken in response to demands from
the public, trade unions, regional and local interests. According to
cynics and the public choice theorists, a government's inclination
to respond to pluralist demands is closely related to its electoral
prospects (Tullock, 1976; Burton, 1979). Within coalition governments sectional interests are often expressed in a direct, immediate
manner, and a government's very ability to stay in power may depend
on its willingness to recognize a crisis that affects the interests of a
coalition partner. The chapters on Sweden and Italy throw up such
examples. Pluralist political pressures for crisis intervention are the
most interesting but often the least tangible factors for analysis. At
one level, of course, they confirm the proper and beneficial workings

of a democratic system. The behaviour of a Swedish government when it observes the traditional priority of keeping unemployment low but uses a subsidy, or of a German federal government that attempts to balance the employment needs of *Länder* (states), appears as a legitimate reaction to trade union and regional political pressures. At another level, a political input into crisis definition can appear destructive when, for instance, Chrysler's ability to secure loan guarantees depends on Mr Carter's electoral calculations or Mr Reagan's need to obtain support in the Senate; or when the top management of Italy's ENI is removed owing to factional infighting between Socialists and Christian Democrats.

The tendency for democratic governments to identify 'market failure' and to override the market is clearly a central concern of this study. Liberal economists and liberal governments have strong objections to subsidies and to 'rescue' or 'bail out' operations. But industrial crises reveal that all governments intervene in the market, that intervention is seldom premised on purely economic arguments, and that routine adjustment processes can be seriously disrupted. Even in Japan, for instance, 'politics can and occasionally will thwart the regular policy consensus process' (Magaziner and Hout, 1980, p. 70): the 1978 rescue of the shipbuilders Sasebo Heavy Industries is an example. The perceived proliferation of apparently opportunistic microeconomic interventions, which are seen as defensive, as impeding necessary structural change and as comprising a dangerous drain on public finance, gave rise to international demands for 'positive adjustment policies' (which are discussed later in this chapter). The question arose of whether such national responses to recession and structural adjustment were generating a policy competition among states that was essentially defensive, a 'new conservatism' based on 'a set of attitudes about our mature, rich societies that favours preserving them much as they are (or were before the recession and the oil crisis)' (Diebold, 1978, p. 579).

DE-INDUSTRIALIZATION AND COMPARATIVE ADVANTAGE

The incidence and intensity of corporate crises could be expected to vary from state to state. Some economies, as the comparative growth figures demonstrate, are more successful and in a better position to cope with corporate crises and sectoral decline. Clearly, questions of comparative economic performance are of almost unreconcilable complexity; statistics as well as explanations are subject to wide differences of interpretation (Hallett, 1981). To provide some comparative perspective, however, it is useful to look at two indicators: relative de-industrialization, and changes in comparative advantage.

The scale of de-industrialization demonstrates the size of the adjustment problem, of which response to industrial crises is only a part. The British debate on de-industrialization suggests three different measures: absolute decline in industrial employment; decline in the proportion of total economic activity accounted for by industrial output; or (the 'Cambridge definition') an ability to finance the full employment level of imports. Thirlwall (1982) argues that the first of these measures is best suited to international comparison because it is unambiguous and causally neutral. Hence the figures of absolute decline in employment, supplemented by unemployment figures, for our subject countries are given in table 1.2.

Table 1.2
Industrial employment and unemployment in OECD countries, 1973–81
(thousands)

	Employment			Changes			Unemployment		
	1973	1979	1981	1973–79	1979–81	1979–81	1973	1979	1982*
						%	%	%	%
United Kingdom	10,484	9,669	8,354	−815	−1315	−13.6	3.2	5.7	12.4
France	8,266	7,670	7,294	−596	−376	−4.9	2.6	5.9	8.2
Sweden	1,427	1,360	1,327	−67	−33	−2.4	2.5	2.1	3.0
Germany	12,448	11,233	11,084	−1215	−149	−1.3	0.9	3.2	5.5
United States	28,045	30,402	29,995	+2357	−407	−1.3	4.8	5.7	8.6
Italy	7,470	7,646	7,748	+176	+102	+1.4	6.2	7.5	9.1
(compare) Japan	19,570	19,140	19,817	−430	+677	+3.5	1.3	2.1	2.2

*First quarter. OECD standardized rates.
Sources: Thirlwall (1982, p. 27); OECD (1982b, p. 153)

As far as loss of industrial employment is concerned, the UK position is outstandingly poor, with a decline from 1973 to 1981 of a remarkable 20 per cent of industrial jobs. At the other extreme Italy has shown consistent gains, with an improvement of 4 per cent over the same eight-year period. Italy performs less well on the unemployment measure. By contrast, Sweden's employment record is exceptionally good: she sustained low unemployment levels throughout 1982. Overall, the figures underline the fact that for Britain individual corporate failures are simply the manifestation of a larger crisis of the whole manufacturing sector. For the other states the industrial employment base has remained fairly resilient, although increasing unemployment during 1981–82 has made large-scale redundancy steadily more painful.

The trends in growth and employment are also reflected in international market share. As far as business failure is concerned, international competition is important as a frequent immediate cause. In the case of industries from footwear to consumer electronics, decline can be attributed to intense competition from imports, competition that reflects the movements in international comparative advantage. Such structural shifts may make protectionist devices an attractive response to crisis for governments. They can be seen to be shielding the firm or sector in trouble in a concrete, politically visible manner. Such an approach is given greater logic when competition takes the form of the so-called 'laser beam' selective marketing. This form of marketing involves an attack on individual products or product groups and has been used successfully by Japan and some of the newly industrialized countries (NICs). Deliberate and highly selective strategies of import targeting also have geographical implications and lead, as the European Commission (1981, p. 98) point out, 'to very rapid increases in market penetration in certain sectors, which are often concentrated geographically. The subsequent high level of regional unemployment has naturally given rise to demands for protection.'

Structural adaptation policies have sought to encourage high value added products, which rely on a comparative advantage embodied in specialized human capital or are fundamental to technological development. Emphasis of public policy is on support for knowledge-intensive industries, and Japan has become a model for such a strategy for countries like France. Germany and France have had some success in this respect, and the European Commission declare that 'the Federal Republic of Germany . . . has a pattern of specialisation which is well adapted to the pattern of demand and to its relative comparative advantage' (European Commission, 1981, p. 99). More recently, the French have also formalized a target list of 'industries of the future', which as a policy goal they seek to promote (see chapter 6, p. 18). By contrast, Italy has increased its share of trade in manufactures but remains over-reliant on low skill products. The USA has performed relatively badly in high-skill exports, although the statistics are of particularly limited value in this case because the US economy is not very open in terms of trade as a proportion of GNP. Notably, however, the USA and Britain have both declined significantly in overall world market share as well as in high-skill products, as table 1.3 illustrates.

Table 1.3   Market shares in OECD imports of manufactures, 1963–79

	1963	1973	1979	Change, 1963–79
	%	%	%	%
United Kingdom	10.5	6.6	6.5	– 38
United States	16.9	13.2	12.0	– 29
Germany	20.9	19.5	17.5	– 16
France	7.6	8.0	8.4	+ 11
Italy	5.6	6.2	7.0	+ 25
(compare) Japan	4.0	6.7	7.0	+ 75

Sources: European Commission (1981, p. 95); OECD (1982a)

The recessionary shocks of 1973-74 and 1978–80 would, therefore, lead us to expect a greater incidence of corporate failure. All economies have jointly experienced recession, and the coincidence of the 'downturn' is indeed seen as one of the prime obstacles to international recovery. Comparatively, however, some economies have fared worse than others and could be expected to have a greater problem of managing industrial crises. The atypical economy has of course been Britain. In a recent virtuoso analysis of British decline, Pollard (1982) charts the exclusion of the UK from the international postwar boom. He points out that, on simplistic present assumptions, Britain would not reach the *present* German level of prosperity until the year 2051. Figure 1.1 reproduces the per capita GNP comparison given by Pollard to demonstrate Britain's anomalous position. Britain and Italy are seen to be the worst performers in terms of GNP per capita. Of course, Italy is held back by the acute underdevelopment of the south — in growth and productivity measures northern Italy is in line with European standards. The other significant poor performer is the USA. Hence over the past 20 years there has been a process of 'catching up' and a considerable degree of economic convergence (again in per capita measures). Within Europe significant convergence took place up to 1973 in terms of output per head. From 1974 divergence is the rule, although Britain's very poor performance distorts overall comparisons (European Commission, 1981, p. 112; Hodges, 1981, p. 8).

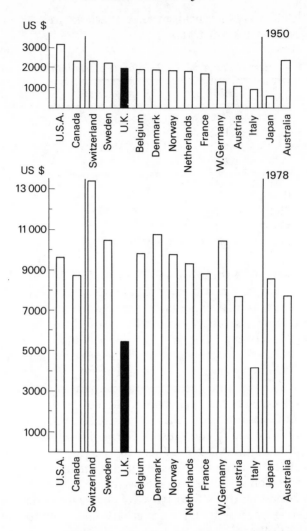

Figure 1.1   Gross National Product per capita, 15 countries,
1950 and 1978
Source: Pollard (1982, p. 5)

These comparisons are little more than a summary of impressions
from an inevitably brief survey. They should simply be regarded as
outlining an overall economic picture that sets a context for the following chapters. In these extremely general terms the picture reveals

Germany and France as the resilient industrial economies, Sweden and the USA as characterized by structural adjustment problems, Italy as successful but not as yet having completed the modernization process, and Britain as an economy that has declined to the point where corporate failure is an extension of a larger and disastrous industrial failure.

THE INTERNATIONAL DIMENSION OF INDUSTRIAL CRISES

A drawback with a collection of country studies is, of course, that international economic forces and policies tend to be overlooked. Given our analytical orientation towards the political and institutional origins of policy, a concentration on the state, and the forces that have shaped the development of its role in different societies, is essential and is the focus of chapter 2. At this preliminary stage, however, some account needs to be taken of the international perspective. As has been pointed out above, corporate crises inevitably will be attributable in part to world trading conditions. The health of the corporation, the sector and the domestic economy will vary with the prosperity, comparative advantage, exchange rates and industrial support policies of major trading partners. This study suggests that the management of industrial crises, for instance types of policy instrument utilized, will be shaped primarily by domestic political factors that are rooted in ideology, institutions and the character of capitalist development. Domestic political factors mediate the relationship to the international economy (Katzenstein, 1978, p. 306).

The oil shock of 1973–74 clearly constitutes the dominant event in the international economic context. It produced a policy response from the OECD countries of seeking to avert protectionism and competitive devaluation or deflation. The impact of the oil price rise was accentuated by three further factors. First, the major OECD economies were already moving into a recessionary phase after the 1969–73 (peak-to-peak) business cycle. The leading indicators in Japan, the USA and Europe were all distinctly pointing downwards in the second quarter of 1973. Second, the recession was unusually coincidental, and the simultaneous downturn was, of course, consolidated by the jointly experienced rise in energy costs. The third factor was self-inflicted. As Allsopp (1979, p. 417) confirms, policy reaction to 'oil price deflation' was unduly restrictive. Western governments tightened fiscal and monetary policy to limit imports, and additional distortions were produced by *ad hoc* energy-saving measures, from petrol rationing to switches to less economic domestic fuel sources.

The business failures that arose in large part from the recession were in many cases international in manifestation as well as in origin. International manifestation of industrial decline and crisis can be structural and diffuse, as in steel, textiles, shipbuilding or basic chemicals; or corporate and concentrated when, for instance, a transnational corporation faces bankruptcy. The motor industry provides several examples of international corporate crisis: for instance, Chrysler's European divestment, the international rescue of Massey Ferguson and the prolonged financial problems of International Harvester. In the case of the structural crises, the central problem has emerged as a global over-capacity that is the product of a fall in demand, competitive and over-optimistic investment or competition from NICs — or, indeed, a combination of all three factors. Perhaps the oldest structural crisis is in textiles; the most serious and controversial, because of its huge employment implications, is in steel; and one of the most intractable is in shipbuilding. When a transnational corporation is in commercial difficulties over-capacity may be only part of the problem, and consistent losses may also reflect a mistaken corporate strategy. International corporate failures have in practice been seen primarily as a problem for the private sector, partly, no doubt, owing to the liberal postures of their home governments (usually American or British).

Logically enough, international business failures have given rise to international crisis definition and responses. Such responses can be envisaged on one or more of three levels: agreements between companies, between governments, or under the auspices of an international organization. Historically, agreements between companies — 'cartels' — have been regarded with suspicion. US anti-trust legislation and EEC competition provisions prohibit market-sharing and collusion over pricing. Such cooperation does, of course, take place. It is the essence of oligopoly, and in most international industries controlled by large companies it exists as informal understandings and patterns of behaviour. In one or two cases, however, modern cartels have taken on a formal existence. They have been approved by governments and operated through government regulation that seeks to control production and prices and hence to stave off crisis. Examples include IATA (International Air Transport Association), the European steel cartel (Eurofer), and the European synthetic fibre producers, who have negotiated informal agreements on capacity reduction and have signed a cartel agreement, although it failed to gain ratification by the European Commission (Tsoukalis and Silva Ferreira, 1981, p. 131).

International agreements between companies, or, more correctly, between financial institutions, have also taken place in relation to specific corporate failures. The rescue of Massey Ferguson was an example of a genuinely international crisis that was resolved in January 1981 by agreement between about 250 financial institutions, mainly banks but including also insurance companies and other lenders. Massey's problems originated in the deep recessionary trough of the highly cyclical farm machinery market; they were exacerbated by a heavy debt burden, high interest rates and misconceived diversification into construction equipment (*The Times*, 19 January 1981). Although it is a Canadian-owned corporation, only 6000 of the workforce of 47,000 were employed in Canada. Its huge Coventry tractor plant (the biggest in the West) and its Perkins diesel engine plants, also in Britain, employed about 16,000; there was also a significant manufacturing presence in Italy, France and Germany. The rescue was orchestrated by Barclays, the Bank of England and the Canadian Imperial Bank of Commerce, which had C$380 million, equivalent to 30 per cent of its equity, in outstanding loans to the Group (*Financial Times*, 19 January 1981). The rescue package, worth C$720 million, involved a conversion of bank loans into equity and new equity guaranteed by the Ontario provincial government and the Canadian federal government. Canadian government guarantees amounted to C$200 million and were motivated by a desire to protect Canadian financial institutions, by the 'national champion' sentiment about Massey, and by the fact that the financial problems were in any case concentrated in North America. The rescue was fortunate for the British Conservative Government, which had distanced itself from the negotiations but encouraged the Bank of England to take an unusually active role. If the Massey Group had been dismembered, there would have been some very difficult rescue decisions to have been made about the large and valuable British factories. For the banking community the extent of unsecured indebtedness had come as a shock. No one bank or supervisory authority had a picture of Massey's overall debt burden. The banks were thus 'locked in'. Bankruptcy appeared more costly than rescue. All the same, the complex rescue package demonstrated an impressive potential for international public and private sector cooperation which is likely to be tested further. By mid-1982 Massey had cut its workforce to 32,000, was continuing to make substantial losses, and was reported to have breached the conditions of the rescue agreement (*The Guardian*, 27 August 1982).

The second possible level of international response to industrial crises — agreement between governments — is rare in OECD countries. When sectoral discussions have taken place, for instance for textiles or shipbuilding, they have been conducted through the OECD machinery or the General Agreement on Tariffs and Trade (GATT). Systematic bilateral contact has been transient. For instance, Mr Callaghan and Giscard d'Estaing established an Anglo-French 'Committee for Industrial Co-operation' at the end of 1977 to discuss aerospace, issues such as collaboration between BL and Renault and problems of declining industries (*Financial Times*, 14 December 1977; 22 February 1978). The Committee appears not to have survived the fall of the respective governments. In relation to individual corporate crises such as Lockheed/Rolls Royce or Talbot/Peugeot/Citroen, governments have tended, rather surprisingly, to stay aloof from bilateral discussion.

The third possibility is action by international organizations to manage decline. Textile agreements are the oldest example. The Multi-Fibre Agreement negotiated under GATT in 1973 and revised in 1977 and 1982 provides a mechanism for allocating market shares and, in theory, for avoiding sharp dislocations of production. Active coordination and forceful leadership backed in some instances by sanction are also provided by the OECD and the EEC, particularly the European Coal and Steel Community (ECSC). Two important aspects of their activities are represented by the doctrine of 'positive adjustment' and the management of the steel crisis.

The prescriptive concept, or 'doctrine', as Pinder (1982, p. 258) calls it, of positive adjustment was evolved within the OECD during 1978. The doctrine endorses positive action by governments to encourage adaptation to the market by transfer of resources towards competitive sectors of the economy. It seeks to alleviate the impact of structural decline rather than to defy the market by protection of, or subsidy for, declining industries. The concept was formulated in direct response to the proliferation of defensive subsidy of jobs in public and private undertakings in Britain, France, Sweden and Italy during the mid-1970s. The main advocates of positive adjustment within the OECD were the USA and Germany. Nevertheless, the concept was received sympathetically by most member governments, especially those like Britain that had experienced a political move to the right. Within the European Community the positive adjustment concept also struck a sympathetic chord, and the Commission's attitude to subsidy underent a distinct hardening. In its recent analysis of economic issues the Commission defines 'positive adjustment measures [as] those aimed at making the productive system more flexible and more capable of adapting to change, as opposed to "negative" adjustment measures which maintain the status quo, preserve inefficient structures and introduce new distortions and rigidities into the operation of the economy and into trade'. The Commission adds that 'all government measures must therefore be reviewed in the light of the contribution they make to positive adjustment' (European Commission, 1981, pp. 151–2). The OECD documents on positive adjustment are made up of similar platitudes with little concrete recommendation of policies or institutional mechanisms (OECD, 1979). It is difficult to see in the doctrine much more than a reassertion of the values of the free market and free trade. It has perhaps succeeded in providing a slogan to popularize such values, and as such reinforces market criteria of crisis management.

In the case of steel, and in blatant disregard of the concept of positive adjustment, no government has been foolhardy enough to allow global over-capacity, falling domestic demand and 'dumped' imports to liquidate its home industry. The issue of steel unemployment is explosive. The French steel riots in Lorraine were followed in the spring of 1982 by strikes and civil unrest in Belgium over steel closures, and it seemed that the very survival of the state was under threat. It is not, therefore, difficult to find overwhelming political reasons for the maintenance of over-capacity in steel. Even so, large numbers of jobs have been lost. Steel consumption fell off dramatically after 1974, while capacity in developing countries and the OECD continued to expand as a consequence of long-term capital investment and modernization programmes. The international efforts to manage the acute financial difficulties that faced all OECD steel industries had three facets. First, the OECD formed a steel committee, which began to meet in 1978 but failed to agree on an international system of market sharing, primarily because of US opposition. The Committee has been retained as a monitoring forum but is seen as unlikely to give birth to an international cartel (Crandall, 1981, p. 151). Second, therefore, the three major producer groupings each developed their respective crisis management measures. In the USA a 'trigger price' system was adopted: it restricted imports that were priced below an index of Japanese prices, but was seen towards the end of 1981 as providing inadequate protection. There followed the threat of massive tariffs on European steel imports as one aspect of the Europe–USA 'trade war' over steel and European exports for the Soviet gas pipeline, which was conducted during 1982. Hostilities over steel were resolved, at least temporarily, by the signature in October 1982 of an agreement between the USA and the EEC that restricted the export of a wide range of steel products to the USA over a three-year period. The agreement constituted a substantial victory for the American steel firms whose allegations of unfair subsidy and dumping were upheld by the American International Trade Commission. The powerful American steel lobby (see chapter 3 below) was able to use its legal advantage to force the US government to tighten its negotiating stance and to extend import restrictions to steel alloys and tubes. The Germans in particular regarded the final agreement as particularly onerous and unfair but were unwilling to breach the solidarity of the European negotiating position and ratified the agreement at the eleventh hour (*The Economist*, 23 October 1982).

The European approach to managing the steel crisis was to adopt a regime of weak cartelization that has been supported by mandatory ECSC regulation. The Japanese have pursued a strategy of state-led capacity stabilization that has contained a problem that was in any case less severe than elsewhere owing to the Japanese producer's ability to operate profitably at lower levels of capacity utilization. The Japanese steel industry is the world's lowest-cost producer and, although import controls have prevented it from increasing exports, it has benefited from increased export prices. The third facet of the international steel crisis measures is the restriction of imports from NICs into Europe by a system of base import prices and bilateral negotiations over volume. Overall, the impact of these assorted initiatives has amounted to a 'damage limitation' exercise, in which the arguments of market logic, the domestic pressures for aid and the overriding concern not to provoke outright trade retaliation have been balanced by each state in a complex and unstable political equation. The most striking aspect has been the development of a concerted European approach to the problem.

The European attempts at crisis management for the steel industry have drawn on the unusually powerful terms of the Treaty of Paris, which established the European Coal and Steel Community. In 1980, five years after having been first asked by the French, and after strong resistance from the Germans, the Commission declared a 'manifest crisis' under article 58 of the Treaty of Paris (Woolcock, 1981, pp. 73–4). This measure empowered it to set production quotas and to widen the system of minimum prices first established in 1978.

Between 1974 and 1980 EEC crude steel capacity had increased by 12 per cent. At the same time the industry's capacity working had fallen from 80 to 55 per cent, and employment had fallen from 792,000 in 1975 to 605,000 in 1980, a cut of 24 per cent (*Financial Times*, 3 March 1981; *The Times*, 26 February 1981). The problem was obviously intense. From the late 1970s European producers who account for 95 per cent of European production have been organized into 'Eurofer', a grouping that has been variously described as a cartel, a club or a 'rather weak lobby' (Woolcock, 1981, p. 72). It has in the past reached voluntary agreement on prices and quotas but has been poor at imposing them. There have been extensive wrangles, especially with the smaller Italian producers, about compliance; the quotas proved very hard to police. Self-regulation was weak, and in June 1981, when the 'manifest crisis' was renewed, the Germans agreed to a fresh combination of compulsory quotas and a voluntary restraint pact, but only in return for an agreement and a timetable for 'subsidy disarmament' from the rest of the Nine (*The Times*, 26 June 1981). During 1982, therefore, there was in operation an agreement to end virtually all government aids to national steel-makers on a timetable that prohibited emergency (crisis rescue) aid after June 1982 and prohibited aid for restructuring after 1985. By the end of 1982, however, the combination of even lower demand than forecast and poor compliance with importing, pricing and capacity rationalization measures was calling the European steel strategy into question. Commentators were gloomy, and it appeared unlikely that states would be able or willing to phase out subsidies (*The Economist*, 20 November 1982, p. 72). In November 1982, for example, the Commission approved German government loans of DM 150 million (£38 million) to Arbed Saarstahl, the first of several German steel companies meeting steadily more severe financial problems.

European efforts at managing the steel crisis have, therefore, been unusually energetic. They reflect the exceptional powers of the ECSC as well as the personal commitment of the Industry Commissioner, Viscount Davignon. There has been some success (if that is the appropriate term) in raising prices and restraining imports, but little success in dealing with the core of the problem, a reduction of capacity and an allocation of that reduction among the Community producers. In the absence of international economic expansion, problems are taking on the quality of a sustained crisis. The ban on government subsidy should oblige industries to shed capacity. However, national governments will find it very difficult to resist pressures for aid. It has been argued that Europe should adopt Japanese-style 'recession cartels', which fix production and prices only on condition that capacity is also reduced (Pinder, 1982, p. 262). Such prescriptions, of course, beg questions about the structure of the industry (Nippon Steel is dominant in Japan), about the interventionary philosophy of governments (MITI is prepared to guide industrial development), and about the policy instruments available to government, especially a fragmented supra-national European government (Magaziner and Hout, 1980). The following chapters focus on such questions of national capacities for management of industrial crises. This focus stems from a recognition that the individual state remains the key centre of industrial policy decisions.

REFERENCES

Aaronovitch, S., Smith, R. *et al* (1981), *The Political Economy of British Capitalism*, London, McGraw-Hill.

Abernathy, W., Clark, K. and Kantrow, A. (1983), *Industrial Renaissance*, New York, Basic Books.

Allsopp, C. (1979), 'The International Demand Management Problem', in D. Morris (ed.), *The Economic System in the UK* (2nd edn), Oxford University Press.

Brittan, S. (1977), *The Economic Consequences of Democracy*, London, Maurice Temple Smith.

Buckley, P. and Casson, M. (1976), *The Future of the Multinational Enterprise*, London, Macmillan.

Burton, J. (1979), *The Job Support Machine*, London, Centre for Policy Studies.

Central Policy Review Staff (1975), *The Future of the British Car Industry*, London, HMSO.

Chandler, A. D. (1977), *The Visible Hand: The Managerial Revolution in American Business*, Cambridge, Massachusetts, Harvard University Press.

Corden, W. M. (1976), 'Conclusions on the Logic of Government Intervention', in W.M. Corden and G. Fels (eds), *Public Assistance to Industry: Protection and Subsidies in Britain and Germany*, London, Macmillan.

Crandall, R. (1981), *The US Steel Industry in Recurrent Crisis*, Washington, DC, Brookings Institution.

Diebold, W. Jnr (1978), 'Adapting Economies to Structural Change: The International Aspect', *International Affairs*, October.

Downs, A. (1964), *Inside Bureaucracy*, Washington DC, Rand Corporation.

Edelman, M. (1977), *Political Language: Words That Succeed and Policies That Fail*, New York, Academic Press.

European Commission (1981), *European Economy*, vol. 9 (Brussels), July.

Grunberg, L. (1981), *Failed Multinational Ventures*, Lexington, Massachusetts, D. C. Heath.

Hallett, E. C. (1981), 'Economic Convergence and Divergence in the European Community: A Survey of the Evidence', in M. Hodges and W. Wallace (eds), *Economic Divergence in the European Community*, London, Allen and Unwin.

Hannah, L. (1976), *The Rise of the Corporate Economy*, London, Methuen.

Hodges, M. (1981), 'Liberty, Equality, Divergency: The Legacy of the Treaty of Rome?' in M. Hodges and W. Wallace (eds), *Economic Divergence in the European Community*, London, Allen and Unwin.

Hood, N. and Young, S. (1982), *Multinationals in Retreat: The Scottish Experience*, Edinburgh University Press.

Katzenstein, P. (1978), 'Conclusion: Domestic Structures and Strategies of Foreign Economic Policy', in P. Katsenstein (ed.), *Between Power and Plenty*, Madison, University of Wisconsin Press.

Magaziner, I. and Hout, T. (1980), *Japanese Industrial Policy*, London, Policy Studies Institute.

Mottershead, P. (1978), 'Industrial Policy', in F. Blackaby (ed.), *British Economic Policy 1964–74*, Cambridge University Press.

OECD (1979), *The Case for Positive Adjustment Policies*, Paris, OECD.

OECD (1982a), *Main Economic Indicators*, Paris, OECD.

OECD (1982b), *OECD Economic Outlook*, Paris, OECD (July).

Peacock, A. (1979), *The Economic Analysis of Government and Related Themes*, London, Martin Robertson.

Pinder, J. (1982), 'Industrial Policy in Britain and the European Community', *Policy Studies*, April.

Pollard, S. (1982), *The Wasting of the British Economy*, London, Croom Helm.

Sampson, A. (1981), *The Moneylenders*, London, Hodder and Stoughton.

Shonfield, A. (1980), 'The Politics of the Mixed Economy in the International System of the 1970s', *International Affairs*, January.

Simon, H. (1976), *Administrative Behaviour* (3rd edn), New York, Free Press.

Thirlwall, A. P. (1982), 'Deindustrialisation in the United Kingdom', *Lloyds Bank Review*, April.

Tsoukalis, L. and Silva Ferreira, A. da (1981), 'The Response of the European Community' in S. Strange and R. Tooze (eds), *The International Politics of Surplus Capacity*, London, Allen and Unwin.

Tullock, G. (1976), *The Vote Motive*, London, IEA Hobart Paper.

Wilensky, H. L. (1967), *Organisational Intelligence*, New York, Basic Books.

Woolcock S. (1981), 'Iron and Steel', in S. Strange and R. Tooze (eds), *The International Politics of Surplus Capacity*, London, Allen and Unwin.

2

The Cultural, Ideological and Structural Context

Kenneth Dyson

Industrial crises have become a pervasive and striking feature of advanced industrialized societies. Moreover, they have emerged as a central, complex and intractable issue on the political agenda of these societies. The USA has experienced the crises of the Douglas and Lockheed aircraft corporations as well as of Penn Central, of International Harvester and of Chrysler. Britain has suffered a shock-wave of industrial crises, of which the most prominent examples are Rolls Royce, British Leyland, Chrysler UK, British Steel and the computer giant ICL. France has developed a formidable structure of inter-ministerial committees to process a growing case-load of industrial crises that include the textile industry of the Vosges and the steel industry of Lorraine as well as spectacular crises like that of the Willot empire. West Germany's rapidly mounting list of industrial crises has ranged from the traditional heavy steel industry of the Ruhr and the Saar (notably Arbed Saarstahl) to the electronics giant AEG Telefunken. These crises posed the question of whether government could continue to rely on a private sector mechanism of crisis management. Sweden's catalogue of industrial crises has encompassed the shipbuilding, steel, electronics and timber industries, has cast doubt on the country's traditional reputation for an anticipatory policy style, and led to a greater extension of public ownership in six years of 'bourgeois' governments (1976–82) than in four decades of social democratic governments.

These industrial crises have similar characteristics: the threat of bankruptcy of a large employer and of a 'knock-on' effect to other industries and to whole regions; the threat of social crisis as the costs of industrial adjustment are borne disproportionately by unskilled, foreign and older workers; and intense political pressure on industrial policy-makers. The latter are confronted by threat both to election prospects and to central policy objectives (like employment, regional balance and technological independence); and they face a requirement of urgent decision on the basis of a paucity of reliable knowledge. Industrial crises are the instances of drama that are thrown up by the pressures of industrial adjustment. While the drama may be conditioned by the 'script' of economic structure and development, its stage management remains both interesting and important and draws attention to the character and role of institutional arrangements.

Industrial crises present, of course, a complex picture. Advanced industrialized societies have had a wide range of experience of such crises in the 1970s. Thus, Britain and Italy were characterized by a scale and intensity of industrial crises that did not occur in West Germany. The British media were absorbed by industrial crises even before the urban riots of 1981 focused attention in a dramatic way on the social and political consequences of rapid and concentrated 'de-industrialization' for traditional industrial areas. Industrial crises encompassed not just declining sectors like textiles and shipbuilding but also, and more ominously, growth sectors such as aerospace (Rolls Royce) and computers (ICL). By contrast, West Germany appeared to face a rapidly changing international economy with a modernized, 'knowledge-intensive' and adaptive industrial structure. The international success of Germany's industrial structure and its dominance of European markets prompted a different conception of industrial crises from that in Britain. German debate about industrial crises in the 1970s was less concerned with specific cases of the collapse of giant corporations and more preoccupied with the general social crisis of employment. Rapid modernization produced a more rapid loss of jobs in German manufacturing industry than in most other advanced industrialized societies and, correspondingly, was seen as the motor of an emerging social crisis (Scharpf, 1980). Industrial crisis in this broad sense was caused by modernization and existed also in Britain. However, the scale and intensity of British industrial crises was more often related to *a failure* to modernize and a consequent threat both to the survival of corporations and to the jobs and economic and social opportunities of their workers. West German observers were prone to define industrial crisis broadly as a social problem, to emphasize the social crisis of industrial modernization and to blame a neo-corporatist approach of formal and informal collaboration among management, trade unions and government. A 'selective' neo-corporatism appeared to reward skilled workers and to penalize others in the interests of modernization (Esser *et al.*, 1978). British observers were more inclined to concentrate on the discrete crises of corporations, to emphasize the local social crises that are created by their collapse because of failure to modernize, and to blame an antiquated capitalist society that exhibits institutional inertia. Thus, blame was attached to an 'anarchic' system of industrial relations that encourages contest between management and workers, to a banking system that fails to provide sufficient long-term credit for industry, or to the lack of will of governments which have not ensured that the common interest in modernization was realized. While conceptions of industrial crisis reflect the ideological disposition of the observer, they reveal also contrasting contexts of economic structure and development.

Variety of national experience suggests that the term 'industrial crisis' is not likely to be amenable to rigorous operational definition. According to the Concise Oxford Dictionary, crisis means a 'turning point' or 'moment of danger or suspense'. Crisis is clearly a perceptual affair. Industrial crisis has different faces in the sense that a particular crisis is likely to consist of a set of interlocked crises: a managerial crisis, perhaps occasioned by inadequate management accounting or by the failure of organizational structures or styles to keep pace with changes of strategy (for instance, the attempt to combine product or geographical diversification with continuity of family control or a personalized management style); a technological crisis, caused by neglect of research and development and product innovation; an employment crisis, the product of large-scale redundancies; an 'industrial policy' crisis, as the collapse of a sector or firm casts doubt on the credibility of government's sectoral or regional policies; and a financial crisis, when banks or governments threaten to withdraw their support.

This multi-dimensional character of industrial crisis is only one reason why it is difficult to specify objective, universally applicable criteria for describing them. Usage of the term 'crisis' to describe industrial events is conditioned by political history and structural context. Advanced industrialized societies appeared more 'crisis-prone' in the 1970s because more was expected of government. The propensity to define industrial crises varies with the changing roles and responsibilities of government. The terms of debate about industrial crises have also been transformed by the structural context of increasing concentration of industry. Chandler (1977) identifies a transition from market economies to managerial economies; the 'invisible hand' of the market has been replaced, or at least supplemented by the 'visible hand' of the large corporation. These corporations manage technical change over a broad geographical and product range. Consequently, according to Chandler, they substitute a hierarchical allocation of resources on the basis of a conscious strategy for the allocation of resources by the impersonal price mechanism of the market. In practice, corporations are caught between the dangers of internal managerial failure and the harsh, ultimate and uncertain judgement of the market.

Even if Chandler overstates his case, the performance and fate of corporations has become so important for political, social and economic objectives that governments cannot afford to ignore them. The collapse of corporations, for whatever reason, threatens to create a vacuum that the market may not be able to fill effectively (for instance, because markets may be bad at managing complex technological change). Industrial crisis is the story of dramatic encounters among institutions whose various perceptions are bound by time and structural and cultural context.

Industrial policy-makers exhibit variations not just over time but also cross-nationally in their conceptions of industrial crisis. Thus, in France and Italy ideologies of government–industry relations emphasize the problem of market 'failure'. Their industrial policy-makers are correspondingly sensitive and responsive to industrial crises and tend to take a broad view of them. French and Italian policy-makers attempt with varying success to monitor the difficulties and dangers that face industries and large corporations. Their approach to managing industrial crises has an anticipatory character. Anticipatory policy style is, of course, not to be equated with will and capability to manage industrial crises, as the different experiences of France and Italy illustrate.

By contrast, when ideologies of government–industry relations emphasize the virtues of the free market as the efficient allocator of resources, management of industrial crises tends to take on a narrower meaning. For example, in the USA industrial crisis refers to the *ad hoc* reactions of legislatures and executives to the dramatic troubles of giant corporations. The broad and flexible range of policy instruments for crisis management in France and Italy contrasts with the preference for the loan guarantee in the USA. An important part of the New Deal programme of President Roosevelt in the 1930s was the transformation of the new Reconstruction Finance Corporation into a flexible instrument of crisis intervention. Its abolition in the early 1950s meant, however, that the federal government could manage industrial crises in the 1960s and 1970s only when they had broken — when a corporation declared that it could not meet the demands of its creditors and the banks were unable or unwilling to continue their support.

In West Germany too, government tends to react to the reactions of the banks. However, respect for the market and a preference for the loan guarantee as a policy instrument is tempered by the importance that German political ideology attaches to the 'social principle'. This principle finds its expression in the concept of the 'social market economy', in the welfare policies of the 'social state', in the theory and practice of 'social partnership' in industry (notably worker participation in supervisory boards and the rights of works councils), and in a broader conception of industrial crisis than that in the USA. Crisis management involves elaborate social plans that are carefully and laboriously negotiated with works councils and that aim to give the worker time to adjust to the threat of redundancy. Government and the 'social partners' display a greater concern for an 'acceptable' distribution of the costs of industrial crises. Thus Toni Schmücker (1976), chief executive of Volkswagen in the 1970s, referred to the corporation as 'association of interests' whose effective integration depended on a reconciliation of commercial and social principles. This conception underpinned the attempt by Volkswagen in the mid-1970s to manage its crisis in an anticipatory and 'socially responsible' manner so that mass redundancies could be avoided. Priority was given to elaborate social planning on the basis of consent and to special regional action programmes in the management of the Saar steel crisis and of the Volkswagen crisis. These crises provide examples of a horizontal coordination of different policy instruments that has not been characteristic of crisis management in the USA or even Britain. Crisis management by such 'package deals' suggests a neo-corporatist approach that emphasizes collaboration rather than competition of interests.

In contrast to France, West Germany and the USA, government-industry relations in Britain have been plagued by ideological instability (Grant, 1982). During the periods 1964–70 and 1972–79 the emphasis of industrial policy was sympathetic to government's attempts to tackle market failures: crisis interventions were acceptable. During 1970–72 and after 1979, the stress was on market forces and 'disengagement' of government from industry: crisis interventions were seen as exceptional. This ideological oscillation has broken the confidence of industrial policy-makers, who, in part as a consequence, failed to develop an organizational capacity for an anticipatory management of industrial crises. Over time, Britain has lacked a coherent conception of industrial crises. Its approach was muddled, confused and confusing; the dominant feature of crisis management was hesitancy.

INDUSTRIAL CULTURE

Despite problems of definition, industrial crisis provides a useful heuristic device for comparing industrial policies. Analysis of the management of industrial crises reveals the impact on policy of contrasts of industrial structure, of historical processes of industrialization, and of conceptions of law and public authority. In particular, management of industrial crises provides an interesting insight into the different legal and political traditions of the Anglo-American and continental European societies (Dyson, 1980). These traditions of public authority find their expression within industrial cultures through their embodiment in institutional structures. Hence they help to explain some of the deep and subtle differences between the character of government–industry relations in Britain and the United States on the one hand, and France, Italy and West Germany on the other.

In the Anglo-American legal and political tradition, there has been a tendency to view the rights of the individual as the product of birth: hence the historical importance of the phrase, 'the freeborn Englishman' and of the American creed, 'We hold these truths to be self-evident, that all men are created equal . . .' Industrial culture is formed in part by the conception that the individual has priority and precedence over social and political arrangements. Correspondingly, representation and voluntarism have been central ideological themes; principles of autonomy and self-government have formed the basis of institutional life; an adversary procedure of contest has dominated the law, parliament and industry; and the conception of good citizenship has incorporated a spirit of stubborn independence and a willingness to resist 'arbitrary' authority. The effects of this distinctive Anglo-Saxon liberal tradition are notably apparent in the administrative culture of government. A preference for 'arm's length' government combines with a scepticism about government's competence in industrial affairs and an unwillingness to act in advance of political pressures to do so (Shonfield, 1965). Although government has expanded greatly in function and size, neither administrative nor business culture has absorbed the concept of a benevolent 'public power' — the state — acting in the name of the common good.

In the continental European legal and political tradition, the rights of the individual and of the group tend to be seen as the product of recognition by the state. The peculiar importance that is attached to the state derives from its role in the formation and regulation of social life. Despite vociferous attacks, the mainstream of politico-legal tradition has resisted as radical a concept of the individual or group outside the framework of the state. Correspondingly, the state has been a central ideological theme, alongside community and unity; the state has been expected to exhibit interest in the welfare, even 'happiness' of its citizens, whether by regulation of the exercise of private power in the form of the elaboration of an 'economic constitution' (as in West Germany) or by direct and detailed intervention in industrial affairs (as in France and Italy); principles of integration, order and consistency have formed the basis of institutional life; the norm of objectivity and respect for technical argument pervades the law, parliament and industry; and the concept of good citizenship emphasizes the precedence of public obligations over the private concerns of 'selfish' individuals (Dyson, 1980). Industrial culture accords priority to the value of order, accepts readily the importance of common or corporate interests, and assumes the need for legal regulation of social relationships. This type of industrial culture supported the emergence of formalized institutional structures, of an 'organized capitalism' that was concentrated and bureaucratized and symbolized by the cartel. Examples of the influence of collective attitudes are provided by the French concept that government has a strategic mission in industrial affairs, the Italian concept that public enterprise has such a mission, and the German and Swedish concept that the 'social partners' must collaborate in the interests of social responsibility.

The response of public policy to the emergence of the large corporation in 'state' societies differed from that in 'stateless' societies (Dyson, 1980). The continental European concern for 'orderly' social relations was reflected in a tendency to view the emergence of the large corporation as the creation of a set of new authority relations. Authority relations were seen to require systematic legal regulation, even if they were located essentially in the sphere of civil society. The Anglo-American politico-legal tradition has been more suspicious of the idea that the character of private corporate authority was a suitable or desirable object of public regulation. Public regulation concentrated more on the uses of corporate power. Regulation of processes of industrial decision-making in 'state' societies is an example of the priority that is accorded to the regulation of the exercise of private authority relations in the interests of order, equity and consistency in social relationships.

This concern of public policy with the 'constitution of the firm' contrasts with the concept of industrial decision-making as a private and voluntary matter in Britain. The classic model of the attempt to ensure the public responsibility of corporate decision-making remains the German model of the representative supervisory board (*Aufsichtsrat*) alongside, and in contrast to, the executive management board (*Vorstand*). Similarly, the emphasis on social planning by corporations in conjunction with their works councils contrasts with the *ad hoc* approach of British corporations. A concern for the social dimension of managing industrial crises has, of course, been exhibited by some British corporations like ICI. However, this concern has been primarily pragmatic rather than rooted in a public requirement of moral responsibility within capitalism. The social conscience of American and British corporations is more the outcome of their own recognition of their industrial power and of their long-term economic interest in an image of responsibility.

Of particular importance for managing industrial crises is the role of law in assisting firms in trouble. Britain's bankruptcy laws are strikingly inflexible. In particular, they have not encouraged the emergence of a group of 'company doctors' who would be able to exert control over a corporation before it goes bankrupt. The Bankruptcy Act of 1883 and subsequent legislation make the interests of the creditors the major reference point for the work of the receiver when he replaces management upon insolvency. This narrow concept of interest contrasts with the flexible and quick procedure in France and Germany. There, a corporation can manage its financial restructuring in advance of bankruptcy by applying to the courts for control (as AEG Telefunken did in 1982). The USA's Bankruptcy Code has absorbed the notion of court protection for corporations. However, the concept of interest remains narrow, as in British law. In French and German law the survival of a corporation takes precedence over the protection of creditors. Legislation recognizes also the 'knock-on' effect of insolvency on employees and customers as well as on shareholders and seeks to guarantee their interests in financial restructuring. Corporations can gain an immediate moratorium by proposing a settlement with creditors under the supervision of a court. According to French law, if the saving of a corporation is in the national interest, the plan for its financial reorganization that is prepared by a court-appointed administrator may not even require the approval of creditors. In short, corporation law and the law of insolvency rest on a concept of the firm as a community of interests and reject a strictly contractual notion of employment. The 'soulful' corporation of Britain and the USA operates on the basis of a more utilitarian concept of its own character. Indicative of the different styles of managing industrial crises in Britain and West Germany was the rejection in 1982 by AEG's works council of the proposed partnership with GEC in the capital goods field. It feared that a more abrasive and utilitarian managerial style would be imported.

The contrast between 'state' and 'stateless' societies is, of course, forceful and bold, invites numerous qualifications, and is more important as a mediating than as an explanatory factor for crisis management. For instance, the fraternalism of social democracy and the Tory tradition of hierarchy and concern for stability distinguish Britain from the USA and introduce a greater concern for welfare into industrial policy. The revolutionary tradition of resistance to authority introduces a powerful counter-current into French industrial culture. Correspondingly, France's system of industrial relations lacks the collaborative values and institutional integration of West Germany. While formal ideology within Italian industrial culture is profoundly influenced by the state tradition, political and administrative practice is affected by the centrifugal factional pressures of patronage politics. Hence the state tradition of authority is more of a facade than in other West European countries. More generally, concentration of ownership within industry combines with political democracy to force attention in all countries on collectivist solutions to the problems of industrial power. Nevertheless, this contrast of political tradition has deep roots in law, culture and political experience (Dyson, 1980) and makes comprehensible important differences of general approach to managing industrial crises in Britain and the USA, on the one hand, and in continental Europe, on the other. In Britain and the USA, policy-makers display a reluctance to assume responsibility for managing industrial crises. The Americans are disposed to a radical equation of 'crisis intervention' with 'socialism', the British are inhibited by a deep cultural aversion to 'interference' with the firm. In continental Europe the state assumes responsibility for managing industrial crises, either by direct and detailed intervention or by public regulation of private sector management of crises. The German aversion to allowing free rein to the individualism of the market represents the major contrast between the market economies of West Germany and the USA. West Germany is not a 'market society'. Management of industrial crises is, therefore, embedded in very different legal and political traditions.

In the preceding analysis emphasis has been on the complexity of industrial crises and contrasting national approaches to their management. At the same time, common forces are at work and suggest that, despite differences of structure and culture, no advanced industrialist society is likely to be able to escape a problem of managing industrial crises. The various factors that have combined to put industrial crises high on the political agenda were the subject matter of chapter 1. Emphasis on this common context of economic forces can, however, distract attention from the distinctive ideological, institutional and cultural inheritance of societies and the impact of that inheritance on their capacity to manage industrial crises. The character of processes of managing industrial crises is obviously shaped also by factors of industrial structure and development. Nevertheless, the thesis of economic determinism needs to be qualified by attention to variations of industrial culture. Management of industrial crises reveals different styles of problem-solving and of accommodation of interests. Styles of managing industrial crises are embedded in industrial cultures, which reflect and are reflected in institutional structures and ideologies of government–industry relations. Industrial cultures exert subtle but important constraints on the way in which industrial crises are managed, and they embody different traditions of public authority as well as contrasting processes of industrialization.

In addition to offering a more explicitly political analysis of industrial crises, one that focuses on comparison of the character of its management, it is important to counter the tendency of political scientists to study industrial policy 'from the top down'. Political analysis of industrial policy has tended to emphasize the elite interaction of ministries, industrial and employer associations, trade unions and a few 'national industrial champions' within specialized and rather exclusive 'industrial policy communities'. The politics of the firm has been neglected. Analysis of the role of the firm has been the preserve of microeconomics, with its formal analysis of firms in various markets, and of economic history, whose growing interest in business history has been largely neglected by political science. In fact, advanced industrialized societies display fascinating contrasts in the politics of the firm, contrasts that are cultural as well as economic. Political tradition and industrial development have thrown up different industrial cultures and, within these industrial cultures, contrasting concepts of the firm and of its relationship to the wider capitalist society. An industrial culture embodies a particular body of beliefs, values and attitudes by reference to which behaviour is evaluated and organizational structures attain their meaning. It provides a common vocabulary that facilitates communication. One way of distinguishing industrial cultures is by reference to their characterization of the firm. Management of industrial crises illuminates contrasting conceptions of the firm and the political and economic factors that have supported such conceptions.

Traditionally, interest in the politics of the firm focused on the issues of ownership and control and, in particular, on the difference between economies with little public ownership (such as Sweden and the USA) and economies with considerable public ownership (such as France and Italy). Analysis of industrial policies assumed that public ownership could provide important levers of control for industrial policy-makers. Hence an important issue in research on public enterprise was the effectiveness of their political control in the public interest. However, it is notable, and significant for this argument, that in Britain the political problem of public ownership tended to be viewed as one of 'excessive' control or 'interference' in the affairs of public corporations. Implicit in British debate about public enterprise was a preoccupation with their autonomy of action, a preoccupation that was typical of the wider industrial culture of Britain. Extension of public ownership proved less important to the development (or rather to lack of development) of an industrial policy network in Britain than the character of the industrial culture. This culture has proved remarkably resilient to changes of ownership and transcends the publicly and privately owned sectors of industry. As we have seen, industrial culture involves attitudes towards the proper structure, functioning and behaviour of firms. In Britain the traditional emphasis within industrial culture has been on the self-sufficiency of the firm, the independence of its management in taking and implementing decisions, and the periodic need for resolute action from 'heroic' industrial leaders. Cross-national comparison highlights the extent to which attitudes within British industry (and outside it) are resistant to a concept of the firm as enmeshed within a web of institutional interests, whether those of public agencies (France and Italy), of the complex financial holding companies of Belgium and France, of commercial banks as in Sweden (for instance, the famous Wallenberg family bank–industry interests) and Germany, or of trade unions (West Germany). British industrial culture exhibits intense suspicion of, for instance, the complex spider's web of relationships that bind together German banks, insurance companies and firms through cross-shareholdings, and the role of elite bankers in supervisory boards and that bind together French ministries, banks and firms through a common elite background in the public service (education in a *grande école* and membership of one of the few *grands corps*) and through the practice of transfer of members of the elite corps to the private sector and nationalized banks and enterprises (*pantouflage*). In contrast to Britain, state engineers moved into key areas of French private industry from the 1890s, and the central role of the *grandes écoles* as a source of recruitment of elite technicians to senior posts in industry was soon established. The style of managing industrial crises is not, therefore, related simply to the issue of ownership. It is more deeply rooted in industrial culture and in the extent to which that culture stresses a 'private' concept of the self-sufficiency of the firm or a 'public' conception of the firm as interlocked with a network of institutional interests.

Industrial cultures are complex and variegated and, in large part because of their qualitative character, are often treated as an extraneous variable for the purpose of comparative analysis of economic performance or of economic and industrial policy making. Both market economists and Marxists have tended to neglect the concept of industrial culture. The argument of this chapter is that, even if priority is attached to the causal influence of market and technological factors or of 'the forces and relations of production', industrial culture continues to be important as a mediating factor in the policy process. More seriously, when questions about the formation of industrial cultures are posed, they are often answered simplistically so that the sight of the multi-dimensionality of industrial cultures is lost. An example of a one-dimensional approach has been the emphasis placed on socio-structural explanations that focus on elite strategies in the context of the relations between new industrial elites and traditional elites. Clearly, the terms of elite accommodation in Britain had an important influence on industrial culture. An important aspect of the accommodation of new and old elites in the nineteenth century was the reform of the public schools and of the Oxford and Cambridge colleges. These reforms consolidated the social prestige of the aristocratic model of the gentleman and the 'gifted amateur' within elite education (Armstrong, 1973; Wiener, 1981). Both reforms of the civil service and the development of state education were in turn deeply influenced by this elite education model. The children of industrial families were assimilated into this elite structure on terms that denied industry of talent and that isolated industrial culture as 'northern' and philistine. Industrial culture was subordinate and peripheral to the establishment circle of Whitehall, the City, Oxford/Cambridge and the public schools. The governmental world of Whitehall and the financial world of the City maintained an arm's-length relationship to industry. By contrast, the pre-eminence of business values was made possible in the USA by the absence of traditional elites. Hence business provided a role model for both education and the civil service, and business executives enjoyed great social prestige and political influence. However, focus on elite strategies is liable to distract attention from the political and legal arrangements that form the context of such strategies. Elites are assimilated into, and their strategies formed against the background of, political and legal arrangements that predate the Industrial Revolution and that involve ideas and assumptions established by earlier religious struggles and experiences of state-building rather than by later economic struggles of class interest (Dyson, 1980). Strategies of social elites appear so important in the Anglo-American tradition because of the flexibility of their representative institutions. In France and Germany it was not so much the nature of relations between social elites as the military requirements of a beleaguered state, and growing recognition of the importance of industrial strength to military power, that led to an emphasis on the technician in elite education. Technical education acquired a social prestige unknown in Britain and of different character from that in the USA. Whereas British family firms sought the prestige of public school education for their children, the French family firm sought the prestige of the *grandes écoles*, which trained their children as technicians with greater respect for managerial values.

Fascination with socio-structural explanations of industrial culture has tended to distract attention from politico-legal explanation in terms of contrasting attitudes towards public authority and economic explanation in terms of the 'requirements' of capital mobilization for industry. Styles of managing industrial crises indicate the importance of politico-legal and economic as well as socio-structural explanations of industrial culture.

MANAGING INDUSTRIAL CRISES?

The heading 'Managing Industrial Crises?' implies two questions: whether industrial crises *should* be managed, and how effectively industrial crises *can* be managed. Although the two questions are distinct and appear different in character, they are interdependent. The answer to the one question is likely to influence the answer to the other. Thus, the view that industrial crises should be managed is encouraged when mechanisms that promise an effective management of industrial crises exist — for instance, France's various important inter-ministerial committees for industrial rescue and the *grands corps* network that knit together ministries, banks and industry.

Conversely, as in the case of Britain, ideological support for managing industrial crises tends to founder when mechanisms of crisis management appear to fail repeatedly to tackle problems of industrial adjustment and confidence in collective action is weakened — witness the abolition of the Industrial Reorganization Corporation in 1970. In other words, advanced industrialized societies are likely to be characterized by virtuous or vicious circles of industrial crisis management. In the 1970s Britain's record of managing industrial crises displayed intellectual muddle and lack of organizational continuity or development. From different ideological perspectives, France and West Germany exhibited a more consistent approach and possessed or developed sophisticated mechanisms of crisis management. At the same time, such stability is precarious. Sweden's 'market-oriented' approach and reliance on private sector mechanisms of crisis management left industrial policy-makers seriously exposed and ill-informed in the 1970s when the scale of crises exceeded the capacity of the banks. A similar danger of collapse of confidence in traditional mechanisms and styles of crisis management emerged in West Germany in the early 1980s. The powerful coordinating role of the Treasury in France and its close links to banks and industry suggested a capacity for more flexible and rapid response, for the state to bring more strategic weight to bear on management of industrial crises.

The question of whether to manage industrial crises is clearly normative and involves ideological issues. From the perspective of theorists of the market (whether of the 'pure' market or of the 'social' market), industrial crisis is a false and dangerous label to describe what is no more than a necessary aspect of the normal functioning of a market economy. 'Crisis' interventions are likely only to delay or even distort the functioning of the market. Hence, the onus is on the 'interventionists' to prove that support of a firm or sector will maximize net social welfare. 'Crisis' interventions are expected to be exceptional situations. From a contrasting ideological perspective, theorists who endorse selective intervention are disposed to view industrial crises as a symptom of market imperfection or of failure by the market — for instance, to provide satisfactory information about consumer preferences on which to base costly investment decisions with long lead-times, to generate high levels of long-term credit for growth industries, or to account for the social and political costs of industrial adjustment (Grant, 1982). Contrasts of dominant ideologies among societies suggest differences in the cultural readiness to support and develop a range of institutions and policy instruments whose function is to tackle industrial crises as a continuous problem of the capitalist economy. Thus France has an ideology of *dirigisme* and Italy an ideology of social reconciliation, both of which legitimate an important role for institutions of selective intervention. Such institutions have no real parallel in Britain or the USA.

The second question, how to manage industrial crises, appears at first glance technical. It requires the identification of the political and organizational conditions for an effective management of industrial crises. In fact, this question is far from technical. It raises the political issues of the criteria by reference to which 'effective' crisis management should be assessed, an issue to which we return in the conclusion. In practice, industrial policy-makers have tended, with varying degrees of emphasis, to focus on the economic criterion of 'positive' adjustment to changes in the international economy. This criterion of crisis management provides, therefore, a useful starting point for analysis, albeit a controversial one. Effective crisis management in the narrow sense of an orientation towards international competitiveness and structural modernization requires sound commercial judgement about markets and technology. In addition, effective crisis management requires institutional arrangements that encourage anticipation to reduce the extent of surprise, coordination of objectives, and measures to ensure unified action and monitoring of implementation. These elements of crisis management depend for their effectiveness on strong inter-organizational linkages, which are in turn facilitated by close social networks that bind together informally decision-makers in the worlds of government, banking and industry (for example, the French *grands corps* and Germany's senior bankers) as well as by a neo-corporatist style of 'concerted action' that emphasizes stable forms of collaboration among affected interests in the design and implementation of comprehensive rescue packages (such as the use of the 'crisis cartel' in the West German steel industry). Inter-organizational linkages and corporatist styles are typically selective in the sense that they favour certain interests over others. In France the trade unions are marginal or are excluded from the collaborative system of crisis management; in West Germany incorporation of the trade unions has meant priority to the interests of a core workforce that is skilled, German and male. Despite this selectivity and consequent limitations, strong inter-organizational linkages increase the level of operational preparation of policy-makers by provision of an institutional structure of communications and control that facilitates agreed, rapid and unified action. The policy process for crisis management benefits from the flexibility of direct communications outside channels and acquires a potential for early warning and assessment of threat that reduces the element of surprise in crisis.

A manifestation of this collaborative style of crisis management is an ideological consensus among the participants — supported by the structure of party political power — that mechanisms of elite collaboration are important in order to disseminate respect for norms of integration and objectivity within the industrial culture. This elite consensus emphasizes concepts like *Sozialpartnerschaft* and *concertation, Sachlichkeit* and *technique*. In addition to ideological consensus, and party political support, a collaborative style of crisis management requires an institutional structure that insulates policy-makers from the political pressures of sectional interests — for instance, the centralization within West Germany's industrial unions and the 'relative' autonomy of the French executive. These structures develop a vested interest in collaborative styles. A collaborative style of crisis management is also associated with a concept of industrial crisis as ultimately a technical issue, which can and should be resolved in a dispassionate spirit of objectivity. This concept is particularly hostile to the public politics of confrontation that has been a distinguishing feature of management of industrial crises in Britain and the USA. Their industrial crises have been managed in the glare of publicity. The existence of a traditional neo-corporatist policy style of collaboration is a major reason why a politicized style of management of industrial crises has proved such a source of disillusion and pessimism in Sweden. Such a disjunction between norm and reality is more readily accepted in Italy, where structures appear more abstract affairs, and where political and economic survival rather than effectiveness of policy is the fascination. In Italy the potential for collaborative management of industrial crises that is provided by the patronage of the dominant Christian Democratic Party is not realized because of elite fragmentation and factional politics and the pursuit of short-term sectional interests.

The extent to which elite ideology is market- or intervention-oriented helps to explain important differences in mechanisms of crisis management. Thus, in West Germany management of industrial crises is normally left to the bank–industry nexus in order to emphasize the 'private sector' character of industrial decision-making. A more active role is played by the state in France (in the form of the *grands corps*) and in Italy (in the form of public enterprise). However, more important for the character and effectiveness of crisis management is the type of policy style. Policy style reflects both traditions of public authority and character of economic development. As 'state' societies, France and West Germany approximate closest to a collaborative style. Inter-organizational linkages on the basis of social networks and a neo-corporatist practice provide, in both of these cases, a different institutional framework of integration and of political and financial support for large firms. This framework has come to play a major role in their strategic calculations. Firms seek entry into the charmed and privileged inner circle by the devices either of the *grands corps* officials within the firm in France or of the bank representative on the supervisory board in Germany. For reasons that are deeply rooted in political tradition and industrial development, elite ideologies and institutional structures have not encouraged integrative norms within the industrial cultures of Britain and the USA. Correspondingly, a de-politicized management of industrial crises has proved impossible.

It must be emphasized that elite consensus *per se* does not facilitate effective management of industrial crises. Elite consensus about a liberal, market-oriented industrial system has, by and large, prevailed in the USA without the emergence (outside the privileged military industry complex) of a collaborative style of crisis management. It is the nature of elite consensus that is important, not its existence. It must also be emphasized that, while elite ideology and industrial culture may motivate industrial policy-makers, they are neither autonomous nor sufficient explanatory factors. The central thesis of this chapter is that the character of elite ideologies, of styles of crisis management and of industrial cultures are rooted not just in social structure and in political and legal tradition, but also in the historical conditions of industrialization. In particular, 'later' developers like France, Germany, Italy and Sweden were typically confronted by a problem of capital mobilization for industry on a scale that was qualitatively different from an 'early' developer like Britain. This problem became acute if their industrialization focused on capital-intensive and technologically sophisticated heavy industries, whose firms could not be expected to finance increasingly 'lumpy' investments from their own resources (Gerschenkron, 1965). Provision of industrial credit could not be tied to a restrictive criterion of self-financing if such industries were to be encouraged. In these cases industrial cultures were marked from an early stage by explicit or tacit acceptance of the need for specialized institutions and policies. Thus, the industrial investment banking of the Pereire brothers in France, and later Germany's 'universal' banks, provided models for other continental European societies like Italy. Germany used tax concessions for medium-term savings with banks in order to encourage long-term and large-scale bank finance for industry, while France emphasized public subsidy in order to encourage ample low-cost industrial credit. The ideological rationale of such institutions and policies was to overcome the problem of capital mobilization for industry in these countries. Another response to the problem of economic backwardness was the state's espousal of formal education as a device for mobilizing productive skills and knowledge. France, Germany and Sweden created a hierarchy of technical schools for this purpose.

Capital and skill mobilization were not seen as a problem in all branches of continental European industry, particularly in traditional craft and retail businesses where the pre-industrial values of the family firm (self-sufficiency, security and thrift) remained strong. Indeed, the strength of affective ties to the family firm as a way of life inhibited entrepreneurship, notably in France. Despite (and in part because of) the strength of these ties, the political imperative of national security, military power and economic strength ensured that heavy industries were at the forefront of the industrialization process of most 'late' developers. The prestige of elite and institutional support ensured that their practices, rather than those of the family firm, provided the model for economic development. 'Late' developers tended to evolve not only technologically oriented ideologies (like the Saint-Simonism of the Pereire brothers) but also institutions (like investment banks) and policies (like technical education) that assumed the need for organized development (whether by banks or government) of firms in strategic industries in order to tackle the problems of capital and skill mobilization. These institutions and policies were later to provide flexible and anticipatory instruments for managing industrial crises as a routine rather than exceptional aspect of the functioning of the industrial system.

In Britain and the USA political ideology, institutional development and the formation of policy networks were not as dominated by the problems of capital and skill mobilization for industry. These problems were not as central to their early industrialization. In the case of many 'late' developers, the political priority of the problems of capital and skill mobilization was the product of the alliance or collusion of the strategic interests of governments and of related private interests, for instance of the agrarian Junker-heavy industry coalition in imperial Germany. The political imperative of these problems generated an explicit, articulated moral code that attempted to inspire collaborative norms within the industrial culture. In particular, it lent a messianic quality to their elite ideologies. 'Late' developers were more likely to emphasize the moral mission of managers, bankers and the state in economic development and to espouse a Saint-Simonian conception of the importance of technique for social progress.

At the same time, the USA presents an interesting contrast to Britain. It suggests that an explanation of the character of industrial culture only in terms of the economic conditions of industrialization does insufficient justice to its complexity. Comparative absence of support for pre-industrial values from a native aristocracy provides an obvious and important contrast with Britain. Technocratic values of business rationalism were able to take deeper root, particularly in the prestigious business schools. At the same time, conditions of industrialization and traditional political ideals combined to generate a powerful tension at the heart of American industrial culture. Economic abundance offered great opportunities for expansion to new industrial corporations, so that the USA emerged as the proto-type of managerial capitalism (Chandler, 1977). It also offered opportunities for speculative development and corruption. As a consequence, the new corporations became hungry for capital and often ran into legal as well as financial difficulties. Many corporations were forced to sacrifice self-sufficiency to investment banks that specialize in mobilizing capital and were expected to bring greater order into corporate affairs. At the end of the nineteenth century the growth of large corporations was paralleled by the rise of powerful investment bankers like J. P. Morgan. The lending policies of the investment banks were, nevertheless, based on a short-term and speculative rather than long-term and managerial perspective. Despite the greater complexity of banks and corporations in the USA, finan-cial control of large corporations appears considerable compared with Britain. This financial control is also remarkably concentrated. However, the major instrument of this control after the 1930s was the trustee stock holdings of the big commercial banks like Chase Manhatten Bank, Morgan Guarantee Trust, Mellon National Bank and First National City Bank (see chapter 3, p. 95 below). By the 1970s the Chase group alone controlled over 10 per cent of the largest 200 corporations, including Boeing and TWA.

On the other hand, the entrenched political ideal of economic individualism — represented by entrepreneurial heroes like Henry Ford and the Rockefeller family — was expressed in a powerful undercurrent of cultural hostility to 'bankers' control'. A combina-tion of this hostility with an enormous variety of economic interests inhibited the development of the intimate capitalist self-organization that was characteristic of Germany. Congressional investigations, legislation (especially in the 1930s), regulation by the Securities and Exchange Commission and anti-trust litigation in the late 1940s broke the power of the investment banks and constrained that of the commercial banks. At the same time, the American economy contains a vast diversity of economic interests, and this diversity has prevented the formation of a coherent public policy towards industry. Relations between banks and industry are neither as intimate nor as mutually supportive as in West Germany. Moreover, the character of the big commercial banks like Chase Manhatten contrasts with that of the big German banks. The big American banks tend to be controlled by the descendants of the industrial capitalists (like the Rockefellers) who earlier presided over the creation of the giant corporations. They tend to be developments or extensions of corporate power. The banks did not preside over industrialization, and their entrepreneurial ambitions were inhibited by a critical and questioning public.

The relationship between political tradition and economic development in the formation of government–industry relations was clearly complex. 'State-oriented' societies like France and Germany did not derive their political tradition of priority for the role of the state simply from the process of industrialization. The heritage of Roman law and of the political process of unification in the context of threat, from home and abroad, fixed attention on the concept of state (Dyson, 1980). State was associated with an emphasis on values of unity, community and solidarity. In particular, it drew attention to the importance of a moral framework of order for society that was expressed in the development of public law and in a systematic civil law. However, the problems of capital and skill mobilization for industry gave an added dimension to concern for the state. They reinforced the 'state orientation' of 'late' developers. Conversely, the 'society orientation' of the British and American political tradition involved an emphasis on the autonomy and voluntary self-regulation of the institutions of civil society. The consequence was an ideological resistance to political identification of problems of capital and skill mobilization for industry. Their identification suggested a role for the state that clashed with the mainstream of political tradition. 'Society-oriented' governments were, therefore, likely to be poorly equipped with respect to institutions, social networks and policies to tackle industrial crises. In the face of industrial crises, they suffered from institutional and cultural disadvantages whose roots are in an inheritance of political tradition and industrial development that has tended to isolate governments and bankers from industry — and to make their crisis interventions reactive, defensive and ill-prepared. Hence, American and British industrial policies have been heavily influenced by the outcomes of crises: and both their industrial policies and their crisis interventions lack coherence of development and of presentation.

CONVERGENCE OR DIVERGENCE?

It is difficult to find evidence of convergence among advanced industrialized societies in their styles of managing industrial crises after 1973. This absence of convergence is to be understood in terms both of the different nature of the economic problems that confronted them (the objective context) and of contrasting political traditions and industrial cultures (the subjective context). In the case of Britain, there has been a poor handling of industrial crises, a lack of consensus about how they should be handled, and a large number of them. It is, however, by no means clear whether Britain's problems of managing industrial crises — ideological, institutional and cultural problems — are more a cause or consequence of poor economic performance. Management of industrial crises is shaped by a complex pattern of economic and non-economic factors, objective and subjective factors, that are interwoven and difficult, if not impossible, to disentangle. The importance of the objective context must, nevertheless, be emphasized.

Industrial Structure

The character of the problems of managing industrial crises that an industrial society faces will be greatly influenced by two objective factors: first, whether, as in the case of the USA, a large expansive domestic market provides a dynamic and vigorous environment for industry and permits an internal specialization and variety within the industrial structure, which in turn enhances flexibility and competitiveness; and, second, whether the structure of its industrial system is well fitted (like West Germany) or ill fitted (like Britain) to changing patterns of international market opportunities. Industrial crises appear as a manageable problem in societies that are characterized either by an internal 'politics of plenty' (like the USA) or by a position of dominance in world markets (like West Germany), which endows their products with a favourable image, facilitates market success and so encourages investment and innovation. By contrast, Britain's concentration of resources of capital and labour in industries that suffered from comparative disadvantage and from the lack of an expansive and large domestic market meant industrial crises on a wide and intense scale. Britain's problems of industrial adjustment were apparent as early as the 1860s. However, they were shielded and exacerbated by a concentration of trade on captive imperial markets that were neither as challenging and invigorating nor as expansive as, for instance, the West European market, which provided the context of German industrialization. All advanced industrialized societies are, of course, experiencing declining competitiveness in a growing number of sectors (ranging from textiles and footwear to bulk steel and shipbuilding) as a result of the emergence of the newly industrializing countries. However, Britain appears also at a disadvantage in its competition with other advanced industrialized societies.

Clearly, the wider the scale of industrial crises and the more intensely they are experienced, the more difficult and intractable become the problems of managing them. Structural economic decline increases the complexity of the problems of industrial adjustment and the level of conflict among interests and reduces the availability of resources to restructure industry. Industrial structure has, therefore, provided contrasting objective contexts in which industrial policy-makers have had to consider problems of managing industrial crises. For instance, the French state, and to a greater extent the Italian state, have had greater problems than German bankers in managing industrial crises, because their industrial structures have squared less adequately with patterns of international demand. The experience of Sweden in the 1970s illustrates that intense specialization in a limited range of sectors for the international economy can produce a structural 'over-commitment' that creates vulnerability to industrial crises. Also, owing to the geographical concentration of such sectors as pulp, shipbuilding and steel, structural vulnerability is intensely focused and expressed by cross-party political interest. In Sweden the sudden scale and intensity of industrial crises overwhelmed the resources of the traditional private sector mechanism of crisis management and revealed that the government was unprepared with respect to institutions, policy networks and ideology for the new issues that it confronted. The failure of the bank-led rescue of AEG in 1982, and the threat of industrial disengagement by the banks in order to prevent a banking crisis, suggested that West German government could be similarly overwhelmed by industrial crises in the 1980s. Clearly, industrial structure is immensely important for explanation of the quality of crisis management.

Britain is paying the price of early industrialization, of being the pioneer among industrial societies. Its style of crisis management continues to reflect the conditions of that industrialization and its impact on industrial culture. In Britain the pacemakers of industrialization were the small firms, whose priorities were autonomy and self-reliance. Their vitality depended on the personal skills of practical tinkerers on creative individuals, rather than on professionalized management structures. The emergence of a sturdy, individualistic spirit of self-reliance was possible because early industrialization concentrated on consumer rather than producer goods. Their production could be more easily financed out of internally generated funds (augmented by help from close personal associates and a proliferation of small local country banks) and later (mainly from the 1880s) by the addition of equity capital. On the one hand, the formal capital markets of Britain have been seen as a means of escape from the loan dependency that has been associated with the relative weakness of the equity base of many French, German and Italian firms. On the other hand, the London stock market had little experience or information on which to base an assessment of new and untried industries with growth potential like electrical engineering and chemicals and later motor vehicles (Kennedy, 1976). The institutional structure that was generated by early industrialization to raise funds was not sensitive enough to the capital requirements of the heavy industries. Lack of institutional development for capital mobilization was largely due to lack of growing demand for external finance by large firms, and this deficiency of demand was in turn influenced by a pattern of behaviour that had been established in the early phase of industrialization (Cottrell, 1980, p. 270). Britain's adaptation to the age of capital-intensive heavy industries was, therefore, hindered by a tradition of industrial self-reliance. This tradition was associated with a suspicion of state action in technical education as well as in finance for industry; and both of these fields were increasingly important ingredients of success in the emergent international industrial system.

The moral code of the autonomous, self-reliant firm was also congruent with, and gained strength from, the tradition of voluntary self-regulation that was characteristic of institutions in British society. Firms expected to organize their own affairs. Hence, to a greater extent than any other European society, Britain resisted the idea of public regulation of the decision-making structure of the firm in the manner of Germany. In particular, British firms engaged in consultation with their employees in a haphazard and irregular manner.

Managements oscillated between a hesitant, suspicious approach to industrial change and resort to dramatic *fait accompli*. Very often they found that they had to invent procedures in order to manage industrial change. In the absence of uniform and agreed rules, industrial relations comprised a bewildering variety of practices and tended to gravitate towards the confrontational style of collective bargaining (Jacobs *et al.*, 1978). The preference for private, closed decision-making structures made it difficult to co-opt trade union support at times of industrial crisis, for instance in the form of the 'crisis cartel' that managed the Saar steel crisis of 1978. British management displayed a strongly tactical, 'fire-fighting' approach to managing industrial change, an approach that gave little scope to technical values in the decision-making process.

Britain's relatively poor resources of applied technical skills, her scarcity of venture capital and her comparatively weak relations between industry, trade unions, financial institutions and government reflect, therefore, in part the character of her early industrialization and the cultural tradition that it spawned. These traditional features of the British industrial system are at the heart of Britain's contemporary problems of managing industrial crises, and are notably expressed in the disjunction between financial and industrial capital. Quite simply, the British have not learnt how to manage large industrial corporations and their complex internal and external relations effectively. The 'family capitalism' of Britain proved tenacious (Hannah, 1980). In the inter-war period and beyond, many of the major British corporations (for instance, in the steel industry) were federations of family firms under a holding-company umbrella. The consequence was parochial outlooks and inhibition of change. Despite the emergence of professionalized management structures, the management style of the corporation was that of the small firm 'writ large'. By the 1980s British managers and workers were the least professionally qualified in the EEC. Values of technological rationality and of inter-organizational collaboration found only weak representation in the administrative styles of Britain's industrial corporations, trade unions and government departments. The occasional emergence of support for technological and neo-corporatist values from the political party arena or from employer or industrial associations foundered quickly against the strength of these administrative styles: witness the fate of the Mond–Turner proposals in the 1920s, of the Labour government's commitment to a 'white-hot' technological revolution in 1964, and of the National Industrial Strategy from 1975. Successive director-generals of the National Economic

K. Dyson

Development Office (NEDO) have preached these values into a political vacuum that has been created by institutional 'parochialism' within the industrial culture.

The character of the industrial culture has also shaped the process of professionalization within management. At the level of the firm, the importance that is attached to short-term profit (in order to satisfy shareholders and to finance investment from retained earnings) has meant that accountants have tended to take precedence over engineers as a professional group, in contrast to France, Germany and Sweden: their skills are more relevant to the nature of the capitalist environment within which British industry functions. More generally, technicians are less integrated into the structure of British firms. They are usually found outside line management and follow different career structures, which emphasize loyalty to profession rather than to firm. The British employer, traditionally, was a general director who was rather narrowly concerned with financial targets and the general objective of profit and who, therefore, looked to accountants as chief advisers. By contrast, the German employer was traditionally an industrial technician. The authority of line management rested firmly on technique; organizational planning and control and man management focused on the technical requirements of production (Landes, 1960; Childs *et al.*, 1981). The respect for technical skills that was implicit in the integration of technicians into line management facilitated the consolidation of the concept of the firm as a community.

THE STATE AND THE ADAPTIVE CAPACITY
OF THE INDUSTRIAL SYSTEM

Economic structure and comparative advantage do not provide a sufficient explanation of problems of managing industrial adjustment, of vulnerability to crises and of managing crises. These problems are not simply a function of good or ill fortune. An effective relationship between industrial structure, on the one hand, and market demand and technological opportunity, on the other, will also be shaped by the adaptive capacity of the industrial system. Adaptive capacity refers to the ability to modernize industrial structure in order to become competitive in the international economy and to achieve continuing economic growth. The relationship between industrial structure and adaptive capacity is symbiotic. Inherited structures can of course inhibit strategies of adaptation, and market and technological factors can generate dramatic and radical change that may threaten to overwhelm policy-makers. At the same time, external agencies like government or financial institutions can break structural 'log-jams'. While market, technological and structural factors appear to be paramount, they do not necessarily determine the nature and timing of crisis management. The major differences among Western capitalist economies are to be understood by reference to the manner in which the external progenitors of change are mediated by institutional structures and policy styles.

Adaptive capacity in the interests of international competitiveness and economic growth raises a hornets' nest of problems, some of which are considered in the final chapter. Here, the focus is on the political contribution to adaptive capacity of the industrial system. In Western Europe adaptive capacity is strongly influenced by the 'subjective world' of attitudes towards industrial organization. Adaptive capacity is clearly encouraged by an industrial culture that supports a high valuation of economic logic in political and industrial argument, as reflected in managerial arrangements based on respect for technical function. It is also encouraged by simultaneous support for values of collaboration, as reflected for instance in corporatist arrangements for 'social partnership' that aim at an acceptable distribution of the costs of industrial adjustment. Pursuit of economic efficiency is threatened by the prospect of a political counter-attack on 'technocracy' and gains greater acceptability if flanked by political concern for problems of social justice and consent. Industrial cultures encourage 'positive' adaptation if they favour arrangements for decision-making within the firm (such as the West German 'codetermination'), and for reorganization of firms in crisis (as in French and German composition procedures), that recognize the right of various social interests to participate in corporate policy. The attempt to achieve a greater representation of external interests in corporate decision-making through the appointment of non-executive directors in Britain has proved of little importance. They have been 'ornamental' directors who lack the access to levers of power that are possessed by French public officials or German bankers. Technocratic and corporatist values exist in a complex state of tension. On the one hand, the macroeconomic orientation of technocracy supports the collaborative norms of corporatism. On the other hand, corporatism's technocratic face creates fears that 'fair' distribution will be sacrificed to the economic rationality of capitalism (Esser and Fach, 1979).

Adaptive capacity of the industrial system depends in particular on the extent to which the macroeconomic costs of industrial adjustment are shouldered by public authorities or other supra-firm institutions and the social costs of industrial adjustment are correspondingly reduced. Other advanced industrialized societies have been notably more successful than Britain in taking the 'related costs' of industrial adjustment from the individual firm — for instance, by the provision of social capital like technical education and training or of cheap long-term credit for industry. The consequence has been a more flexible and a more optimistic attitude within industry. Their corporatist and technocratic industrial cultures acquire a more human face. Thus Sweden pioneered the 'active' labour market policy to provide extensive retraining and to promote occupational and regional mobility in the interests of a 'socially responsible' modernization. France gave priority to subsidized credit for industry, while West Germany pursued reconstruction by reliance on the traditional expertise and contacts of its banks.

The continental European tradition of 'mixed' or 'universal' banking has meant that commercial banks are much more important actors in the management of industrial crises than in Britain or even the USA. In contrast to the specialized banking system of Britain, their multi-purpose commercial banks combine retail deposit banking with investment banking. Correspondingly, their financial interests are closely and directly interwoven with those of industry. Banks like Société Générale in France or the Deutsche Bank in Germany take an active, selective and long-term interest in the fortunes of a cluster of important industrial firms. They regard it as their duty to organize comprehensive rescue operations. The provision of long-term credit to industry is combined with the issuing of shares of, and floating of debenture loans for, the forms concerned. According to Riesser (1910, p. 364), the active role of the banks in the capital market was 'the keystone of the vast structure of industrial relations between banks and industry' in Germany. Banks may also function as major shareholders in key firms, and — particularly important in Germany — have representatives on their supervisory boards. Hence, when faced with a massive problem of postwar reconstruction, West German government built upon the established industrial knowledge of the commercial banks by augmenting their activities through the new Reconstruction Loan Corporation (Kreditanstalt für Wiederaufbau). The Reconstruction Loan Corporation was entrusted with the value of money represented by Marshall Aid and was expected to act as a bankers' bank. The commercial banks were the channel for sifting claims on its behalf and making recommendations for low-cost loans. In this ingenious way the strengths of the banks were put to best effect. The banks were also a central part of a 'multi-tiered system of long-term export finance', which included central bank provision of cheap credit lines for export accounts to the commercial banks and the banks' own consortium, the Export Credit Company (Ausfuhrkreditgesellschaft, AKA), in a concerted export promotion (Hankel, 1975, p. 117). Under political pressure from the Social Democratic Party in the 1970s, and with the support of the Federal Research and Technology Ministry, the banks established the German Risk Financing Company (Deutsche Wagnisfinanzierungs-Gesellschaft) to assist innovation by new small and medium-sized firms. In short, the German banks have established themselves as channels that can deal comprehensively with the problems that are faced by their industrial clients. British banks have moved in this direction in the 1970s, to some extent with official prompting. They have acquired merchant banking interests, participated in the government's new loan guarantee programme for small businesses, and established 'intensive care' units. During the early 1980s it became also clear that some German banks, notably the Dresdner, were trying to reduce some of their industrial shareholdings from fear of over-exposure. Such evidence of convergence must, however, be seen against the context of the different traditional assumptions of British and German bankers, particularly with respect to crisis management.

Historically, the contribution of the 'universal' banks has been double-edged. On the credit side, the banks could be invaluable channels of wealth into heavy industry, especially when the supply of capital was limited or hard to mobilize with respect to increasingly sophisticated and costly technology. By their policy of supporting the shares of firms for which they acted as banker they could have a stabilizing influence. Banks could help firms in new and high-risk growth sectors to weather short-term storms and to maintain a long-term perspective. Thus, in the growth sector of electronics in the late nineteenth and early twentieth centuries, Siemens enjoyed the close support of the Deutsche Bank, and AEG gained the support of Deutsche's rivals. The Deutsche Bank maintained its close involvement in the Mannesman steel products corporation from its troubled early days through to its phase of huge success. The promotive role of banks in industry meant that investment decisions were motivated less by considerations of short-term profit and early returns than by mobilization of financial and technical resources to secure market share and to improve the long-term cost structure of the firm. Helped by the industrial expertise, contacts and wide range of services of its *Hausbank* (literally, 'house bank'), a firm could expand easily and more easily sustain adversity without direct government intervention (witness Krupp in 1967 and AEG in the 1970s). West Germany's big three banks — Deutsche, Dresdner and Commerzbank — undertake analysis of the profit rates within different sectors of industry as the basis of their industrial lending decisions. The traditional flexibility of lending criteria, informal methods of risk assessment and concern with formal 'security' in British banking contrast with the reliance of German banks on their intelligence departments for assessment both of the 'standing' of a firm in relation to industry, area and national averages and of the relation of a particular loan to 'bank strategy' (Economists Advisory Group, 1981, pp. 197–9). Consequently, compared with Britain, government is better insulated by a de-politicized system of self-organization of capital from the difficult process of managing industrial crises and, in particular, from the tortuous problems of reconciling the 'high' and 'low' politics of crisis management (a problem that is returned to in the final chapter). The 'bank-oriented' system of external finance also reduces reliance on the takeover bid as a solution to a firm's problems. The role of the takeover bid within American and British business practice reflects the importance of the stock market. This 'sledgehammer' method of enforcing corporate change contrasts with the continuing and active role of German banks in financial advice and executive recruitment.

On the debit side, the banking system itself could become highly exposed and vulnerable to crises if the banks over-extended their illiquid industrial credits during booms and failed to diversify these credits. Industrial crises can rapidly escalate into a spectacular financial crisis and provoke the entry of the state to rescue both banks and industry, as in Italy in 1933. The great achievement of British banking has been the pursuit of a type of banking that avoided financial crisis. At the same time, their 'arm's length' approach to industry has weakened the system of industrial crisis management. Finance for Industry (1981), the leading British institution for long-term industrial finance, has emphasized the dangers that are implicit in the higher level of gearing in continental Europe than in Britain; the equity of British companies rarely falls below 50 per cent of total assets (a debt-equity ratio of 1:1). During protracted recession firms find themselves with a heavy burden of debt interest; and banks face the dilemma of whether to disengage from 'loan-dependent' firms and to risk political unpopularity for the sake of short-term financial caution or to rescue firms and to risk their own financial crisis for the sake of long-term economic interest. The economic anxiety that pervades countries with a tradition of investment banking is in part to be understood by reference to a historical experience of the rapid escalation of industrial crises into a financial crisis of the banking system. Thus Austria and West Germany combined comparatively successful industrial performance in the 1970s with an anxiety about industrial crises that had more to do with their potential financial effects than their contemporary scale and severity. 'Organized capitalism' is especially vulnerable to the 'knock-on' effects of industrial crises. Of course, there is not an inevitable escalation of industrial crises into bank crisis in these countries. Banks that are effective capital-mobilizers may be efficient capital-allocators (like the Deutsche Bank) or inefficient capital-allocators (like Austria's Länderbank, which had to be rescued by the state in 1981). As in the early 1980s in West Germany, banks may become more cautious about bold private sector solutions for corporations in crisis. Their greater reluctance to take risks was reflected in a partial disengagement from shareholdings (notably by Dresdner) and by their concentration on preservation of the viable parts of such corporations by finding strong industrial partners for them (for example, the involvement of Grundig, Bosch and Mannesmann in a potentially profitable part of AEG's operations).

Management of industrial crises is also shaped by the internal politics of industry itself. In Austria, Switzerland and West Germany branch industrial associations and chambers of trade and industry (in which membership is compulsory) are often capable of acting as instruments of risk reduction, and thereby encourage long-term investment horizons. They encourage a 'competitive equilibrium' among their members, an industrial culture of support for the idea of an industrial 'common good' and the emergence of industrial statesmen. The past character of state action has been particularly important to the development of this sense of industrial solidarity. Thus when, as in Germany and Switzerland in the late nineteenth century, the state resorted to protection at time of crisis, industrial associations were strengthened by government's need for detailed information about individual sectors. Industrial associations have attracted the support of their members not just because of their protective and regulatory functions, but also because they developed functions that supplemented the market (such as research and development). Self-organization of industry gives industrial associations a potential to coordinate an intra-industry adjustment that shifts resources from uncompetitive to competitive products of an industry (Ackerman and Steinmann, 1981). By contrast, in Britain and the USA the development of industrial associations has been impeded by the cultural tradition of the self-sufficient firm (witness the withdrawal of GEC, one of Britain's most important industrial corporations, from its branch industrial association in 1981). Corresponding to this tradition has been the absence of a substantial history of government's use of these associations to manage industry. The formation of the British Iron and Steel Federation in 1934 as a government-sponsored cartel appears at first sight an exception. However, it failed to achieve even a minimal amount of collaboration in reducing the costs of the industry. In the USA the strength of political support for anti-trust legislation ruled out the possibility of 'crisis cartels' and thereby worked against the development of powerful industrial associations. Against the background of industrial culture, American and British industrial associations did not acquire the wide range of functions and the integrative role that would have enabled them to preside over an intra-industry adjustment.

In France, crisis management was influenced by the emergence of large industrial groups (like Saint Gobain) that were tied together by very powerful financial holding companies and a complex of interlocking directorates. Their rationale was the requirement of external finance. These financial holding companies served to spread the impact of industrial crises and to shelter firms by assistance from other members of the group. More generally, the rise of the large multi-divisional corporation has meant that intra-firm adjustment has assumed increasing importance for management of industrial crises. Conglomerates function as mini-capital and mini-labour markets and identify their interests less with a particular product or industry and more with survival and expansion. Changes of demand or of cost structure are likely to encourage them to change their self-conception. Thus in the 1970s oil companies sought to transform their image to that of 'raw materials' or energy companies. Conglomerates like General Electric in the USA are able to meet or prevent crises by internal shifts of their product mix towards new sectors. In Germany intra-firm adjustment has exhibited a paternal concern for a 'core workforce' of skilled, male German workers. In this case it is possible to identify a paternal system of 'welfare corporatism' in large firms that attempt to guarantee lifetime employment based on an intra-enterprise career and training system, formal mechanisms for employee participation, and the continuous nurturing of corporate loyalty and culture. By contrast, large firms in Britain have tended to cling to a market-oriented employment system that is premised on the mobility of employment and a limited commitment of the worker to the firm. Unlike in Austria, Switzerland and West Germany, the social costs of industrial adjustment are not assumed to be a prime responsibility of the firm. Intra-firm adjustment is more likely to be delayed or even prevented by the priority of loyalties to class, craft or trade rather than to the firm as an organic, evolving community. In such a context the development of trade unions did not focus on the firm or industry. They sought to further the welfare of their members through political means that aimed at the creation and extension of the 'welfare state' as an alternative to a 'welfare corporatism' that found little support within management.

Management of industrial crises is further facilitated by the existence of social networks. These networks transcend the boundaries of institutions and provide a capacity to anticipate and communicate crises, to respond to them with carefully designed packages of policy measures, and to monitor the implementation of these packages. Firms gain access to a continuous and systematic flow of information and advice. In France the efficiency of the informal and pervasive practice of administrative guidance rests in large part on an intricate social network that is united by the assumption that government must play a guiding role in industrial affairs. Members of the elite *grands corps*, notably finance inspectors and engineers, transfer to senior managerial posts in public and private corporations and in banks while maintaining their official contacts through retention of membership of their corps. This practice of *pantouflage* provides a network of close personal relations between government, banks and industry that has no parallel in Britain and the USA. Even during the period of Giscard d'Estaing's 'organized liberalism', the private banks were drawn into government's discussion of rescue plans for various firms. After the election of a Socialist president, Francois Mitterand, and a Socialist majority in the Assembly in 1981, the nationalization of 36 of these banks was seen as a device to force a closer interest of the banks in the management of industrial crises. West Germany lacks such a close social network based on the public service. In its place is the intimate bank–industry nexus, which contrasts with the 'arm's length' relationship between bankers and industrialists in Britain, and which functions to keep government out of industrial crises (witness Krupp in the 1960s and AEG in the 1970s). In Britain it is rare for full-time clearing bankers to serve as part-time directors of companies. Clearing banks seek information about developments in industry by inviting full-time directors of companies to become part-time members of their boards (Economists Advisory Group, 1981). In West Germany in 1975 the private commercial banks held 179, or 14.9 per cent, of the seats on the supervisory boards of the top 100 companies (notably in chemicals, engineering, metals and construction). Only 25 of these companies had no bank representative, and in 31 cases a bank provided the chairman (Dyson, 1982). Of the 66 large companies examined by the Gessler Commission, 59 had bank representatives on the board and 51 had more than one representative. The voting rights of the banks (including proxy voting rights) amounted to 26 per cent of the total in the top 100 companies. However, the influence of German banks on crisis management is a consequence of seats on supervisory boards rather than of their shareholdings. Banks are subject to strong pressures to display solidarity with management. They experience greater involvement with 'their' firms and are useful not just for their financial advice but also because they provide a network for recruitment of senior executives.

Large firms in France, Italy, Sweden and West Germany are closely interlocked with other institutions. Their decision-making structures are penetrated by public officials, bankers or trade unionists; and on occasion these external actors may have an incentive to collaborate to safeguard their mutual interests in a firm. Thus a firm's *Hausbank* may insist on a social plan as a condition for its loans and thereby promote the role of the trade unions. The effectiveness of institutional interlocking and penetration of decision-making structures for crisis management depends on the capacity of the 'inner circle' to provide market leadership. West German bankers and the French state have proved better able to offer such leadership and inspire confidence than the faction-ridden networks of Christian Democratic patronage in Italy. Large firms in Britain and the USA are also involved in a complex web of direct, informal contacts to politicians and officials at many levels and especially at times of crisis. In particular, they have become conscious of the importance of the 'government relations' function in order to coordinate their external contacts. However, outside the privileged defence sector, the cultural and institutional context of the interaction of government and industry has precluded the development of the kind of social network that has facilitated management of industrial crises in France and West Germany. The emergence of the 'government relations' function in the form of specialized units within firms has been a substitute for membership of such a social network, an advertisement for the problem of access to government that firms experience. At the same time, firms have not developed the German form of capitalist self-organization that bypasses the need for state action by provision of a private sector capacity for crisis intervention. The importance of the interlocking directorships of British merchant banks was always reduced by their traditional 'arm's length' relationship to firms and by their limitations of function and scale. Britain has not developed a sophisticated system of 'political self-government of capital' (Ronge, 1980) as an effective alternative to state intervention. Financial institutions have maintained a distance from industry, an attitude of professional detachment, rather than the managerial engagement that parallels the character of government–industry relations.

Debate about the degree of difference between bank–industry relations in Britain and continental Europe (especially West Germany) has been intensified by protracted recession and has involved counter-allegations. Indeed, as early as 1911 the British clearing banks were being criticized for 'failing' industry (Cottrell, 1980, p. 236). Observers like Landes (1960) and Shonfield (1965) have emphasized the managerial engagement of German bankers in contrast to the closed world of British bankers. More recently, this contrast has been rejected as an oversimplification (Economists Advisory Group, 1981). This re-evaluation reflects in part the political problems that have been faced by the banks in both countries in the 1970s. In West Germany economic recession and industrial crises like AEG have 'exposed' the industrial power (real or potential) of the banks and forced them to disclaim publicly the existence of such power. Emphasis has been placed on the low involvement of the German banks in direct shareholdings in industry and on variations of this involvement across sectors. In Britain, economic recession and industrial crises like Stone Platt engineering in 1982 seemed to 'expose' the lack of bank support for firms in crisis and invited unfavourable contrasts with Germany. British banks feared that their lack of an active industrial role could become a major political issue and could reinforce demands for their public ownership. Hence they sought publicity for the changes that had taken place in the relationship between banks and industry since the 1960s. In part, the re-evaluation of the contrast between British and German banking reflects a changed reality of closer links with industry in Britain. The greater involvement of banks in corporate finance began in the 1960s as a consequence of increasing competition from foreign banks in the City for corporate customers (especially in the development of North Sea oil) and as a response to government's concern for the requirements of higher productivity and growth. In particular, the property and secondary banking crisis of 1974 encouraged the clearing banks to establish corporate rescue units. Barclays Bank formed a special headquarters team of about 40 people who, by summer 1982, were handling approximately 600 rescues (of which about 15 per cent involved direct regular contact). In summer 1982 the Midland Bank, traditionally the bank closest to industry, had 70 companies in the intensive care unit of its corporate finance division. Eleven of these companies (with 35,000 employees) had no prospect of early improvement. In the face of this problem the Midland Bank took the unusual step of announcing that it had done all that it could for them by restructuring of loans and deferred payments on capital, and that their survival depended on government loan guarantees (see chapter 5 below). Both Barclays and the Midland had to double their provision for bad and doubtful debts in the first half of 1982. These new procedures, and the new emphasis on debt conversion rather than receivership as a cure for corporate crises, were a response to pressures from the Bank of England for a 'responsible', caring attitude by the banks and to the dangerous political exposure that they gained from cases of receivership (like Midland Bank and Stone Platt in 1982). Political reactions to the banks' 'neglect' of industry could range from calls for extra taxation of bank profits to demands for public ownership. Also, receivership was often not an attractive option for banks; when industrial assets were at a low level, buyers were more difficult to find.

The image of British banking changed in the 1970s. They appeared to shift towards the model of 'universal' banking. Clearing banks developed or acquired merchant banks, engaged in more term lending, leasing and factoring and formed corporate finance divisions and intensive care units. Nevertheless, the 'arm's length' tradition remained intact in the sphere of industrial crisis management. The intensive care units depended on the initiative of local bank managers and found that referrals of crisis were typically late so that their room for manoeuvre was limited. Crisis management by the banks continued to lack the close personal contacts to industry that were enjoyed by German bankers through membership of supervisory boards.

Despite the greater prominence that was given by British clearing banks to corporate finance, the provision of this function took place in a pluralistic framework that required complex negotiation and great patience by firms. Corporate finance in Britain was traditionally characterized by a division of labour between small merchant banks like Lazard Brothers, Hambros and Hill Samuel and big clearing banks. Neither provided the comprehensive range of services of the German *Hausbank*, although both have tried to broaden the range of their corporate finance activities since the 1960s. Traditionally, the big clearing banks provided overdrafts for short-term financing and, to a lesser extent, term loans: the merchant banks handled new equity issues and provided or organized loans. Both types of bank avoided taking up equity holdings, although merchant banks like Lazard Brothers established grapevines by accumulation of directorships. Even then, the merchant banks were late in the formal development of their corporate finance function and were unprepared or unwilling to adopt a role of market leadership, for instance by assuming a responsibility for technological diffusion.

The fragmentation of the corporate finance function, coupled with the 'arm's length' relationship between clearing banks and industry and political pressures for assistance to industry, prompted the Bank of England into a more important role in industrial crisis management than had been played or needed to be played by the Bundesbank in West Germany. Also, the traditionally close links between the merchant banks (with their company directorships) and the Bank of England (whole Governor usually has a background in merchant banking) has made the central bank more conscious of the problems of industrial crisis management. Hence during the 1930s Montagu Norman, Governor of the Bank, sought to encourage the clearing banks to play a role in the reconstruction of basic industries like steel and shipbuilding. The Bank itself rescued Armstrong Whitworth. Similarly, during the late 1970s under Gordon Richardson, a former merchant banker, the Bank increased its concern for industrial finance (an executive director was appointed with this function) and attempted a 'discreet orchestration' of the financial institutions in the form of *ad hoc* 'industrial lifeboats' (for example in the case of Laker Airways). Restructuring plans for sectors like steel castings and iron foundries were prepared: Lazard Brothers played an important role in these negotiations. The Bank put pressure also on the big pension funds and life assurance companies, which had preferred to take a 'backseat' role. Their involvement in the firms in which they had a financial interest was typically aloof, pragmatic and concerned with the good character rather than the technical efficiency of their management. In 1982 the Bank's approach was apparent in the establishment of Sheffield Forgemasters as a new joint venture to rationalize special steels. Under the orchestration of the Bank, the government, British Steel, City institutions and the clearing banks provided finance for this restructuring.

CONCLUSIONS

There is little evidence of convergence of mechanisms of crisis management. Management of industrial crises exhibits the closest features cross-nationally in the realm of national security. Here interests of state are readily recognized. Governments are prepared to take a more active interest and to develop close personal relations with corporations in defence and defence-related industries. As in the cases of Douglas and Lockheed, governments are willing to take exceptional measures, measures that in the USA would normally be labelled 'socialist'. More generally, emphasis on the self-sufficiency of the firm in American and British industrial culture helps to explain differences in the language of industrial crisis management as well as the lack of inter-organizational collaboration. Such is the aversion to 'interference' at the level of the firm that crisis interventions cannot be readily accepted as a technical issue. Crisis interventions are characterized as 'rescues' or 'bale-outs', terms that suggest force of circumstance rather than planned, rational action. By contrast, the German *Sanierung* (reorganization) is a more neutral term, which evokes an image of collaborative effort in a technical (*sachlich*) exercise of restructuring industry. In the absence of the high cultural valuation of the self-sufficient firm, the language of industrial crisis is less distinguished by emotive, even pejorative, terms which may, as in the British case, serve to drive out technical analysis of problems of industrial adjustment.

The problems of crisis management that confront an industrial society can be understood only very partially by reference to social networks and inter-organizational collaboration between 'key' firms and institutions that have a capacity for market leadership. The relationship between inherited industrial structure and the international market will determine the load of cases that face policy-makers. As in Italy, Sweden and Britain, a high and escalating load means increasing intellectual complexity, greater problems of bargaining, and diminishing resources for effective response. Even a sophisticated social network as in France is subject to the usual vagaries of human communication, including organizational and personal interest, and a tendency to specialization and factionalism as the industrial system grows in complexity. Nevertheless, social networks can facilitate a more precise handling of industrial crises, a form of crisis management that is more likely to anticipate and lead events in the market-place. Social networks help to overcome the forces of organizational inertia and to achieve a broad mobilization of resources for crisis management.

Management of industrial crises has revealed the extent to which government, banking and both sides of industry in Britain function as separate spheres. This separation is to be understood by reference both to a political tradition that has emphasized organizational differentiation and voluntarism and to the pattern of industrialization and its legacy of the self-sufficient firm. Circumstances of economic history (notably reliance on capital accumulation rather than capital mobilization) and the character of political and administrative ideologies have combined to prevent the establishment of a policy network, whether French- or German-style, that rests on an interlocking between firms and institutions that are capable of market leadership. In the absence of such a policy network, and constrained by a political tradition and moral code of organizational self-regulation, government has not been able to establish itself as a reliable and competent partner of industry or to work with and through the banks to shape industrial decision-making. Industrial leaders have often favoured government intervention: for instance, the 'rationalization' movement of the 1920s and 1930s aimed to achieve state support for a system of industrial self-government and planning; the 'modernization' movement of the 1960s focused on central industrial planning (through the new Department of Economic Affairs' ill-fated National Plan of 1965) and restructuring of industry (through the activities of the new Ministry of Technology and of the Industrial Reorganization Corporation); and the 'regeneration' movement of the mid-1970s sought to draw greater attention to the detailed problems of industrial sectors into the annual budgets of the Treasury through the mechanism of the National Industrial Strategy. However, they wanted government action on terms of 'intervention without interference', which were likely to prove self-defeating. An 'arm's length' intervention limited government's capacity to learn from experience and to achieve the precise, light touch of the French *grands corps.* Despite a secular increase of selective intervention in the 1970s, British industrial policy-makers have not learnt from an 'experience curve' of intervention in the manner of the French state or German bankers. Hence, industry's experience of government, especially in the 1930s and 1960s and 1970s, consolidated the traditional idea that the firm must depend on its own resources. The central, and mutually reinforcing, supports of Britain's industrial order have, therefore, been the autonomy and self-sufficiency of the firm and the perceived incompetence and unreliability of government. This industrial order has been periodically disturbed by the continuing failure of British firms to compete successfully in world and domestic markets, only to be reconsolidated by the ineffectiveness of government. The complex of industrial and official attitudes that underpin the industrial order have frustrated organizational development for crisis management. France's sophisticated network of inter-ministerial committees — linked by the Trésor — have no real parallel in Britain.

From one perspective, Britain's industrial culture appears to embody a worthy moral code of stubborn independence that has withstood the test of time longer than its temporarily more 'successful' competitors. Britain's industrial culture has been shaped by a process of development of the capitalist economy different from that of most other industrial societies. However, it is not merely a reflex of that distinctive economic development. Britain's industrial culture derives its historical strength and resilience from its embodiment of a political tradition that predates industrialization. From another perspective, Britain's industrial culture is characterized by institutional and cultural inertia and paralysis of policy-making and implementation. Industrial culture has failed to keep pace with rapidly changing economic and industrial problems despite alarm signals and proposals for reform that go back to the 1860s. The symptoms of the 'British disease' include intellectual muddle and puzzlement and lack of institutional development. By contrast, France and West Germany display a consistent approach and possess sophisticated policy instruments for intervention. The peculiar character of the 'British disease' lies not simply in structural factors (see pp. 46–50 above) but also in the nature of elite accommodation, political tradition of public authority and the conditions of industrialization. In particular, early industrialization did not offer a challenge of capital mobilization that could 'force' collective industrial responses. Later industrial problems of adjustment could not be easily surmounted by institutional development in the absence of a political tradition that intimated 'activist' government (as in France) or collaborative arrangements of neo-corporatism (as in West Germany). The intractability of the 'British disease' was the product of the gulf between the objective nature of contemporary industrial problems on the one hand, and the responses from government and from within capitalism on the other. These responses are conditioned by the cultural mould that has been created by political tradition and process of industrialization.

Ideologies of government–industry relations and industrial culture reflect and support patterns of behaviour that are no longer in touch with contemporary problems. These problems are capital mobilization for industry and access to world markets. Yet neither government nor capital itself is willing or able to organize capital mobilization on a large scale or to develop an active, aggressive negotiation of access to world markets. The obstacles to tackling these problems lie within an industrial culture that rejects the conception that 'outsiders' (government, bankers and unions), who do not 'understand' industry, should 'interfere' in decisions that are properly a matter for management. Britain's policy-makers are entrapped not just within political tradition (Shonfield, 1965; Dyson, 1980), but also within an inheritance of industrial culture that accords conceptual priority to the self-sufficiency of the firm. Development of a capacity for an anticipatory management of industrial crises would, of course, require more than a major change in the terms of political debate about industrial policy. There would have to be a willingness to confront the economic and social costs of the self-sufficient firm and to shoulder heavy short-term political costs for the long-term task of transforming industrial culture.

REFERENCES

Ackermann, C. and Steinmann, W. (1981), *Strukturen des Schweizerischen Verbändestaats*, Zürich, ETH.
Armstrong, J. A. (1973), *The European Administrative Elite*, Princeton, New Jersey, Princeton University Press.
Chandler, A. D. (1977), *The Visible Hand*, Cambridge Massachusetts, Harvard University Press.
Childs, J. *et al.*, 'Corporate Goals, Managerial Objectives and Organisational Structures in British and West German Companies', *Organisational Studies*, 2, 1-32.
Cottrell, P. L. (1980), *Industrial Finance 1830-1914*, London, Methuen.
Dyson, K. H. F. (1980), *The State Tradition in Western Europe*, Oxford, Martin Robertson.
Dyson, K. H. F. (1982), 'West Germany: The Search for a Rationalist Consensus', in J. Richardson (ed.), *Policy Styles in Western Europe*, London, Allen and Unwin.
Economists Advisory Group (1981), *The British and German Banking Systems: A Comparative Study*, London, Anglo-German Foundation.
Esser, J. and Fach, W. (1979), *Konfliktregulierung durch Kartellbildung: Die Stahlkrise an der Saar*, Berlin, Wissenschaftszentrum.
Esser, J., Fach, W. and Vath, W. (1978), 'Die sozialen Kosten einer modernisierten Volkswirtschaft', *Politische Vierteljahresschrift*, no. 9, 140-68.

Finance for Industry (1981), *The Capital Structure of Industry in Europe*, London, Finance for Industry.

Gerschenkron, A. (1965), *Economic Backwardness in Historical Perspective*, New York, Praeger.

Grant, W. (1982), *The Political Economy of Industrial Policy*, London, Butterworth.

Hankel, W. (1975), *Der Ausweg aus der Krise*, Düsseldorf, Econ.

Hannah, L. (1980), 'Visible and Invisible Hierarchies in Great Britain', in A. Chandler and H. Daems (eds), *Managerial Hierarchies*, Cambridge Massachusetts, Harvard University Press.

Jacob, S. E. *et al.*, (1978), *Approaches to Industrial Change in Britain and Germany*, London, Anglo-German Foundation.

Kennedy, W. P. (1976), 'Institutional Response to Economic Growth: Capital Markets in Britain to 1914', in L. Hannah (ed.), *Management Strategy and Business Development: an Historical Comparative Study*, London, Macmillan.

Landes, D. S. (1960), *The Structure of Enterprise in the Nineteenth Century: The Cases of Britain and Germany*, Berkeley, California, Institute of Industrial Relations.

Riesser, E. (1910), *Die Deutschen Grossbanken und ihre Konzentration*, Jena.

Ronge, V. (1980) (ed.), *Am Staat vorbei*, Frankfurt, Campus.

Scharpf, F. W. (1980), *Beschäftigungsorientierte Strukturpolitik*, Berlin, Wissenschaftszentrum.

Schmücker, T. (1976) 'Die Unternehmung als Interessenverbund: Theorie und Realität', *Betriebswirtschaftliche Forschung und Praxis* no. 1, 13–26.

Shonfield, A. (1965), *Modern Capitalism*, Oxford University Press.

Wiener, M. (1981), *English Culture and the Decline of the Industrial Spirit 1850–1980*, London, Cambridge University Press.

3

Market Ideology and Corporate Power: The United States

Martin Edmonds

> Each corporate crisis has to be assessed on its merits, political and economic. . . . This unpolicy has worked rather well.
>
> *T. Murphy, President, General Motors*

The United States is distinguished from other advanced Western industrial societies by scale, history and, above all, ideological emphasis. Its economy generates a gross domestic product roughly equivalent to the combined total of Japan, West Germany, France and Britain; it is almost twice that of the Soviet Union. It has a domestic market that alone is sufficiently large not only to enable US industry and commerce to operate at an optimal level, but also to treat exports as a bonus to normal business operations. The scale of domestic production immediately places US manufacturers in an advantageous competitive position in world markets, especially in high capital-intensive, high value added products such as computers, aircraft and heavy machinery.

In a wider, and more political, perspective it might be preferable to see the USA as the amalgam of 50 separate state economies, each with its own gross domestic income and expenditure pattern, and legislative, executive and judicial machinery. Moreover, some states, such as New York, California and Texas, generate a domestic product in excess of that of most of the world's independent states, including many in Europe. The 50 states of the union exercise varying degrees of economic, fiscal and political independence from the federal government, and it is only the provisions in the US constitution and statutory law, which provide for regulation and uniformity of practice and policy between and within them, that enables discussion and analysis of either an economy or an industrial policy of the USA as a single entity. The interventionary dispositions of the various state governments range from activist programmes of industrial promotion to a strictly free market approach. Analysis of industrial policy in such a federal system poses many problems, resolved here by restricting discussion to the federal level.

The size of the US economy has significant implications for the structure of the US economy and, in particular, for its industrial sector. For example, the US home market has afforded extensive opportunity for business enterprises to take advantage of economies of scale, both from mass production and from amortizing research and development costs over large production runs. Consequently, there has been a persistent tendency towards a high concentration of industrial and economic power, a trend that, despite fears of the economic and political implications, has increased markedly over the past three decades. This concentration has also focused increasingly on a handful of larger states, thus distorting the distribution of power and influence within the political system.

A distinction has been drawn between the percentage share of output enjoyed by a small number of the largest firms in specific US industries — market concentration — and the degree of control that a number of large corporations exercise over more than one industry, product or market — aggregate concentration (Adams, 1971). Market concentration has changed little over the past 20 years, while the level of aggregate concentration has steadily moved upwards following the pattern of corporate mergers during the 1960s and 1970s. Of significance, however, is the tendency for large corporations to merge with, or to acquire, enterprises in other industries, which explains why aggregate concentration has steadily increased and market concentration has remained relatively stable. Hence US industry has seen the emergence of 'conglomerate' corporations, with enormous economic power and influence, yet which are not necessarily either monopolist or oligopolist. None the less, through interlocking interests the extent of aggregate concentration within certain US industries is greater than merely the number of corporations within them would suggest.

The structure of US industry is especially relevant to the specific question of policy towards industrial crises. A structure that comprises large, diverse industrial corporations, each with extensive economic power, is less likely to generate situations of crisis proportions, excite widespread public interest or create excessive concern. The explanation is self-evident, and well reflects US attitudes towards business enterprise and economic management: large, diverse and heterogeneous US corporations with interests spanning numerous industrial sectors have the influence or resources either to look to their own salvation or to shift operations internally to more profitable areas. For this reason, high aggregate concentration has become accepted in the USA, especially when the advantages of scale, flexibility and adaptability can offset ideological concerns to curb monopolies, cartels and trusts. The conglomerates correspondingly project an image of social responsibility, of working in the public interest and not merely to maximize profits (Galbraith, 1971, pp. 119–35).

The trend towards conglomeration also has its disadvantages. Where US industries have declined, or their products have ceased to be competitive or profitable, it is the smaller companies that have been vulnerable and borne the brunt of the cycle. It is they who have found themselves in financial difficulty, forced to file for bankruptcy or ceased to operate. Over the past 15 years, the number of US businesses filing for bankruptcy increased to a point where the bankruptcy courts could no longer cope. In 1975 Congress was obliged to report on the situation and in 1977 it introduced legislation to change and simplify bankruptcy laws. Although the economic recession during the 1970s contributed to the annual 35–45 per cent increase in business failures, the shift towards aggregate concentration hastened the process.

While such magnitude brings certain rewards and promotes efficiency of scale, where it accompanies market concentration it encourages inflexibility and a vulnerability to industrial decline. Those corporations that dominate the market tend to think that, by their own efforts, their market influence and the injection of capital, they can halt the decline or ride out the situation; invariably, their confidence proves ill-founded, but their collapse disrupts the industry of which they were a major part.

It is fortuitous, perhaps, that the level of market concentration in the USA is relatively small; were this not the case, many industrial sectors would be vulnerable to the scylla of monopoly control and the charybdis of bankruptcy. Industries in which there tends to be high market concentration are those of a more traditional nature, which require heavy capital investment. Depending on how industries are defined, those with high market concentration include locomotives, airframe and aero-engine manufacture, telephone apparatus, steam turbines, railways, steel and motor cars. Many corporations in these sectors have, in recent years, attempted to diversify or balance contracts between the commercial market place and government work. The distinction here is the steady cash flow generated by government work, despite its comparatively low profit margins.

THE PHILOSOPHICAL BASIS OF INTERVENTION

The distinctive structure of the US economy and domestic market, which features huge corporations spanning horizontally across industries more than vertically within an industry, reflects an age-old paradox in American ideology. On the one hand, the philosophy is one of freedom and equality of opportunity, free enterprise and the economic logic of the market. Bankruptcy and failure is merely the formal process of recording that, either through inefficiency or because the market no longer exists, or both, a business enterprise is no longer viable. The 1978 Bankruptcy Act is stringent in specifying the circumstances and conditions under which companies may or may not trade, despite opposition from the credit industry who maintain that it is too weak. Within this philosophy, deep-rooted in the American folklore of how their political economy should function, there is no such thing as an industrial 'crisis' *per se*. Any sectoral decline, corporation bankruptcy or industrial collapse is the natural outcome of immutable economic laws, and consistent with the philosophy of the American 'system'.

There is just as deep-rooted a conviction that, in order to guarantee free enterprise, the operation of the market and the opportunity for all citizens to enter the market, the constitution has to lay down certain ground rules, and the three branches of government have to ensure that these basic requirements are respected and enforced. However, since these principles were codified, two hundred years ago, the US political economy has expanded, the market has widened, products have become more complex, and industrial and business practices have become more sophisticated. The ground rules necessarily have had to be constantly both emphasized and modified, and the interventionary role of government expanded. Even so, the USA, in contrast with other Western countries, is relatively free of government intervention in the direction of business interests and practices. None the less, it falls far short of the ideal that most liberal Americans believe is the key to both their personal hopes for wealth and success and their freedom from central interference in their everyday lives (McKie, 1980, p. 72).

The basic principle behind legislation to regulate free enterprise is that of equal opportunity. It did not take long for Americans to realize that the free market mechanism, far from being perfect, actually encouraged industrial collusion, market manipulation and monopoly. To counteract these tendencies a succession of anti-trust laws were passed, most notable of which were the Sherman Act of 1890, the Clayton and Federal Trade Commission Acts of 1914, the Robinson–Patman Act of 1936, and the Celler–Kefauver Anti-merger Act of 1950. Essentially this anti-monopoly legislation lies at the heart of the American socio-political philosophy, 'which believes in the decentralisation of power, a broad base for the class structure of society and the economic freedom and opportunity for new men, new ideas and new organisations to spearhead the forces of progress' (Adams, 1971, p. 465). It is this philosophy and this legislation that seeks to check excessive private power, and that works against market aggregation. The sentiment was well summarized during debate on the Federal Trade Commission Act by Senator Cummins: 'We have adopted in the country the policy of competition. We are trying to preserve competition as a living, real force in our industrial life; that is to say, we are endeavouring to maintain among our business people that honourable rivalry which will prevent one from exacting undue profits from those who may deal with him.' And then he added, pertinently, 'We are practically alone, however, in this policy' (Adams, 1971, pp. 465–6).

US anti-trust legislation has focused on prescribing the behaviour of companies, policing the market place and imposing certain rules and regulations. It has not been intended to direct or mould the structure of American industry, or to facilitate government involvement in the market. For this reason it cannot be used, and has not been used, by government to postpone or prevent industrial crises or bankruptcies. Attempts to avert industrial crisis by price-fixing, cartels, mergers or market conspiracy are prohibited by law. Anti-trust legislation is enforced by the Department of Justice and by the Federal Trade Commission (FTC), a quasi-judicial administrative agency set up under the Clayton Act. The FTC is the watch-dog of free competition, and has the statutory right to conduct investigations of all registered US companies and corporations where they are thought to be conducting their operations unfairly, deceptively or unlawfully (Liebhafsky, 1971, pp. 228–30). It is therefore well placed to monitor industrial performance over all industrial sectors, and to provide a framework for the US government to identify and anticipate industrial sector decline. However, this practice is not followed because the Commission is independent of government and is there to protect the operation of free enterprise against government interference with the market mechanism.

Although the emphasis is free enterprise over government control, and Americans are brought up to be wary of any government interference of any sort, there is nevertheless extensive government intervention in the US political economy. Much of this intervention has been prompted when the free market failed, or when circumstances are such that the government feels it has no option other than to take the initiative. Increasingly, the government has felt, or has been persuaded to take, a responsibility to correct market failures or assume roles 'in the national interest', in respect of which both major political parties, with differing degrees of enthusiasm, have accepted the principle of government intervention. Both, however, adhere to the primacy of the principle of free enterprise and the market, but differ on the desirability and form of intervention to deal with contemporary political, economic and social problems. They accept wholly that in some areas intervention is necessary — defence is a case in point, energy another — but while the Democrats envisage extensive intervention, especially on social problems, Republicans tend to be more pragmatic, treating each issue on its merits.

The most visible form of intervention in the US political economy is regulation. The majority of instances where regulation has been found necessary has been in sectors where there has been either high market concentration or where necessary public services were being provided. This has been predominantly in the sphere of public utilities and fundamental services to the free market system. In the USA, a public utility is a corporation 'offering an essential service — essential in terms of contemporary living standards — that operates under conditions approaching natural monopoly, i.e., where monopoly is irresistably more efficient than competition' (McKie, 1980, p. 78). Within this definition, suppliers of electricity, water, gas and transport are commonly included. The government regulates utilities in order to guarantee minimum standards of service, and a uniformity across the 50 states. To exercise these regulatory functions, a number of quasi-governmental agencies have been established, including, among others, the Civil Aeronautics Board, the Federal Aviation Administration, the Securities and Exchange Commission and the Interstate Commerce Commission. While preferring to regulate through such agencies, all branches of government have come under pressure to nationalize some public utilities.

A special case of the government's role as regulator and promotor is that of the Small Business Administration (SBA). Concerned that the larger corporations could, through cross-contracting, effectively starve small businesses of a market, the SBA was established in 1953 to ensure that small firms not only had access to markets but also had adequate financial support and access to government contracts. Irrespective of the economic advantage of using big contractors, the SBA can intervene to give small businesses financial protection loans and access to specific markets.

Other forms of regulation by the US government have been classified as 'new-style' regulation (Lilley and Muller, 1977), and have been introduced to cover areas where the market system is neither responsible nor responsive. Following public pressure and persistent lobbying, overarching regulations have been introduced which apply to all industries and cover such considerations as conditions of employment, equal opportunity and environmental protection. Under this category the various Acts of Congress concerning consumer protection and trade descriptions would also be included.

But the US government is not merely the regulator of the competitive market and of business conduct; it has also assumed, where the market has failed, the role of promoter, supporter and, albeit reluctantly, operator. There is no more important element in the free market system than credit and finance; to ensure stability in financial affairs, the government has intervened with extensive powers. Not least among the institutions concerned with the stability of the US economy is the Federal Reserve System (FRS). Established in 1913, the FRS was made responsible for controlling the supply of money and credit in relation to output and employment. Federal and state commercial banks are members of the system and maintain deposits in 12 federal reserve districts into which the reserve system is divided, as does the US Treasury. Through the practice of clearing cheques between banks, issuing loans, issuing paper money, adjusting discount rates, altering the reserve ratio, changing minimum lending rates and trading in government securities, the FRS can influence the level and pace of economic activity. Although ostensibly independent of government, convention requires its policies to be consistent with that of the administration's overall economic policy, as formulated by the President's Council of Economic Advisors (Liebhafsky, 1971, pp. 543-54).

The FRS can be used selectively by government to influence not merely the US economy as a whole, but specific industrial sectors. It is not the only mechanism at its disposal: the Export–Import Bank gives financial support for exports; federal subsidies may be granted in special cases; loan guarantees are possible to assist firms or industries in difficulty; and hidden subsidies are available to industrial sectors that either are working on government business or are acting in the public interest. Nowhere, perhaps, can the government intervene to an industry's advantage more effectively or directly than in its role as tax collector: shifts in policy on tax credits, levels of corporation tax and tax exemptions can affect the fortunes of corporations and whole industrial sectors almost instantly.

In recent years, attention has become focused on the selective use of tariff protection to assist industry (Krasner, 1978, p. 84). There are two principal reasons for this development, which fundamentally runs contrary to the US free market ethic: one is opportunity and the other, justification. The opportunity for selective use of tariff protection for US industry and domestic markets arose as a result of the 1974 Trade Act. Originally intended to clear the way for US participation in the world-wide GATT negotiations, the Act authorized the President to alter import tariffs and surcharges to counter balance of payments deficits and to ease unemployment where foreign imports were deemed to have been an 'important contribution'. It also provides 'adjustment assistance' to industries adversely affected by imports. To advise the President in the execution of the Bill, a federal agency, the International Trade Commission (ITC), was established, replacing the old US Tariff Commission but with increased powers.

Justification for a new approach to tariffs and relief to US industries affected by foreign competition came less from any change in US philosophy than from the painful experience of US industry failing to match foreign goods in price or quality at home, and the social, economic and political consequences that followed. In searching for answers to why US firms were losing ground to foreign producers, the explanation was frequently to be found in the policies and practices of foreign governments in providing assistance to their own industries and to exports. In US terms, this was manifestly unfair competition; to make the rules of the international market-place compatible with the US domestic market, compensation through tariffs and import relief was considered wholly justified. In 1979, the 1974 Trade Act was extended to meet additional unfair practices, such as dumping (*Congressional Quarterly*, 1979, pp. 293–4).

An important, and perhaps unique, feature of the American 'mixed economy' are the industrial sectors that, though in private hands, are almost entirely dependent on government contracts for their viability. Most conspicuous of these are the armaments industries, which research, develop and produce new weapons for the Department of Defense (DOD). As monopsonist, the DOD alone generates the demand for the arms industries products, defines what is to be produced and determines quality and quantity. The economies of over half the states rely on defence contracts, which provides the government with extreme influence (Burns, 1971). The power of the government as monopsonist is not confined to the Defense Department: nuclear energy is another major sector. The manner in which the government meets its procurement needs may vary, but the potential to influence the health and the direction of the industry through them is ever-present. In some instances, the government supplies the facilities and owns the capital that private industry then uses to meet government contracts (GOCO). In others, the government provides the raw materials that industry employs.

To assume non-government involvement in the pace, structure, direction and operation of the US political economy would clearly be fallacious. It is fully recognized that government regulation, promotion and management are all interrelated and that each approach can be employed to influence or direct the political economy. 'Planning', in the sense of giving direction and pace to the political economy, has become a feature of US government over the past 20 years, earning the USA the classification of a 'mixed' system, 'mixed in that it blends private and public enterprise, individual initiative and government promotion, personal responsibility and public regulation' (Burns and Peltason, 1963, pp. 694–5). Nowhere is this overall planning role more evident than in the Office of Management of the Budget, which has responsibility for formulating the government's legislative programme, coordinating policies and determining the budgetary requirements of the various federal agencies.

The historical ideological restraint that makes politicians, government officials and legislators reluctant to interfere too dogmatically or pervasively in private enterprise is matched by an equal resistance in private industry to government interference. Indeed, even where it is unavoidable, such as in the defence industrial sector, there is an instinctive feeling that the situation is unnatural and not conducive to efficiency (Melman, 1970, pp. 22–4). The American corporate executive distrusts his state and turns to it only as a last resort (Vogel, 1978).

There is, therefore, a fundamental dichotomy in US political and economic life: a preference to leave business in private hands, against an acceptance that government has an interventionary role to play. The instinctive style of US government is to leave well alone. Where necessary, the preferred option is to appoint federal agencies to regulate the workings of the economy, and leave decisions which involve federal spending, regulation or management to the political processes surrounding the three branches of government — legislative (Congress), executive (Presidency and government departments) and judiciary (Supreme and federal courts). For this, a large and complex lobby system around Washington has emerged and forms an essential function in the US political economy.

MECHANISMS OF CRISIS MANAGEMENT

Each industry, profession, commercial enterprise or promotional group has its Washington lobby, or has access to one. The lobby is the medium between unrestrained *laissez-faire* capitalism on the one hand and centralized control on the other. Sensitive and responsive though the lobby system is in articulating the interests and opinions of the private sector to government, it, in itself, is wanting in respect of the ideals of fair competition. As scale is a characteristic of the structure of US industry, so the effectiveness of a lobby is closely related to its political and economic 'clout'. Despite some disillusion during the 1970s with big business and corporate scandals, the big corporations' voice in Washington is more effective in securing government compliance than that of smaller fry.

A clear picture of the structure, mechanisms and working of the US political economy is essential if adequate appreciation is to be made of US government policy towards industrial crises. Because Americans slavishly adhere to the principle of the separation of powers, accept the systematic fragmentation of central power among quasi-independent federal agencies and believe in the maximum freedom of economic manoeuvre and choice for private individuals, politics in the USA has become characterized by confrontation and competition, bargaining processes and institutionalized back-scratching. Rivalry and competition in all its manifestations is not confined however to the relationship between public and private interests; it also includes executive departments, federal agencies and the three branches of government. The situation has been aptly described as a manifestation of a 'certain riotous pluralism in US public life' (Shonfield, 1965, p. 323).

Intra-governmental competition for influence and resources goes some way to explaining why the principle of 'anti-planning' has pervaded US politics. Leaving ideology to one side, the growth pattern of US government has been to devolve much responsibility to federal agencies or executive departments; but when these institutions endeavour to take initiatives outside their terms of reference, they are likely to face challenge from Congress. If an agency's policies are acceptable to Congress, it has then to contend with the powerful private sector lobbies which speak for their constituencies. Executive departments and federal agencies generally endeavour to operate with the maximum freedom of action and to extend their influence; their policies are formulated without there necessarily being close reference to the administration or its long-term policies. Integrated policy planning is not seen as the prime responsibility of government, as in Europe; such central policy as exists is invariably the outcome of the countervailing forces that seek to satisfy sectoral interests through bargaining processes.

This pluralism *in extremis* provokes such categorical statements as 'the Carter administration, like the Nixon, Ford and Johnson administrations before it, does not have an industrial policy', and that 'this freedom is an American strength' (*The Economist*, 11 August 1980, p. 73). As the alternative, therefore, to *dirigiste* central planning, industry is left within the framework of law, to operate freely and in directions of its own determining. No mechanisms within either government or industry exist whereby the interests of one are reconciled with the other, except through the Washington lobby, the power the federal budget gives to the administration to encourage compliance, and the political style, popularity and leadership of the President.

When an industry is faced with a crisis, the initiative to do something about it would most likely come from within industry, or from the White House Executive Office. Generally, the expectation is that industry would be the first to take an initiative. This normally takes the form of lobbying the government — administrative departments, federal agencies or Congress — to intervene by modifying aspects of the economy within prescribed limits, by introducing changes to regulatory practices, or by lending direct assistance. Depending on the nature of the difficulty, the strength of industry's case, the public support that can be generated, the reaction of Congress and the interests of the administration, so the tactics will differ, as, also, will the odds against success. Essential to all industries and corporations, whether powerful and secure, declining or expanding, is a reliable lobby in Washington, capable of articulating the industry's interests effectively on both macro- and microeconomic issues and policies.

The US administration has, basically, two major weapons at its disposal. First, it can introduce economic policies at the macro-level, such as changes in interest rates, levels of taxation and the supply of money, to stimulate or dampen the economy as a whole. These policies affect all industries in the private sector, and are invariably too general and too slow to have the desired impact — unless, of course, the difficulties had been identified several years in advance. Even in these more favourable circumstances, there is still no guarantee of success. To an ever-increasing degree, the limitations of macroeconomic measures to assist industries in difficulty is being recognized and more discussion and analysis of sectoral policies has been evident in recent years. Second, therefore, is the range of microeconomic options. Each falls within the general concept of intervention, and can take any one of several forms: promotion, regulation, management or assistance. Which is to be employed depends on the nature of the problem and the economic, political and social circumstances surrounding it. As a matter of course, the scope of discretionary action afforded federal agencies is sufficient to enable them to shelter many firms and industries from the worst of the rigours of the free market system. The Civil Aeronautics Board, for example, closely supervises the air carrier industry not only in the interests of the travelling public, but also with a concern for the long-term economic health and vitality of the industry. Similar interest is exercised by other federal regulatory agencies in other industrial or commercial sectors.

Arguably the most powerful influence on industry is the massive federal procurement budget, of which the defence element is by far the largest and most important. By distributing federal contracts for research and development, as well as the procurement of goods and services, executive departments are in a powerful position to stimulate certain industrial sectors, protect them and influence how they manage and conduct their affairs. To protect government contracts against possible abuse and industry against unfair loss, the Renegotiation Board was instituted to review all contracts referred to it by either side for arbitration and settlement (Edmonds, 1972). The role of the DOD is important in respect of government intervention in industry. In addition to the size of the defence research, development and procurement budget — over a third of the total federal budget — Acts of Congress have defined national security as being of such fundamental importance that prescriptions governing the conduct of the political economy are invariably secondary. Consequently, where economic, political or social circumstances are thought prejudicial to national security, the DOD has discretionary powers to intervene. In an industrial context, this has been interpreted as a justification for awarding uneconomic contracts to firms deemed necessary for national security — by allowing heavy subsidies, to defence contractors for example, including leased capital machinery and GOCO facilities. Similarly, when industrial sectors concerned with defence face commercial ruin, rescue operations can be mounted under the umbrella of the 'V' loan system of aid to firms essential to US security.

On balance, the system of separation of powers, political bargaining and selective intervention has worked well. The somewhat puritanical business attitude of most Americans is epitomized in the phrase, 'you can't get something for nothing', and is given intellectual credence by the economists' assertion that, in Milton Friedman's words, 'no-one gets a free lunch' (Friedman, 1975). Any suggestion that one group has unfair advantage is roundly condemned, and no more so than if it is with public money. Conversely, there is a fundamentalist conviction that hard work and enterprise should be fairly rewarded whereas laziness and inefficiency should be penalized. Indeed, nothing is more likely to generate public criticism than the suggestion that private corporations in trouble are to be helped with public money. On such occasions the Washington lobbyists more than justify their existence.

In an ideal world of free enterprise firms would get into difficulty because they were inefficient or no longer viable; they would be forced out of the market or, other things being equal, move into new areas. Investment would be put where there was the greatest potential. But the ideal is far from reality. Immediately, there are the omnipresent political, social and economic realities of industrial failure: political, in that congressmen from constituencies where there is industrial decline have an interest in re-election; social, in that the knock-on effect of unemployment consequent upon industrial collapse creates problems for which central government would not want to assume further responsibility; and economic, in that major sectoral decline might well cause loss of confidence, industrial dislocation and budgetary strain. Equally important is the perception of crisis, even if the realities of industrial failure are not immediately evident. Against a strong reluctance to use public money to assist industry in crisis is the equally powerful force of pragmatism, which argues that the costs of doing nothing exceed the costs of intervention. Which attitudes prevail cannot be decided by reference to ideological prescription, statutory provision or convention; the outcome depends on the interplay of political forces conditioned by the realities of the day.

Some generalizations, however, can be made. First, there are relatively few crises, as distinct from the cycle of difficult times or

difficult economic circumstances which affect all firms and industries. When there is an industrial crisis, it is invariably defined by a
set of circumstances wherein a major corporation or a whole industry
faces the predicament that it can neither meet its liabilities nor raise
credit or capital in the money market. Industrial crises in the USA
are closely associated with bankruptcy and collapse. A second point
is that industrial crises are not usually associated with inadequate
support for industries to realize growth in sectors of perceived economic potential. The US political economy is much better attuned to
market opportunities, new products and risk than it is in lending a
sympathetic ear to firms in trouble: success remains the name of the
game. A final point is that industrial crises are essentially financial;
the political battle between intervention and non-intervention tends
therefore to be fought in and around Congress, which holds the purse
strings; and has to be persuaded. It is on Capital Hill, therefore, that
clues to US policy on industrial crises must be sought.

US government help to different industrial sectors, whether
through decisions of federal agencies within their discretionary
powers, shifts in federal spending within the annual budget or discriminatory practices, do not necessarily indicate either industrial
crises or policies to avert industrial crises. They are, for the most
part, decisions consequent upon the daily flow of interest articulation, political management and day-to-day administration. The term
'industrial crisis' must be reserved for those few occasions when the
government is confronted, usually without much warning, with an
enterprise that requires short-term help, all other avenues having been
foreclosed. The atmosphere of 'crisis' in these occasions emanates
from a situation in which the government's hand has been forced.
A decision has to be taken on an issue that exposes the inherent
contradictions in the US political and economic system, lays bare
some of the hypocrasies of the major actors, and, in all likelihood,
polarizes opinion in both the public and the private domain. For
the analyst, these are the very occasions when the essence of the
US political and economic system is revealed, and when the major
political forces enter the arena to do battle.

A distinctive feature of the USA is the place of the 'public authority'. In the USA the relationship between the state and the public
authority is more complex than in Europe, not merely because of
the federal constitution but also because of the manner in which the
country developed and incorporated new townships. Thus, towns
and cities can be seen as incorporated entities which own their own
facilities and have wide discretion in the conduct of their own affairs.

When they need finance, it is not the state's responsibility but their own, and for this reason they can face financial crisis in much the same way as any other private enterprise. The experience of New York has illustrated that they can confront the federal administration with the same set of problems as firms in financial difficulties (see p. 89 below).

The criteria for defining an industrial crisis in the USA therefore are: situations that require federal action, whether perceived or real, other avenues having been exhausted; a relatively short amount of time before industries or large corporations would have to cease operations or radically reorganize; and repercussions that would have a significant impact on US industry as a whole, state and regional economies, levels of employment, long-term industrial and economic prospects, national security or wider public confidence in US government and institutions. Since 1967 there have been several crises that meet these criteria, the more revealing of which are: the Douglas Aircraft Corporation, 1967; Penn Central Railroad, 1970; Lockheed, 1971; Pan American Airways, 1974; NE and Mid-west Railroads, 1974; New York City, 1975; W. T. Grant and Co., 1975; the US steel industry, 1978; and Chrysler, 1979.

US EXPERIENCE OF INDUSTRIAL CRISES

Chronologically, the first recent industrial difficulty of 'crisis' proportions was that which confronted the Douglas Aircraft Corporation in 1964. Douglas's problems were caused, paradoxically, by its being too successful. In the early 1960s the company developed two new civil aircraft, the DC8 and DC9, in response to the US domestic airlines' requirement for new jet airliners to meet a massive increase in demand for air travel. Although in direct competition with Boeing, Convair, the British Aircraft Corporation and the French Sud Aviation, the world and US markets were sufficiently large for all to succeed. Consumer resistance to foreign aircraft and the size of the US domestic market together guaranteed Douglas, traditionally a major US civil aircraft supplier with long experience and an extensive support infrastructure, a major share.

However, the market for civil aircraft is both large and volatile; domestic air carriers — the US airlines — operate on relatively slim profit margins in what is a tightly regulated industry, and shortfalls on delivery dates carry severe financial penalties. Old and slow production methods, traditional producer–customer relations that were increasingly anachronistic, quality control processes and poor financial management combined, with short-falls on contractually specified performance, to put the Corporation well behind on delivery. In an industry characterized by high debt–equity ratios, long lead-time products and negative cash flow problems, Douglas soon found itself starved for credit and with mounting liabilities. When the private finance market lost confidence, despite full order books, Douglas found itself unable to meet its financial obligations.

Douglas's saving grace was its position as a major defence contractor. Although steady-stage payments on defence contracts contributed to the cash flow of the Corporation as a whole, it was not allowable legally, not to mention ethically, to provide such cash for civil work. The government, however, was reluctant to allow a major defence contractor to file for bankruptcy. Douglas had a large Navy contract to produce 'Skyhawk' fighter-bomber aircraft, and in the ostensible interest of national security the DOD responded to Douglas's appeal for assistance by invoking the 1950 Defense Production Act to grant Douglas a 'V' loan. The 'V' loan was originally incorporated into the 1950 Defense Production Act to provide public finance to enable firms to shift production to defence requirements during the Korean War emergency and was strictly for national security purposes. The Douglas loan involved a generous, if loose, interpretation of the Act. None the less, the additional finance bought Douglas time to resolve the outstanding problems with the DC8 and DC9. Soon after, it merged with the more dynamic McDonnell Corporation, and the reorganized company was able better to exploit Douglas's strong market position.

If Douglas's problems came as a surprise only to those not intimately involved in civil aircraft manufacture, the announcement in May 1970 that the Penn Central Railroad was in financial straits was totally unexpected. In common with Douglas, Penn Central enjoyed public respect; both were traditional, established companies and epitomized business stability. Despite a love–hate relationship between Penn Central and the travelling public over lack of punctuality, unreliability, discomfort and an air of genteel chaos, the company's symbolic position as a major utility with a long history, on which the big north-eastern industrial states depended, was never questioned. But Penn Central, like Douglas, had not moved with the times. Too little attention to investment, traditional methods, poor financial control and, as it later became evident, bad and corrupt management determined that the company faced bankruptcy in early 1970. Its creditors were prepared neither to support an expensive, ailing railroad, nor to defer calling in their loans.

The precedent of Douglas 'V' loan established the DOD as a first point of reference after the commercial banks had refused further credit. Under Section 301 of the Act, the DOD could guarantee commercial loans to businesses necessary to national security. Penn Central was deemed to be one such essential service because it was responsible for the movement of strategic materials throughout the eastern United States. The initiative to guarantee loans to Penn Central of up to $200 million was first taken by the Transport Secretary, John Volpe, and Treasury Secretary Kennedy, with the participation of Arthur D. Burns, President of the Federal Reserve Bank; only later was the DOD informed of what had then become government policy. Its first move was to confirm that the proposal — for which it would be financially liable — came under the authorization of section 301 (Department of Defense, 1970). Then, two weeks later, Deputy Defense Secretary Packard added a note of caution, demanding that the proposed loan to Penn Central be given congressional support. The time available from the crisis to final agreement from Congress was barely one month — time that Penn Central could not afford.

To cover Penn Central's immediate problems, the Navy Department, the service most dependent on Penn Central, was directed at short notice to prepare the necessary papers for 'V' loan guarantees while the larger $200 million loan guarantee for congressional approval was being assembled. It was intended that the 'V' loans would be paid off as soon as the $200 million loan guarantee was finalized and should not, therefore, exceed that figure. The first guarantee, requested by the First National City Bank of New York through the Federal Reserve Bank, was for $50 million, to be secured by Penn Central assets and paid after 29 June 1970 (Federal Reserve Bank of New York, 1970).

It was at this juncture that the US administration found that the checks and balances of the political system still operated. The use of public money, however legal, to assist private industry without the support of Congress invited challenge. In Penn Central's case, the resistance came from the chairman of the powerful House Committee on Currency and Banking, Wright Patman. Piqued at being excluded from the secret meetings between Penn Central, the administration and the banks, he initiated investigations of his own as to the legality of the use of the 1950 Defense Production Act to issue 'V' loans to companies in difficulty. His findings were that the Act was 'never intended to prevent the insolvency of a large corporation only tangentially involved in defence contracts' (House Committee on Banking and Currency, 1972, p. 12). His investigations further revealed that the DOD had not determined the security of the government loan, and that the Office of Emergency Preparedness, which officially administers the 1950 Defense Production Act, doubted the legality of the 'V' loan expedient (*Business Week*, 6 June 1970). He quickly made known his feelings about the manoeuvre, by holding over the banks, Penn Central and the administration the threat of stopping the subsequent $200 million loan guarantee legislation. The effect was immediate: the group of nine banks that had gathered in New York expecting to sign the 'V' loan agreement with the Secretary of the Navy, John Chaffee, on 19 June waited in vain; the papers did not arrive (Loving, 1970, p. 104).

The Administration's case for 'V' loan was weak, and its behind-the-scenes tactics ill advised; but neither mistake could disguise the parlous state of Penn Central. In putting its case to the Federal Reserve Bank, Penn Central had estimated a loss for 1970 of $271 million and for 1971, $221 million. Income from other sources would realize only $103 million, which indicated that, even if a $200 million loan guarantee had been forthcoming, insufficient capital would be available to effect improvements in Penn Central's operating efficiency. The Federal Reserve Bank of New York had independently concluded that, at best, neither $200 million worth of 'V' loans nor a $200 million loan guarantee would do other than postpone Penn Central's bankruptcy and inflict substantial losses on the guaranteeing agency. This opinion was made public two days before the 'V' loan meeting on 19 June 1970.

When interim financing was not forthcoming and the drastic plight of Penn Central had been exposed, the fate of the company was sealed. Under Section 77 of the Bankruptcy Act the Interstate Commerce Commission (ICC) was required to investigate the company and plan its reorganization. No one thought, or had the stomach, to seek guaranteed loans under the 1958 Transportation Act, and Penn Central was left to register bankruptcy on 21 June 1970 and hand over to the ICC.

The administration's attempt to bypass Congress with the Navy 'V' loan had immediate implications for the Lockheed Aircraft Corporation, which was facing enormous financial problems at the same time. Indeed, both Penn Central and Lockheed affected each other in that they generated widespread public awareness of the potential abuse of public money to protect or bail out private companies. Indeed, with the sustained criticism of the 'military industrial complex' during the 1960s and the mounting unpopularity of the Vietnam War, it was not a time to be seen to 'feather-bed' defence-related companies.

The Lockheed crisis *per se* broke in February 1971 consequent upon the failure of Rolls Royce in England to deliver its RB211 engines to specification and on time for the Lockheed L1011, Tristar (Edmonds, 1983). So heavy was Lockheed's investment in the L1011 programme, and so indebted had it become on several major fixed-price defence contracts, that, despite full order books for well over three years, it could not absorb any setback. The RB211 failure came at a time when the company had a huge negative cash flow, $1.4 billion in sunk costs on the L1011, a fixed loss agreed with the DOD one day before the Rolls Royce announcement on three major defence fixed-price contracts totalling $484 million and, as one commentator described it, the world's 'largest glider'. Estimates at the end of 1970 put Lockheed's financial obligations at four times its stated capital assets.

Lockheed's predicament was further complicated by the British government's stipulation of a US government financial commitment to the L1011 as a condition of the Rolls Royce RB211 programme continuing (MacCrindle and Godfrey, 1973, pp. 316–17). No other engine at that juncture could easily, or economically, be substituted; this left Lockheed the option of either filing for bankruptcy, or seeking a loan guarantee from the government both to satisfy the British condition and to placate the company's and the L1011 customers' bankers. The perception of 'crisis' was made more acute, first, by the unexpected suddenness of the Rolls bankruptcy; second, by the contrast of the predicament with the euphoria following the settlement only days before of the apparently intractable problems over Lockheed's defence contracts; third, by the urgent need of the domestic airlines to introduce the L1011 into service to head off their own financial problems; and, last, by the Penn Central experience, which had closed all avenues of temporary financial help through the Defense Production Act. But worst of all was the DOD condition of its arrangement with Lockheed over defence contract over-runs that $600 million financial support would be guaranteed by the company's bankers; the collapse of the L1011 programme therefore also brought down Lockheed's deal with the DOD.

As the DOD had expected the commercial banks to come to Lockheed's support on its civil project as a condition of agreement over its defence contracts, so, when the L1011 project faced collapse, the commercial banks looked to the administration for support in the interests of defence and national security. The options before the administration were limited: it was either to let Lockheed go bankrupt, reorganize the company's defence side and sell off the civil work, or to seek from Congress authorization for the loan guarantee requested by the banks and the British government. The pros and cons of either course of action were equally balanced; Assistant Secretary of Defense, David Packard, summarized the situation succinctly: 'our defense programmes would be less troublesome if the company survives [but] it is not an absolute disaster if it goes the other way' (Senate Committee on Banking, Housing and Urban Affairs, 1971, p. 166).

The administration chose the former course, as much because the President's home state, California, would be most affected by Lockheed's demise, as for any other reason. The initial Bill, prepared by the Federal Reserve Bank President, Arthur Burns, emphasized the effect Lockheed's bankruptcy would have generally on public confidence and proposed a $2 billion fund to support private industry with loan guarantees to protect the public interest. In the event, Congress would not wear so radical a course, and the administration modified its Bill only to meet Lockheed's requirement for a loan guarantee of $250 million.

The hearings and debates in both chambers of Congress are instructive, in that they revealed the deep ideological division between supporters of state intervention and those of free enterprise. Further, they exposed the realities of political bargaining, pressure and manoeuvre, which cut across normal party, regional, interest group and ideological boundaries. Though many congressmen assumed firm, immutable positions, a large percentage were at the margin, open to persuasion either way. When the moment came to cast a vote, every hand counted, with the administration's Bill winning the day in both chambers by the odd vote; 1 vote in the Senate and 3 votes in the House (*Congressional Record*, 2 August 1971 and 30 July 1971). Never before, or since, has Washington witnessed such frenzied, uncompromising lobbying. When the excitement had died down, it appeared that the deciding factor had not been one of the principle but a more pragmatic consideration of the effects of Lockheed's demise on regional employment and industrial disruption over a number of states. Treasury estimates put job losses at 34,000, concentrated in the hard-pressed aerospace industry (unemployment level of 14.2 per cent in California), and likely to raise the overall unemployment rate in southern California by 0.5 per cent to 7.9 per cent (Senate Committee on Banking, Housing and Urban Affairs, 1971, pp. 26–32).

Once Lockheed had received its loan guarantee, the commercial banks advanced the necessary line of credit to complete the L1011, and the British had the US government's commitment which allowed public money to be made available for the RB211 engine. Execution of the Act was instituted through a Loan Guarantee Board set up as a condition of the loan. The Board, comprising the Secretary of the Treasury, the Chairman of the FRS and the Chairman of the Securities and Exchange Commission, was authorized to issue loan guarantees up to $250 million until the end of 1973. The performance of the Board and the compliance of Lockheed with the conditions of the Act were to be monitored by the General Accounting Office, a condition with which the Board found disagreement (General Accounting Office; 1972, pp. 3 and 11). Lockheed was required to repay all guaranteed loans, plus interest, by 1975, from which source the Board managed to record a profit.

The time that Lockheed was able to 'buy' was sufficient for it to become profitable within five years of the crisis. On balance, the episode proved successful for all the interested parties without compromising too much the basic principles of the politico-economic system. Moreover, the experience evoked recollections of the Reconstruction Finance Corporation that operated in the Depression, and the World War I War Finance Corporations, each designed to keep companies and industries afloat during difficult times. The reflections were not sufficiently strong, however, to prompt the establishment of a federal funding agency in addition to those specialized ones — SBA, Commodity Credit Corporations, Export–Import Bank, Farmers' Home Administration and so on — already existing.

The significance of the Lockheed loan guarantee should not be under-estimated. Lockheed, the country's leading defence contractor and symbol of technical prowess in weapons development, was a prime candidate for purely executive action. But such a massive injection of public funds was not politically possible, thus confirming the basic principle that industrial crises were a matter for public debate and congressional enactment. The style of government was not to 'manage' industrial crises, but to respond to them as political forces allowed.

The plight of the US railroads did not end with the bankruptcy and reorganization of Penn Central. By 1973 it became evident that the problems of ageing stock, decaying track and the need to modernize operating procedures that had bedevilled Penn Central also applied to the big rail companies of the north-east and mid-west. Indeed, six companies filed for bankruptcy, despite a $100 million congressional loan guarantee to ailing railroads immediately following the Penn Central collapse, and the Trustees appointed by the ICC to run Penn Central simultaneously appealed to the government for a further $600 million in federal aid over four years 'to avoid closing the railroads' (*Congressional Quarterly*, 1973, p. 468). The request was refused, but a combination of pressure from the federal judge presiding over the Penn Central case, strike action by the railway union, and congressional pressure to back an ICC plan to reorganize the whole north-eastern region railway system under a single, non-profit, quasi-non-governmental corporation, was effective. The administration proposed, and Congress passed, a Bill to authorize $1.5 billion in loan guarantees to enable a new Consolidated Rail Corporation (CRC) to take over the operations of the bankrupt companies, repair the track and purchase facilities. In addition, $550 million in federal aid was granted to design a new railway system, subsidize operations, pay off reduntant staff and operate rail subsidiaries. By 1975, the CRC, with federal government representatives on its board, was fully operating.

The unprecedented rail organization introduced new elements into the US government's response to industrial crises. The puritanical streak in American attitudes to business surfaced with government insistence that no one should benefit from past incompetence. If public funds were to be used to help save an industry from collapse, those who worked or managed that industry, whose future employment would be saved, were expected to make some contribution to the rescue either through pay restraint, buying share capital or changing work practices. The policy had the added attraction of giving those concerned a stake in the industry and an interest in its future viability. In all, the Bill was less a plan to save six bankrupt railroads than a comprehensive initiative to modernize and restructure rail transport in the north-eastern United States. The provisions of the Act were specific in what was required, the time allowed, and the terms under which the reorganized system should operate. To assist the new corporation, which was made answerable to the ICC, generous grants and loan guarantees were given for specified purposes. More significantly, the new utility was made exempt from anti-trust laws, bankruptcy regulations and some environmental legislation, and allowed federal loans to states for local rail transport services on a 70–30 matching basis (*Congressional Quarterly*, 1973, pp. 465–7).

Aerospace and railroads were not the only major areas of established life to get into difficulties amounting to 'crisis' proportions. In late 1974 and early 1975, New York City's financial problems escalated to a point whereby, by late 1975, the City authorities would be unable to pay interest on borrowings, raise new capital or meet its financial obligations. The implications were enormous. New York's crisis reached far beyond the City's limits, a naked fact soon recognized by Arthur Burns of the Federal Reserve Bank. Initially, the Ford administration viewed the crisis as another in a long sequence of New York's financial 'scares', and adamantly refused to act. New York, it believed, had been living beyond its means for too long, paying its employees excessively high salaries; New York could find its own salvation. Ironically, even though the City faced bankruptcy, the terms of the Bankruptcy Act made it virtually impossible for the City to file, and no meaningful precedent could be followed. A vain attempt to raise funds by the sale of City 'Big Mac' long-term bonds gave temporary relief, but by September 1975 the short-term future was bleak. What New York sought was a federal guarantee of its bonds to restore confidence.

Pressure was brought to bear on Congress, the administration and the President by the US Conference of Mayors, many of whom projected similar problems in their own cities. Congressmen also took up New York's plight with a variety of proposals. Treasury Secretary Simon gave testimony in late September to the effect that he questioned the impact of a default, but his opinion was challenged by Arthur Burns, who concluded on 11 November that, unless the federal government acted, there was a strong likelihood that the country's financial markets would 'deteriorate noticeably' (*Congressional Quarterly*, 1975, p. 444).

The perception of crisis was heightened as the time leading up to insolvency ran out. In New York's case, only the use of $150 million from the teachers' pension fund deferred default between 17 October and 1 December, a gesture that was agreed with only two hours remaining! With a $286 million cash shortfall and a further $437 million due the following week, New York City would have to default on 1 December 1975. It was also accepted that the state of New York would default soon after. In defiance of President Ford's promised veto, Congress acted. Committee reports from both chambers approved Bills to give federal loan guarantees to the City—Senate $11.5 billion, House $6 billion up to 1978. Although Ford had argued that federal aid to a defaulting city would be a 'terrible precedent', he changed his position on 26 November and proposed a Bill granting short-term loans to New York. The Bill became law on 9 December but was not without its critics, and even those who voted in favour were reluctant to make the future easy for New York's administrators. 'Bankruptcy should be efficient,' said one. 'A Federal guarantee for New York City will make insolvency attractive' (*Congressional Quarterly*, 1975, p. 455).

Perceptions are central to the question of industrial 'crisis', and though a company or a whole industry may be experiencing real or continuing crisis, such as the Massachusetts shoe industry, if the public do not perceive it to be a problem, or if Washington is unconvinced, the industry can effectively die without a trace. Conversely, an industry might be relatively healthy, though facing temporary problems, and through skilful lobbying and public relations create the impression of problems amounting to total crisis. Such was the situation with the US steel industry in 1977.

As has been observed, 'there is a mystique involved in the steel industry that makes it the symbol of economic strength all over the world. . . . For more than a century, both politicians and economists have regarded steel capacity as a measure of industrial progress and a source of geopolitical power' (*Business Week*, 19 September 1977, p. 66). In the USA, the shock of the industry's problems were out of all proportion to the actual figures involved, especially as steel was no longer the foundation of the US economy; but they were perceived to be a threat to the foundation of American industrial might.

The evidence, however, was presented clearly: US steel production was stagnant; anti-pollution legislation had placed a heavy burden on capital investment; foreign steel had captured a 16 per cent share of the domestic market; costs were rising at 10 per cent per annum; the market was shrinking; and profits had been cut to a minimum. 'To an alarming extent, the US steel companies fitted neatly into the standard economic description of a declining industry' (*Business Week*, 19 September 1977, p. 65). Politically, the industry was in crisis, and it looked to Washington for relief. In particular, it singled out unfair competition from foreign, government-subsidized steel companies as a major contributor to its predicament, and demanded some protection. In terms of open competition, the case was well founded; there was evidence of collusion between Japanese and Western European governments on steel marketing strategies along the lines of an international cartel. To arrest the aggressive marketing of foreign steel in the USA, the steel industry, citing Section 301 of the 1974 Trade Act, demanded that a quota be imposed on Japanese steel imports. It further looked for some relaxation in the time scale imposed for the introduction of new mandatory environmental rules in order to alleviate the estimated $4 billion annual cost of these requirements. In some instances, such as Wheeling–Pittsburgh Steel, requests for loan guarantees from the Economic Development Agency were made to help overcome the immediate cash flow problems caused by pollution control obligations.

Steadily throughout 1978, the steel market deteriorated, foreign imports increased, and the demand for steel declined, until pressure on Washington finally prevailed. To halt the worsening situation, in that year government introduced a trigger-price system designed to 'screen out' low-priced steel imports. The effect of the measures, not only on the profitability of the industry but also upon its morale, was almost instantaneous. 'I just hope we are encouraged by what we see,' said one company president, 'we can keep the upward trend going' (*Business Week*, 10 April 1978, p. 31). For the following two years the industry enjoyed what was described as a boom period, suggesting that the initial crisis was, perhaps, more one of perception and emotion than hard economic reality. Nevertheless, the scene was set for more justified and equally successful lobbying for import controls during 1981 (see p. 22 above).

The most recent major industrial difficulty to have reached 'crisis' proportions was the US automobile industry in the late 1970s, whose major companies had been registering losses that were records in the history of US business. Nowhere was this crisis more profound than with Chrysler, the nation's tenth-largest corporation and third-largest motor manufacturer. The reasons for Chrysler's problems were varied, but the principal causes were its over-extended overseas operations; its mistaken strategy following the oil crisis of the mid-1970s, including a failure to anticipate in time the shift in demand to small cars; and, at least according to the company, new government regulations governing pollution, fuel economy and safety. Not least among Chrysler's difficulties was the massive market penetration of Japanese and German small cars.

By 1979, Chrysler had 80,000 unsold vehicles, its van sales had plummeted, and its market share had dropped to a paltry 9.1 per cent. To produce these cars, it employed 130,000 workers in nine US divisions, and 35,000 abroad; the annual payroll was $4.1 billion. Most workers were located in Michigan, but its operations and dealership reached almost every state in the union. Without new models to recapture its share of the market, the future of the Corporation was non-existent; but neither Chrysler's income nor its $800 million line of credit was sufficient to cover the proposed investment programme of $7.5 billion. Worse, credit was being eroded by continuing operating losses, which in the second quarter of 1979 totalled $207 million.

An early initiative was taken by the Union of Auto Workers (UAW) President, D. Fraser, who proposed that the federal government purchase a $1 billion stake in Chrysler, relax the regulations that were prejudicing its auto sales and grant the Corporation tax credits on investment in advance (*The Economist*, 22 September 1979, p.82). The Treasury rejected these suggestions, despite the precedent for tax credits when help was given to American Motors and to aerospace companies when they faced difficulty. However, a promise of up to $750 million loan guarantees was given provided Chrysler worked out an acceptable recovery plan including significant concessions from the unions.

While the governors of those states most affected by Chrysler's problems lobbied the administration, Chrysler worked to put its house in order. Dividends were suspended; a quarter of the workforce were made redundant; the UAW was asked to accept a wage freeze; and its financial subsidiary was sold to suppliers and dealers. Against a federal loan guarantee was the strong lobby that Chrysler should go bankrupt and under the new bankruptcy laws file for protection while reorganization was implemented. None the less, Chrysler President John Riccardo succeeded in getting Treasury agreement in principle to a loan guarantee; he then resigned, leaving the responsibility of the rescue plan to his successor, Lee Iacocca.

Chrysler's second rescue plan for a $1.2 billion guarantee was rejected on the grounds that the private banks should make more funds available. The Treasury was prepared to offer $750 million, but this left Chrysler with a short-fall, after all savings had been included, of $2.1 billion on its estimated $7.5 billion investment programme. In the short term, it also had to handle an estimated loss for 1979 of $1.07 billion and $480 million for 1980. Although parsimonious, the administration's response at least had the effect of mollifying the banks, which did not press their claims when Chrysler defaulted on its $800 million loan repayments.

With what was almost becoming a predilection for 'crises', the government procrastinated until 1 November 1979 when, openly admitting a 'change in outlook', Treasury Secretary Miller doubled the original offer to $1.5 billion, since it was 'apparent . . . that any financial assistance should be . . . sufficient to accomplish the purpose'. The motivation behind the shift in policy was an awareness of the 'serious impact on localities around the country', and the need to 'help the nation avoid such shutdown costs as unemployment benefits, welfare payments and tax loss' (*Congressional Quarterly*, 1979, pp. 285-8). The forthcoming presidential election was also a powerful influence, especially as those states·in which the President was most eager to attract votes were those where UAW membership was strong.

None the less, the conditions of Chrysler's assistance package were stringent, and added new precedents and emphases to policy on industrial crises. First, Chrysler had to secure $4.5 billion in loans itself and raise a further $1.6 billion by selling assets. To achieve the latter condition, Chrysler sold property and subsidiaries, borrowed finance from interested state legislatures, and received $600 million from the UAW and sale of stock. At least the concessions made by the company helped ameliorate opposition when the administration proposed its rescue plan to Congress.

In Congress opinion was predictably divided. To win over the floating vote in both chambers even tougher conditions were added. Consistent with the principle that private individuals should not benefit from public money, the UAW was required to give up $426 million. It is significant to note that the administration seemed to attribute collective responsibility for Chrysler's problems and put the blame for inefficiency on both unions *and* management. Others had also to share in the process. At least $500 million had to come from domestic banks, $250 million from states, $300 million from the sale of corporate assets, and $180,000 from dealers. Further, Chrysler had to issue an employee stock ownership plan, government interest was to be protected, the GAO was to be authorized to audit the company's books, and the $1.5 billion federal guarantee was to be administered by an independent Loan Guarantee Board. The Bill passed Congress on 21 December 1979 and at $3.5 billion overall represented the biggest 'bail-out' package of any private corporation, dwarfing Lockheed's loan guarantee eight years before.

The demanding conditions of the Chrysler Bill has meant that President Carter's signature on 7 January 1980 was not the end of the story, or of the crisis. Chrysler subsequently found it increasingly difficult to comply with the Bill's terms, mainly because the banks were hesitant to advance unguaranteed loans; many thought Chrysler's investment programme too ambitious. Yet their cooperation was necessary for the federal guarantee to take effect. On 16 April a group representing 326 financiers agreed a solution, including $660 million in interest deferrals and an extension to Chrysler's debts. As Lee Iacocca observed at the time, 'Everybody was waiting to see the colour of the bank's money' (*Business Week*, 8 April 1980, pp. 27-8).

Even this expedient, however, did not resolve the crisis; on 24 April 1980 Chrysler had not the cash to pay its wage bill, and still failed to qualify for the federal loan guarantee. Taking draconian measures, it cut back car production to two types and reduced the workforce by a further 20 per cent; meanwhile, the bankers continued to play financial brinkmanship with the federal government. Finally, the government released the $1.5 billion loan guarantees, since when the hapless Chrysler Corporation has endeavoured to set itself on the road to recovery.

The drama of Chrysler's recovery attempts was heightened by its announcement in February 1981 of the largest loss in American corporate history, of $1710 million (£814 million) for 1980. The Reagan administration none the less honoured the loan guarantees, and during 1981 the Corporation pursued an aggressive recovery programme. By July 1982 the flamboyant Mr Iacocca could triumphantly announce the highest quarter's profits since 1976, $107 million for the second quarter. An admiring media reported that 'even financial analysts are cautiously optimistic about the firm's future' (*Sunday Times*, 25 July 1982). It seemed once again that improvisation, loan guarantees and the resilience of American capitalism had secured survival and therefore a relatively favourable outcome. But again, this did not signify any systematic development of policy. As two authoritative participants in the process concluded, 'anyone who observed the actual process by which the loan programme was developed would be bound to conclude that the decision to approve the loan programme was made on an *ad hoc* basis, without regard for any articulated policy' (Freeman and Mendelowitz, 1982, p. 452).

THE RESPONSE OF THE BANKING SYSTEM

For the past six years, but more significantly since 1980, the USA has experienced economic and financial difficulties formidable enough to constitute a fundamental challenge to its politico-economic system. These difficulties, though not an exact replica of the depression of the late 1920s and 1930s, are no less profound in their effect in that they have forced those with the responsibility to make the system work — politicians, administrators, judges, industrialists and financiers — to question basic assumptions. The difficulties emanate from the continuing economic recession that has afflicted the West in general since the mid-1970s. The apparent inability of the leadership to bring the US economy out of the recession, and the failure of financial and economic advisors to find solutions that work, has added to the atmosphere of apprehension, waning confidence and frustration. It is the financial institutions that have, as in the 1920s and 1930s, begun to generate a sense of crisis. When the banks begin to lose confidence, so then does the public have concern for the economy in general. The present concerns of the banking industry do not, however, stem from a lack of government intervention. The 1933 Glass–Steagall Act separated banking from securities, intro-duced regulations to protect small depositors from over-speculation by banks and, with the Securities Act and the Banking Act regulating each industry, ensured that the effect of another stock exchange crash would be confined. Until the late 1970s little changed: 'Very few deposit-taking institutions failed and almost no depositors lost their funds' (Watts, 1982, p. 76). But perhaps the real reason for this was that until the late 1970s the US economy had not been put under serious strain.

These restrictions on commercial banks had other effects, which, paradoxically, made them more, not less, vulnerable during a period of recession: they were cocooned from competition by restricted access to and from other states in the union; the more ambitious were forced to expand by developing business abroad; and they were under no outside pressure to examine their own creditworthiness. More importantly, since they were not allowed by law to hold company stocks, they had been physically separated from industry, which restricted industrial reorganization. Moreover, because of the tax system, ailing industry also had little incentive to redeploy assets. Indeed it has been suggested that the incentive for industrial cor-porations to merge and form conglomerates in the 1960s, and for others to go into quiet decline, is a direct consequence of constraints imposed by banking regulations (Watts, 1982, pp. 67–8).

Since 1980, the USA has witnessed a revolution in the financial services industry. The commercial banks are required to comply with the rules governing interest limits, and consequently have been unable to compete for depositors in a period of high interest rates. Other financial institutions, such as brokerage houses, thrift institu-tions, insurance companies, finance houses and pension funds, have lured away much of their traditional business. In 1982 the banking lobby increased pressure for deregulation to enable them — the bigger ones, at least — to assume a wider range of financial services than they are at present permitted to offer. In the interim, they are attempting to meet the increasing short-term borrowing needs of industrial corporations by specializing in particular markets. Two major banks,

Bank America Corporation and Security Pacific, have led the move to look to their own devices for the future by finding and acting on loopholes in the Glass–Steagall Act provisions; both have moved into discount brokering (*Business Week*, 12 April 1982, p. 52). More will possibly follow while deregulation legislation is pending.

The US banks, all 15,000 of them, have thus found themselves increasingly vulnerable: other financial bodies have encroached on their place as the principle depository institution, and the banks themselves are divided as to the best way to approach the problem to their collective and mutual satisfaction. The two main financial institutions that failed in 1982, Drysdale Securities and Penn Square Bank of Oklahoma, did so as a consequence of high risk loans that turned sour. This was serious enough, but what disturbed investors was not their demise, but the number of commercial banks with established reputations, such as the Continental Illinois Bank of Chicago and Chase Manhattan of New York, that had deposited large sums with one or the other. This experience has raised questions not just about the judgement of banking executives but also about policing of the banking system as a whole.

In the final analysis, the US banking system has been put under immense strain. However, bankruptcies and losses have, to date, been more a consequence of bad judgement than of any major inherent weakness. The recession has laid bare some anomalies in the Glass–Steagall Act, and if the banks are to continue to play a significant role in the US economy, as and when it picks up again, deregulation would now appear to be a necessary development. The critical task is for the administration to bring interest rates down; in the meantime, the banks will have to be prudent about to whom and where they lend. After the costly financial restructuring of International Harvester in 1982, the old traditional industrial giants of the north and east are likely to be avoided in favour of growth industries such as microelectronics in the south and west, although this might not be the best foundation upon which to regenerate growth.

CONCLUSION

The case studies of industrial crises demonstrate essentially pragmatic, *ad hoc* approaches. Depending on the extent of public support, the effectiveness of industrial lobbies in Washington and the merits of each case, the US government has responded (usually) in providing financial guarantees. No standard procedure or policy exists, though trends — both positive and negative — can be discerned. Most evident is a strong reluctance merely to provide a public subsidy or direct federal loans. Somehow, companies and industries have both to be made to suffer and to demonstrate that in time they can be restored as viable enterprises. There is equal reluctance to nationalize or to prescribe how recovery should be effected; the onus is placed on either the industry or the affected corporation. Finally, the private financial institutions are expected to bear much of the risk; they are not to be cushioned by public guarantees. Conversely, any government financial liability is to be protected against prior claim on a company's assets and, where possible, recompensed through interest charges and repayment of administrative costs.

To demonstrate government reluctance to do more than provide aid, the administration of federal help in each instance has been assumed by a federal agency, acting within legally prescribed powers, and accountable to Congress. Each agency has a limited life-span, and the recipients of federally guaranteed loans are expected to have them repaid within a relatively short period. Without these conditions it is reasonable to assume that the latent resistance in Congress to central intervention would prevent any Bill that proposes federal assistance to ailing industries from ever being passed. For similar reasons, Congress rejected the proposal to have a permanent $2 billion fund on the old Reconstruction Finance Corporation model for assistance to industry. Such a course would leave policy on industrial crises too much in the hands of the executive.

Government willingness to come to an industry's aid is conditional upon the political and economic implications of the individual crisis. High in priority is the effect of industrial collapse on national security, unemployment, regional economic stability and public utility. The chain store, W. T. Grant and Co., did not meet any of these criteria, and was left to go bankrupt; by contrast New York City, Lockheed and Chrysler were given help. But whatever the circumstances, and whatever the crisis, one conclusion is inescapable: the precedent of federal aid has been well and truly set. It has been said that, 'once the government gets involved in doing something, it doesn't leave again.' What must therefore be anticipated in the USA, despite Reagan Republican fundamentalism, is not necessarily a predetermined policy on industrial crises, or, for that matter, a new super-federal industrial finance agency, but a steady increase in large corporations 'stumbling around from Congressional committee to Congressional committee seeking a bail-out' (*The Economist*,

24 March 1980). Indeed, they and their professional lobbies have been getting ample practice in recent years.

Central to the analysis of US policy on industrial crises is the perception by the principal actors involved of whether or not a crisis exists. What may objectively be seen as a crisis by a corporation, at least in terms of its financial statements and forecasts, need not necessarily be a view shared either within government circles or by the public at large. The converse is equally possible, that industries may refuse to acknowledge their predicament despite evidence or outside insistence to the contrary. The US steel industry was able, through persistent lobbying, to generate a perception of crisis and ultimately to succeed in securing government legislation to alleviate the financial pressures. The US shoe industry was unsuccessful, in that the crisis that it faced, through massive foreign competition, was not perceived to be in need of remedy, largely because it did not have a wide public image, nor was its demise considered harmful to the public interest. Relatively, the shoe industry was in a more parlous state than steel, but it was steel that was given respite.

Since the solution to industrial crises requires positive action, either directly through the injection of capital or indirectly through manipulation of the market, Congress is the focal point of attention. The chances of industry getting the assistance it asks for, or needs, depends partly on the skill of the Washington lobbies and partly on its finding a suitable 'sponsor' to prosecute, or indeed 'manage', its case through the complex political processes on Capitol Hill. Sponsors include federal agencies, government departments, congressmen and the administration, either its presidential or Executive Office form. Presidential sponsorship is no guarantee of success, though the record of the past 20 years would suggest that a negative attitude on the part of the President is a major handicap while a positive one may or may not be an advantage. However, the record has also demonstrated that the President's hand can be forced, especially if the effects of an industrial crisis or corporate bankruptcy impact on his re-election prospects or upon the political futures of congressmen to whom he has obligations or loyalties. Sponsors alone cannot necessarily achieve the support that industry requires, and support elsewhere has proved necessary to tip the balance. The Federal Reserve Bank has intervened on a number of occasions with the effect either of persuading the President to change policy, or of getting congressmen to reconsider their position.

Whether or not industries find a sponsor on Capitol Hill to prosecute their interests, and no matter how persuasive the case is, it has never been taken for granted that help should be forthcoming. As a political or ideological issue, there remain fundamentalists, in and out of Congress, who would oppose state assistance to industries in crisis on principle. Paradoxically, opposition to government intervention to assist ailing industries is most marked within industry itself; while sympathizing with the plight of another corporation or whole industry, US industry as a whole tends to be antagonistic to what it chooses to regard pejoratively as government 'bail-outs'. This attitude is not found in financial circles, which see government assistance to industries in crisis as a guarantee and a hedge against collapse for their own investment. However, industrial attitudes are changing as the strength and relative isolation of US industry diminishes relative to international competition. Increasingly, US industrialists are looking to greater government involvement in industrial sectors, especially in affording protection against foreign imports and external penetration of the US domestic market. The policy, however, is preventive in emphasis, not curative.

In the past, US industries have faced crisis more as a consequence of managerial inefficiencies and, in some instances, incompetence and corruption than because of structural changes within the market or unfair intervention and discriminatory practices. This, however, is changing, in that industries are increasingly facing difficulties because of regulations that impact unevenly and unfairly (anti-pollution acts, for example), because of the effect of foreign competition and discriminatory protectionism, and because modern high-technology products involve high capital investment, require long lead-times and generate massive cash-flow problems. Inflation, high interest rates and central government deficit financing impact on industries with high debt–equity ratios, rendering them more vulnerable than ever before.

However, industrial crises in the USA should be seen in perspective. As noted at the start, industry has learnt over the years to diversify; aggregate concentration has been increasing; and new arrangements have been introduced to enable corporations and industries to limit risk. Inter-industry subcontracting, leasing, holding companies and multinational operations are some examples. US industry itself has therefore adapted to limit its vulnerability. The likelihood of crises has not been eliminated, however, and it should be recognized that the precedent to afford help is well established; the resources that have been made available have, in relative terms, been modest; the political salience of 'bail-outs' has been minor; and on balance, especially in industries where there has been market aggregation, public utilities or national security connotations, the results of government intervention have been beneficial to the industry and profitable to the public purse. In other words, 'bail-outs', in the forms of loan guarantees, tariff protection and subsidy, are here to stay.

One last caveat, however, must be introduced. Past practices and traditional values should, other things being equal, provide adequate indicators of likely future policy, but these are not normal times. The world recession and a sluggish US economy, coupled with international banking developments, have exposed US commercial and financial institutions to increasing risk. As their sense of vulnerability to influences beyond their control as private corporations has increased, so attitudes towards government protection have mellowed.

There is, today, a discernable increase in pressure to 'buy American first' and there were several proposals before the end of the 97th Congress in 1983 to introduce legislation that: affords protection against imports; ensures the domestic content of goods and services; introduced trade reciprocity with other countries; loosens the Foreign Corrupt Practices Act; boosts American sales abroad through export trading companies; reduces government regulatory powers; and amends the 1978 bankruptcy laws, not merely to make going into receivership more hazardous and less easy, but also to meet a recent Supreme Court ruling that declared the Bankruptcy Courts' powers unconstitutional (*Congressional Quarterly*, 10 April 1982, pp. 805–7; 3 June 1982, p. 1572). Whether any or all of these Bills will become law is open to question; what will be a dominant influence, however, is the speed with which the Reagan administration can regenerate the economy and turn pessimism, deregulation and protectionism into optimism and 'business as usual'. But what is abundantly clear is the increased readiness of industry since 1980 to look to government to help avert or forestall industrial crises, rather than simply to respond to them.

REFERENCES

Adams, W. (1971), 'Public Policy in a Free Enterprise Economy', in W. Adams (ed.), *The Structure of American Industry* (4th edn), London, Macmillan.
Burns, A. F. (1971), 'The Defence Sector: Its Economic and Social Impact', in S. Melman (ed.), *The War Economy of the US*, New York, St Martin's Press.

Burns, J. and Peltason, J. (1963), *Government by the People* (5th edn), Eagle-wood Cliffs, New Jersey, Prentice-Hall.

Department of Defense (1970), Memorandum, Assistant Attorney General, Washington, Office of Legal Council, 4 June.

Edmonds, M. (1972), 'Government Contracting and Renegotiation', *Public Administration*, Spring.

Edmonds, M. (1983), *Tristar: A Biography*, London, Macmillan.

Federal Reserve Bank of New York (1970), *Application for a 'V' Loan Guarantee, Interim Financing of Penn Central*, 17 June.

Freeman, B. and Mendelowitz, A. (1982), 'Program in Search of a Policy: The Chrysler Loan Guarantee', *Journal of Policy Analysis and Management*, 1 (4).

Friedman, M. (1975), *There's No Such Thing as a Free Lunch*, La Salle, Illinois, Open Court.

Galbraith, J. K. (1971), *The New Industrial State* (2nd edn), New York, Mentor.

General Accounting Office (1972), *Report to Congress: Implementation of Emergency Loan Guarantees Act B — 169300*, Washington, 6 December.

House Committee on Banking and Currency (1972), *Penn Central Failure and the Role of Financial Institutions, 92nd Congress*, Washington, Staff Report.

Krasner, J. (1978), 'United States Commercial and Monetary Policy', in P. Katzenstein (ed.), *Between Power and Plenty*, Madison, University of Wisconsin Press.

Liebhafsky, H. (1971), *American Government and Business*, New York, John Wiley.

Lilley, W. and Muller, J. C. (1977), 'The New Social Regulation', *The Public Interest*, 47, Spring.

Loving, R. (1970), 'The Penn Central Bankruptcy Express', *Fortune*, August.

MacCrindle, R. and Godfrey, P. (1973), *Rolls Royce Ltd*, London, HMSO (DTI Report).

McKie, J. W. (1980), 'Government Intervention in the Economy of the United States', in P. Maunder (ed.), *Government Intervention in the Developed Economy*, London, Croom Helm.

Melman, S. (1970), *Pentagon Capitalism*, New York, McGraw-Hill.

Senate Committee on Banking, Housing and Urban Affairs (1971), *Hearing on Emergency Loan Guarantee Legislation*, Part I, June.

Shonfield, A. (1965), *Modern Capitalism*, Oxford University Press.

Vogel, D. (1978), 'Why Businessmen Distrust their State: The Political Consciousness of American Corporate Executives', *British Journal of Political Science*, January.

Watts, J. H. III (1982), 'How US Financial Markets are Distorted by Government Intervention', *The Banker*, August.

4

'Social Market' and Modernization Policy: West Germany

Josef Esser and Wolfgang Fach
with Kenneth Dyson

Since the mid-1970s, the international economy has experienced a deep and protracted crisis that was induced by the two 'oil-price shocks' of 1973-74 and 1978-79. These 'turbulences' have produced different national reactions, which have depended on the particular economic conditions and on the relations of power among interests in each country. With respect to such key indicators as unemployment, price stability and balance of payments, and compared with the performance of other countries, the Federal Republic of Germany initially withstood these challenges so well that the larger of the two parties in the centre–left coalition government, the Social Democratic Party (SPD), used 'Model Germany' as the basis for its federal election campaign in 1976 (Kohl and Basevi, 1980; Markovits, 1982). The priority of 'Model Germany' was economic performance; its personification was Federal Chancellor Helmut Schmidt (SPD); and its instrument was structural modernization of the economy.

By the early 1980s, however, 'Model Germany' had encountered two problems. On the one hand, problems of inflationary pressures and rising unemployment reduced the credibility of the SPD's attempt to associate itself with 'Model Germany' and its electoral appeal and encouraged its coalition partner in the federal government, the Free Democratic Party (FDP), to switch their support in the autumn of 1982 to the centre–right coalition with the Christian Democrats of Helmut Kohl. On the other hand, the social costs that were implicit in the 'Model Germany' ideology generated dissatisfaction within the SPD and fuelled the resentments of the so-called 'alternatives'. In 1981 unemployment grew by 43 per cent and it maintained the same momentum in 1982, with unemployment affecting 10.2 per cent of the workforce by January 1983. In the same year the German Institute for Economic Research pointed out that between 1973 and 1980 900,000 jobs had been lost in manufacturing industry.

'MODEL GERMANY'

Leading Social Democrats identified the central characteristic of 'Model Germany' as a 'goal-oriented', anticipatory planning of social change — as a 'strategic modenization of the economy' (Hauff and Scharpf, 1975). According to these technocratically minded academics and politicians (Hauff was Federal Minister for Research and Technology till 1980), the state was to be a modernizing force that induced and guided necessary change by

(1) a sectoral policy, promoting 'knowledge–intensive' industries and managing the decline of 'old' industries;
(2) a technology policy, securing and developing an international advantage in particular markets;
(3) a social policy, making modernization acceptable by seeking a 'humanization of work' and by financial support for the unemployed;
(4) a policy of accommodation, binding firms and trade unions to economic growth in 'corporatist' forms (cf. Esser *et al.*, 1979; Altvater, 1980).

Like other ideologies, 'Model Germany' presents a partial, even distorted, picture of reality; its illusions have indeed been gradually revealed by political practice. It appears questionable that such a centrally directed structural and technological policy can be realized in a capitalist market economy. This chapter will analyse the management of industrial crises in the 1970s against the background of the influence, the functioning and the limits of 'Model Germany'.

West Germany's record of comparative economic success owes little to state planning. Far more important is the character of its market economy, which functions efficiently on the basis of a traditionally favourable industrial structure (both highly specialized and coherent) and of a banking system that is oriented to the problems and needs of industry. The efficient functioning of this market economy finds social support in a 'cooperative' trade union movement that plays an active part in the process of industrial adjustment. It is supported politically by the state, which helps to finance the process of adjustment and seeks to make it acceptable by carrying some of its social costs. According to one view, state, banks, firms and trade unions take on the appearance of 'a corporatist modernization cartel', united by the perceived and strongly articulated need to maintain West Germany's position as an economic 'great power' in the context of intensified international competition (Altvater *et al.*, 1979). The political appeal and intellectual interest of 'Model Germany' in the 1970s was based on its characterization of the nature of the West German economic system and its development during the postwar period. In particular, 'Model Germany' draws attention to three aspects of that economic system: the 'social market economy', political consensus, and economic adaptability.

The Social Market Economy

Despite the talk of 'zero hour' (*Stunde Null*) in 1945, the German economy inherited and could build upon a relatively intact, technologically modernized and well-developed basis of capital equipment. The West German economy was, therefore, able to take advantage of a long period of expansion of the international economy, an expansion that was assisted by American aid in the form of the Marshall Plan and by the unleashing of demand after wartime privation, and that was further encouraged by the economic boom that was released by the Korean War. In the 1950s and 1960s West Germany experienced a continuous economic growth that was disrupted only by short-lived and small-scale cyclical downturns: even the first real recession in 1966–67 was reversed in a year. The average annual growth rates were 8 per cent between 1950 and 1960 and 4.9 per cent between 1960 and 1970 (Kommission für den Wirtschaftlichen und Socialen Wandel, 1977). Historical conditions enabled German firms to achieve a position of dominance in world markets, in particular as exporters of technologically advanced and high-value investment goods. The German economy was specialized in the production of investment goods, world demand was especially strong for these goods, and the foundation, extension and liberalization of the European Economic Community after 1957 offered new opportunities. During this 'long export boom' West Germany's share of world exports rose from 3.3 per cent in 1950 to 7.3 per cent in 1957 and to approximately 11 per cent at the end of the 1960s. In the same period the share of exports in gross national product rose from 9 per cent to some 25 per cent: on average, exports rose annually by 20 per cent (Vogt, 1964).

Export success was supported by the Bundesbank's policy of undervaluing the Deutschmark, a policy that continued, despite revaluations in 1961 and 1969, till the 1970s. It was also supported by the credit policies of the commercial banks, especially of the three big banks — Deutsche Bank, Dresdner Bank and Commerzbank — which tended to be well represented on the supervisory boards of firms with a high proportion of exports to total sales (Kreile, 1978a, p. 195). The rapid growth of involvement with the international economy led to a dominance of the export industries within the industrial structure, particularly of technologically advanced sectors like vehicles, machine tools, plant construction, chemicals, petroleum, synthetic products and electronics. The West German economy was also characterized by a high degree of interdependence between industrial sectors. The 'interlocking' shareholdings of the banks in industry, the presence of bank representatives on supervisory boards of major corporations and a tendency for major industrial customers or suppliers to be represented on supervisory boards provided an opportunity for an integration of industrial decision-making.

Various factors combined to strengthen the role of banks and insurance companies in the economy: the heavy dependence of German industry on external finance; the potential for control that arose from the banks' direct shareholdings in industry and, more especially, from their role as proxy voters for clients who had deposited their shares with a bank; seats on the supervisory boards of many firms; and the collection and evaluation of information about the affairs and profit rates of firms and sectors. Big banks and insurance companies (like Allianz) appear to have the potential to develop as private mechanisms for direction of investment with the object of strengthening the structure of the economy as a whole — in so far as a planned direction of a market economy is possible at all (Arndt, 1977; Monopolkommission, 1978; Hack and Hack, 1979). Thus the West German economy possesses to a considerable degree the organizational potential 'to be able to coordinate and implement the decisions that are necessary for adaptation to the changed conditions of international competition' (Hirsch, 1980, p. 20).

The German 'economic miracle' was attributed to the success of the social market economy, and the identification of 'economic miracle' and social market economy worked to the electoral advantage of the Christian Democratic Union and its Bavarian sister party, the Christian Social Union. The CDU and CSU were the dominant parties of government from the foundation of the Federal Republic in 1949 to the advent of the Social Democratic–Liberal coalition in 1969. This combination of economic success and continuous Christian Democratic rule lent a great stability to economic ideology and contributed to the conversion of the Social Democratic Party from economic planning and nationalization to acceptance of the social market economy in its Bad Godesberg programme of 1959 (Smith, 1979). Identification with the social market economy lent prestige to particular politicians: to Professor Ludwig Erhard (Federal Economics Minister, 1949–63, and Chancellor, 1963–66), the so-called 'father of the economic miracle', and to Professor Karl Schiller (Federal Economics Minister, 1966–72), who added the Keynesian concept of 'global steering' and was identified with successful recovery from the recession of 1966–67. More significantly, the social market economy, with its emphasis on the market and private initiative, was compatible with a highly 'systematized capitalism' (Hack and Hack, 1979). According to the concept of the social market economy, the state's role was essentially subsidiary: to maintain stability as the precondition of an effective functioning of the market (hence the important role attributed to the autonomous Bundesbank), to complement the market (for example by research policy) and improve the efficiency of its functioning, and to develop social policies that help maintain confidence in the market economy. The Grand Coalition of CDU–CSU–SPD from 1966 to 1969 and the social–liberal coalition after 1969 attempted to reshape the social market economy.

In particular, Schiller became associated with the concept of the 'enlightened' social market economy. The aim of the policy was to create the conditions for a more effective adaptation to changes in the international economy. An attempt was made to improve coordination in the federal system of government Economic policy was to be coordinated by the Anti-cyclical Advisory Council, budgetary policy by the Financial Planning Advisory Council, and regional structural policy, agricultural structural policy and higher education construction by new joint planning committees of the federal government and the states. Instruments for a more 'active' policy in such fields as research, education and labour market policy were also introduced. The shift to a more active, anticipatory and technocratic concept of public policy was to be a highly distinctive aspect of the 'Model Germany' of the 1970s (Hauff and Scharpf, 1975). It represented, however, a reform within the intellectual framework provided by the concept of the social market economy.

Political Consensus

The economic and electoral 'success' of the social market economy confined the terms of debate about economic policy. This constriction of ideological space was also a function of the presence of a very different economic order in East Germany and the bitter political legacy of German partition. The political consensus seemed to reach its high point with the establishment of Concerted Action (Konzertierte Aktion) in 1967. Until the withdrawal of the trade unions in 1977, Konzertierte Aktion symbolized the political integration of the German trade union movement into the social market economy (Dyson, 1982a). It was created as a forum within which government, employers, trade unions and Bundesbank could consider their respective contributions to stability and growth of the economy. In particular, the attention of Konzertierte Aktion focused on wage policy and the need for its subordination to the general interest in economic stability and growth.

Political and economic integration of the trade unions can be traced back to the years after the First World War. The trade unions gave priority to 'economic democracy' and distinguished their own economic functions from the political functions that were the responsibility of political parties, parliament and government. The preoccupation of the trade unions of the Bonn Republic with co-determination (*Mitbestimmung*) was in this tradition. The emphasis on worker participation found expression and some success in the parity co-determination that was achieved in coal, iron and steel (workers elected 50 per cent of the representatives on their supervisory boards) and the weaker form of co-determination that was achieved in the rest of industry in 1952 and then strengthened in 1976.

A framework for a policy of 'social partnership' had been established at the level of the firm in the form of the statutory rights of works councils to be consulted and of statutory regulation of supervisory boards. Konzertierte Aktion was its extension to the level of the economy. Economic prosperity, declining unemployment, rising real wages and improved social benefits seemed to offer additional material incentive to cooperate with a form of capitalism that created widespread improvement of living conditions and, as co-determination revealed, could be reformed from within. The trade unions' commitment to co-determination and social partnership was crucial to the formula 'Model Germany'. At the level of the firm it was the basis of a relatively smooth management of industrial crises, of the willingness to form 'crisis cartels' whose rationale was a socially conscious modernization policy. At the level of the economy, it enabled — indeed, encouraged — the trade unions, who had withdrawn from Konzertierte Aktion in 1977, to engage in the more informal dialogues that Chancellor Helmut Schmidt organized personally as a way of bringing together the 'social partners' and coordinating their policies with that of the government. Similarly the trade unions joined the technology policy dialogue that was organized by the Federal Ministry for Research and Technology (Esser, 1982).

Economic Adaptation

For reasons outlined in the introduction to this volume, the highly organized economy of the Federal Republic found itself under more intense pressure to adapt and modernize from the beginning of the 1970s. A slow-down in the rate of growth of the world economy, high energy costs and new trade restrictions led to import penetration that threatened traditional industries like the clock industry or the textile industry and created structural crises for some technologically higher-value products. Despite occasional expressions of reluctance, the trade unions were carried along by a highly organized consensus about how the economy should respond to the new international challenge. The consensus incorporated the federal government, the Bundesbank, the Federation of German Industry, the Council of Economic Advisers, the economic research institutes and the banks. The core of the consensus was an anti-protectionist and 'offensive' adaptation that would build on West Germany's position of strength within the international economy to secure old markets and open up new ones.

Emphasis was placed on: an active economic diplomacy that was spearheaded by the Chancellor, who maintained very close personal contacts to leading bankers, industrialists and trade unionists; shift of production of unprofitable products to low-wage economies to avoid competitive disadvantage or trade restrictions; industrial concentration to take full advantage of economies of scale; reduction of costs by tax cuts, increased productivity and rationalization; modernization, in particular specialization on 'knowledge-intensive', high-value products and the development, planning and installation of highly complex large plants; and the value of a highly skilled workforce. These priorities were forcefully expressed at political and industrial levels. At the same time, social commentators became increasingly anxious about two developments that might challenge the stable political consensus of West Germany: the emergence of a category of 'marginal' workers and 'unemployables' who could no longer be integrated into society by the trade unions; and the emergence of the 'alternatives', who were choosing to drop out of an industrial society whose 'human' character they questioned.

The strategy of strengthened export orientation through 'healthy' decline was implemented with particular intensity in those sectors that were affected by structural crises (automobiles, steel, shipbuilding, electronics, watches, textiles/clothing, chemical fibres, synthetic products and parts of engineering) and where comprehensive effort was essential if the sectors were to remain internationally viable. As far as the social–liberal coalition government and the Bundesbank were concerned, this strategy took on the character of an 'objective force' (*Sachzwang*). Within this strategic consensus there were, nevertheless, heated disputes about how best to realize the strategy (Dyson, 1981). One dispute concerned the appropriate priorities of the federal government's fiscal policy: the Free Democratic Party, represented in the Economic Ministry after 1972, stressed tax reductions that would encourage industrial investment, while the Social Democratic Party, represented in the Finance Ministry and the Research and Technology Ministry, stressed the importance of a strong supportive role of public expenditure and of an active structural policy. This dispute reached its peak when an open letter of the Economics Minister, Count Lambsdorf, to Chancellor Schmidt was the immediate cause of the downfall of the coalition in 1982. During the 1970s the Research and Technology Ministry was able rapidly to expand its share of the federal budget: its support was heavily concentrated on a few large firms like Siemens and on such high-value export goods as microelectronics, telecommunications, computers and energy technologies. Another major priority was federal support for training, retraining and mobility of the workforce. These two priorities served to reduce the costs and risks of rapid structural adjustment both for firms and for individuals.

The rapid growth of public expenditure and of the size of the budget deficit during the 1970s and the early 1980s generated new tensions within the federal government and between the federal government (especially the Social Democrats) and the autonomous central bank, the Bundesbank. In the context of the political and economic fears about inflation that were a legacy of the experience of the Weimar Republic (1919–33) and that had informed the law establishing the Bundesbank, the central bank enjoyed considerable political freedom to fulfil its legal responsibility to 'safeguard the currency'. Its priority of a strict monetary policy was, however, oriented to the safeguarding of international competitiveness by achievement of price stability at home. Although a restrictive monetary policy and rapid appreciation of the Deutschmark in the late 1970s caused problems for the export-oriented bank–industry nexus, bankers and industrialists were very aware of the competitive advantage that they could enjoy from cheaper energy imports and domestic price stability. As we shall see, the government sought to maintain the consensus about an export-oriented modernization policy through corporatist arrangements (Esser *et al.*, 1979) that incorporated employers and trade unions into the public policy process: for instance, the Saar steel rescue, the technology policy dialogue, the nuclear policy council.

Despite heavy social costs, the trade unions supported this modernization strategy. The condition of that support was a role for the trade unions in the formulation and implementation of the strategy through co-determination at the firm, sectoral and national levels. However, support was maintained despite the failure of the trade unions to realize their economic policy proposals for structural councils and direction of investment at the sectoral and regional levels. The trade unions were able to achieve attention to an anticipatory social planning through *ad hoc* 'crisis cartels' (for example the steel crisis) and through their role on the supervisory boards of industrial corporations, especially in the coal, iron and steel sectors (see also the Volkswagen crisis of 1974–75 and the rescue of AEG).

It was noted earlier that the dominance of the concept and practice of social partnership in union attitudes to management of industrial crises stretched back to the 1950s and had its roots in the Weimar period. Its justification and the unwillingness to consider other options resided in the apparent success of social partnership in raising the real value of wages and social benefits and the higher economic and social costs that seemed to be associated with strategies of conflict in industrialized societies like Britain.

The distinctiveness and self-confidence of 'Model Germany' sprang from a combination of factors: the ideology of the social market economy, which attributed moral force to civil society and a subsidiary, facilitative role to the state; the social consensus that was expressed in the concept and practice of social partnership and the integration of the working class and its organizations, trade unions and the Social Democratic Party; and the economic strength of West Germany, which had the third largest GNP and was the second biggest exporter among advanced industrialised societies and which possessed a highly specialized, technologically advanced industrial structure that benefited from high internal interdependence especially with financial institutions (Kreile, 1978b).

MODERNIZATION POLICY: SOME CASE STUDIES

Management of industrial crises in West Germany can be properly understood only against the background of the ideology of structural modernization that is associated with 'Model Germany'. Modernization policy has had two aspects. First, there has been an emphasis on the management of a 'healthy' decline in those sectors whose traditional products are under severe competitive pressure from, in particular, the newly industrializing countries. The characteristic of crisis management in these sectors has been its political intensity. Spectacular crises have typically called forth a response of 'crisis cartels'. Second, emphasis has been placed on managing the growth of modern sectors, on an 'offensive' expansion with new products into new markets in order to avoid future crises. The characteristic of crisis management in these sectors has been a continuous long-term strategy of crisis avoidance that is 'non-political'.

Management of Decline

Since 1975, the *steel* industries of all advanced industrialized societies have experienced a deep structural crisis that has manifested itself in over-production on the world market, in a massive fall of profit rates in the most important steel-consuming sectors, and in the competitive advantage that has been achieved by some newly industrializing countries in steel production. The subsequent price war in the international steel market threatened the West German steel industry with particularly serious consequences because more than one-third of its total production was exported. Since the early 1970s, the German steel industry has undergone a very effective and rapid adaptation that has involved rationalization, closures, specialization and a concentration of production. Between 1974 and 1980 the workforce was reduced by about 15 per cent (approximately 50,000); crude steel production dropped by 10 million tons and rolled-steel capacity by 50 per cent (8.5 million tons); while, with considerable state aid, the investment rate in modern capital-intensive plant was increased. The German steel industry's continuing strength in European markets made it a reluctant participant in the cartel that was organized by the EEC to restrain national production and thereby reduce competitive pressure on the member states. Political failure to get other EEC members to reduce their very high levels of state subsidy to their national steel industries eventually led the federal government to introduce a steel programme in 1981 to maintain a 'workable' competition. However, this programme was essentially defensive, and West Germany's government continued to cling to the view that adaptation of the steel industry was primarily a matter for the social partners and for the bank–industry nexus.

Although both the German steel regions, the Ruhr and the Saar, shared the commitment to adaptation, the problem of managing industrial decline was much more drastic in the Saar. By 1977 mass redundancies were being announced, and bankruptcy threatened the two major steel producers in the Saar, Roechling Burbach and Neunkircher Eisenwerke. The imminent danger of high social costs resulted from a combination of small plant size, inadequate investment because of a divided structure of ownership, excessive concentration on bulk steel, lack of an associated steel-processing industry and high transport costs for raw materials. Faced by a 'jobs crisis', the Saar state government (CDU) and the federal government (SPD–FDP) agreed that a massive steel rationalization programme was required. While the Saar's political parties conducted an ideological debate about state versus private reconstruction, the state government and the federal government negotiated in privacy with the Luxembourg steel firm Arbed, which already had interests in the Saar steel industry, and with the industrial union IG Metall. This informal 'crisis cartel' brought together public and private actors in the search for a mutually satisfactory political solution that would involve the maintenance of a healthy, internationally competitive core of the industry. IG Metall gained federal guarantees of financial support for a social plan that would protect a core of employment and reduce the hardship of redundancy for others. Arbed gained control of the affected companies and financial aid in return for producing a rationalization programme that was to have the approval of the public accountancy firm, Treuarbeit AG, and to meet certain structural requirements of the CDU state government. In return for this restructuring and for union agreement, the federal government provided massive financial aid of over DM1 billion to cover Arbed's risks and to help finance the social plan. The federal and state governments gained an agreement that did something for the substantive problem of jobs and redundancies, met the test of international competitiveness and took a difficult issue off the political agenda by pacifying IG Metall. The rationalization programme involved concentration of ownership in one large firm (Arbed Saarstahl), integration of crude steel and rolled-steel production at one site and a reduction of the workforce by some one-third. The restructuring agreement of 1978 was also accompanied by a special programme of regional aid for the Saar during the process of redundancies in order to help diversify the local economy.

When in 1981 the problem of over-production threatened mass redundancies and corporate crisis to large steel firms in the Ruhr, the cartel model of the Saar re-emerged. The complex negotiations between Krupp Stahl AG and Hoesch about a possible fusion into a new company, Ruhrstahl, involved IG Metall directly, because of its representation on the supervisory boards of both companies as well as because of the implications of rationalization for its members. They also involved the state and federal economics ministries, which wanted a politically acceptable solution to the problem of over-production and would anyway have to foot the bill for much of the rationalization programme. The Deutsche Bank, which was represented on the supervisory boards of both firms, was another important actor in getting the negotiations underway and in sustaining their momentum.

During 1982 the problems of the West German steel industry gained dramatic momentum. By June the industry had put in requests for government assistance of DM14 billion. The losses of the six major producers mounted, and at the end of the year some half of the workforce were on short-time working. The producers' federation began to speak of 'catastrophe' and to complain bitterly about the misuse of subsidies by their EEC partners who had pledged to use them for restructuring and not for maintenance of existing plant. Negotiations about the creation of Ruhrstahl proved difficult and protracted and were submerged in a growing number of other ideas for cooperation. In January 1983, a commission of three independent 'moderators' delivered its report to the federal government. In return for aid of DM3 billion, the five steel firms of the Ruhr were to be merged into two groups — a 'Rhine group' of Thyssen and Krupp Stahl; and a 'Ruhr group' of Hoesch, Klöckner and Salzgitter. The plan ran into major political opposition from the state government of North-Rhine Westphalia and from IG Metall. By March 1983 only the negotiations about the Rhine group had made much headway.

More dramatically, in November 1982 the new centre-right coalition of Chancellor Helmut Kohl was faced by the imminent bankruptcy of Arbed Saarstahl, the Saar's second largest employer. Although the federal Economics Minister spoke of the failure of the rescue of 1978, the federal government combined with the Saar state government to provide a special bridging loan in addition to the DM2.2 billion that had already been committed. Its strong commitment to the principles of the market led the government to stress the need for sacrifice. At the same time, it recognized that an unemployment rate of nearly 12 per cent in the Saar and the prospect that over 30,000 more jobs could be lost there made the Saar 'a special case' (in German terms). The 'crisis cartel' of government, employers and IG Metall was faced with a failure of the first Saar steel rescue and greater problems of consensus for a second rescue package.

The model of the 'crisis cartel' was not a discovery of the late 1970s. It emerged in the 1960s as a typical mode of crisis management. Perhaps the most spectacular of the traditional 'bank-led' rescues was that of *Krupp* in 1967. In 1966 Krupp had losses of DM50 million; in 1967 its debt to the banks amounted to DM2.5 billion against the background of a turnover of DM5 billion; and at the end of 1966 the banks' own export credit company (AKA) precipitated a crisis by refusing further export credit. In the strictest secrecy, federal Economics Minister Schiller and the President of the Bundesbank conferred about the need for state aid and a reduction of high interest rates to help firms like Krupp that had encountered difficulties. The Bundesbank's reduction of interest rate in early 1967 was indeed christened the 'Krupp discount'. The crisis negotiations involved Berthold Beitz, general manager of Krupp, Hermann Josef Abs of the Deutsche Bank, three other bankers and Schiller. The contents of the resulting agreement (*Vertrag*) indicated the importance that was attached to reorganization and restructuring of Krupp in order to safeguard its important role as an exporter. The federal government provided loan guarantees of DM300 million to guarantee finance for export orders; the banks extended a further DM100 million of export credit; and the state government of North-Rhine Westphalia offered a loan guarantee of DM150 million. In return, the firm was to be transformed from a private empire into a limited liability company and a supervisory board established. The presence of Abs and of a representative of the board of directors of the Dresdner Bank on the new supervisory board was intended to ensure a careful monitoring of the rescue, including the proper use of the government's loan guarantees. As Krupp was a one-man empire, an active role for the unions in the rescue was excluded. But, a member of the new supervisory board was Otto Brenner, head of IG Metall.

By contrast, the coal miners' union, IG Bergbau, was closely involved in the protracted problem of managing the crisis of the *coal* industry. As a consequence of cheap imported coal and of a cheaper alternative energy source in oil, the coal industry experienced its first crisis of over-production as early as 1958. The federal government, which was committed to a cheap energy policy, continued to believe that a gradual decline of the industry could be managed. Its response to the crisis was a duty on heating oil and an unsuccessful attempt at a voluntary self-limitation agreement with the oil companies. From 1964, however, a deeper crisis of over-production struck the industry. It was clear that rationalization of the coal industry required a concentration of ownership combined with heavy state subsidy to ease the problems of adjustment. The formation of Ruhrkohle AG in 1968 from 26 coal mining companies was the product of the collaborative effort by government, firms and IG Bergbau to find a mutually satisfactory solution. Its mode of operation also reflected a style of concerted action. The coal industry's preference for avoiding or managing crises by negotiation was later apparent in the agreement between the Association of German Electricity Companies and the Association of the German Coal Industry in 1977: the supply of coal to the electricity industry was guaranteed and regulated up until 1987. This capacity for self-organization in the face of crisis is characteristic of the ideology and practice of the social market economy and in particular of the highly systematized German economy, whose elements are efficient at organizing and managing their interdependence.

The *shipbuilding* industry, which was the third largest world producer in the 1950s had already begun to feel the effects of Japanese competition before the international economic crisis. Whereas Japan was able to double its share of world shipbuilding between 1956 and 1974 and already produced over 50 per cent of all ships, the German share fell from 17.3 to 6.4 per cent. Thereafter, oil crisis and worldwide recession led to a drop of demand, over-capacity and sharper competition. The subsequent process of decline led to a drop of share of world shipbuilding to 4.4 per cent in 1979. Between 1976 and 1981 capacity fell by 25 per cent, production by some 40 per cent and employment by about 30 per cent. Crisis of the shipbuilding industry was a serious structural crisis for two reasons: the crisis was spatially concentrated in the four coastal states, notably in Schleswig-Holstein and Bremen, and the shipbuilding industry was an important customer for the steel, electronics and engineering industries of other

states. In other words, the crisis had a sectoral and regional 'knock-
on' effect that the federal government, which was faced by important
state elections that could alter the balance of power at the federal
level, could not afford to ignore. In time for state elections in 1979
the federal government produced a programme of aid for the industry (up to the end of 1981) that sought to subsidize modernization
and diversification. In addition, the federal government, state governments, employers and trade unions collaborated to formulate a
'structural programme for the coastal states' that aimed to diversify
their economies. Characteristic for the perspective of the trade unions
was the restructuring programme for the second-largest shipbuilding
company, AG Weser, which belongs to Krupp. In agreement with IG
Metall, AG Weser sought to transform its production from large
tankers to construction of specialized, technologically advanced ships
(such as roll-on-roll-off ships, factory ships, ferries and container
ships). While the workforce was reduced by half by 1980, IG Metall
protected the position of the remaining workforce by a three-year
earnings guarantee. Similarly, in November 1979 the German Trade
Union Federation (DGB) presented a programme of modernization,
accompanied by social planning and proposals for corporatist arrangements, that aimed to maintain the leading position of West Germany
in the market for 'special ships' (13.7 per cent of the world market)
and that accepted the need for modernization. This apparent success
of the shipbuilding industry in adapting its production to maximize
the benefits of its technical expertise owed more to the structure of
the industry than to government policy. Innovation and diversification was assisted by the fact that four of the six largest companies
were general engineering companies. They were able to draw on the
expertise and resources available to conglomerates (Peacock *et al.*,
1980).

The *textile and clothing* industry experienced the increasingly sharp
international competition earlier than steel. Nevertheless, by intensive restructuring and internationalization of production it was able
to maintain its position as the biggest textile exporter in the world.
The industry's export orientation was typical of the 'Model Germany'
ideology; while the policy of liberalization of the federal government
helped competitors in South-east Asia and the Eastern bloc to gain
a higher market share in textiles than for any other advanced industrialized society. Improved technology, increased productivity by
rationalization and more capital-intensive production, the closure of
production of low-quality goods, and a transfer of production of

labour-intensive manufacture to 'low-wage' countries led to a drop in employment of some 40 per cent between 1970 and 1979. The textile industry alone lost over 200,000 jobs and 30 per cent of firms closed. The success of this modernization strategy was revealed by an increase of export share from 21 to 27 per cent and by the fact that 9 per cent more was produced in 1979 than in 1970 despite the decline of employment. Although not as successful, the clothing industry was able to reduce the share of imports in the domestic market and to increase its export share to over 13 per cent. The trade union IG Textil/Bekleidung accepted the fall of employment, sought to reduce its impact by rationalization agreements with employers, and could save further jobs by longer holidays and a shorter working week. While the union strongly supported the international textile agreement of 1973 and its extension in 1977, it accepted fully the export-oriented strategy of the sector.

The *Volkswagen* crisis of 1974–75 was the result of a worldwide over-production in the motor car industry that arose from the recession. The crisis found its expression in tendencies towards stagnation and decline of total production, increased competition, and fluctuating market shares in different national markets. Volkswagen's sales crisis reflected a combination of high export dependence (in 1973 70 per cent of production was exported and in 1975 still 56 per cent), an aggressive multinational character (numerous production and assembly plants in Belgium, Brazil, Yugoslavia, Mexico, Nigeria and South Africa) and a simultaneous decline of demand (especially in the USA, the largest market for VW). The crisis started at the beginning of the 1970s and was eventually precipitated by an 11 per cent fall of sales in 1974. Management of the VW crisis was shaped by the complex structure of interests that were represented on the supervisory board, in particular the federal government and state government of Lower Saxony as major shareholders and IG Metall in the shape of its chairman. The crisis measures combined a strategy of offensive modernization (domestic rationalization and faster transfer of production to more favourable foreign locations) with a social planning that was designed to ease the personal costs of adjustment.

Government's contribution was two-fold: pressure on VW to spread redundancies across plants and abandon the original plan to close whole plants; and a special regional programme to cover the areas affected by heavy VW redundancies. IG Metall cooperated with the plan to cut the labour force by some 40,000 (about one-fourth of the total) in return for a social plan that avoided spectacular mass redundancies. Almost 70 per cent of those affected took advantage of early retirement or of compensation in the form of individually agreed redundancy pay. The works councils participated in the selection of those to be made redundant. This 'corporatist' mode of crisis management brought VW back into profit in 1976. At the same time, the social costs of the internationally oriented modernization policy were carried by older, unskilled and especially foreign workers.

The crisis of *AEG-Telefunken* occurred despite the strong position of the West German electronics industry in the world market and its capacity to maintain that position after 1973. However, the comparative advantage that was enjoyed by Japan and some newly industrializing countries in the field of domestic appliances and of television, video and radio represented a structural change that provided the context for AEG's financial crisis. Although the size of AEG's turnover made it Germany's second-largest, Europe's fourth-largest and the world's twelfth-largest electronics company, it had failed to shift its production on a sufficient scale to high-value, profitable products like data processing equipment and office technology. Instead, expansion focused on consumer goods and power-engineering (over 50 per cent of turnover). Unlike its larger and very successful rival, Siemens, AEG was slow to engage in foreign production. The background to the losses that AEG incurred from 1974 onwards and to the financial crisis that was unleashed by a loss of DM968 million in 1979 was a series of costly and mistaken acquisitions of other companies, mistakes in the fields of nuclear power and computer development, and falling sales of a series of electronic consumer goods. In the autumn of 1979, led by AEG's *Hausbank* — the Dresdner Bank — a huge rescue programme was mounted by a consortium that involved more than 20 banks and insurance companies as well as Daimler Benz, the motor car company. AEG received financial aid of DM3.4 billion in the form of replenishment of its equity capital and of additional long-term loans in return for a restructuring and rationalization programme. Restructuring meant concentration on new products like telecommunications, a doubling of overseas production, closure of unprofitable plants and cooperation with partners. Rationalization meant a loss of 13,000 jobs by the end of 1980 (a cut of 10 per cent): the workforce had already been reduced by some 40,000 (25 per cent) during the last decade. However, continuing losses led the consortium in 1981 to agree to write off DM240 million of their outstanding loans to AEG.

The monitoring of the rescue was to be ensured by the election of Hans Friderichs of the Dresdner Bank as the chairman of the company's supervisory board in 1980. Friderichs brought in a new general manager, Heinz Dürr, whose career had been linked with the engineering company Robert Bosch, which was known to be keen on diversification and which might, therefore, provide an ideal partner as part of the restructuring programme. In 1981 AEG, Robert Bosch and the steel company Mannesmann (which is closely linked to the Dresdner Bank) agreed on a new joint venture in the field of telecommunications. The deal was facilitated by the financial backing of the Deutsche Bank, the Dresdner Bank, the Westdeutsche Landesbank and the Allianz insurance company, who agreed to take equity stakes in the venture. In total, the AEG rescue seemed to display the remarkable capacity for self-organization of German industry, the role of the banks in insulating government from difficult and complex problems and the emphasis on an export-oriented modernization policy. The depth of IG Metall's commitment to this strategy was revealed by their criticism that the firm had failed to listen earlier to their warning — expressed in the supervisory board — that without a radical restructuring AEG would become internationally uncompetitive. They argued that only parity co-determination could ensure a rapid adaptation of the economy to deep structural changes in the international economy.

AEG would have been insolvent in 1979 without a rescheduling of its debts and new loans from the banks. Unfortunately, the problems of restructuring AEG proved obstinate, if not intractable. By 1982 the problems of this sprawling industrial giant had turned into West Germany's biggest ever industrial disaster. The new management was unable to free itself from the burdens that had been imposed by the past phase of rapid empire-building, which had been based on borrowed funds and on the priority of increased sales over increased profits. This inheritance of enormous financial liabilities was aggravated by record high interest rates after 1979. In 1979 the banks had pumped DM930 million into AEG at DM150 a share. By August 1982 the value of AEG's shares had dropped as low as DM22. The strategy of the banks and of management was to concentrate on preserving the viable areas of AEG by finding strong industrial partners for them. After the involvement of Bosch, Grundig and Mannesmann in the profitable telecommunications business, AEG management's restructuring programme AEG-83 sought to split the group into separate companies for capital goods and for household appliances. This programme collapsed in the summer of 1982 when the works council of AEG rejected the proposal that Britain's GEC should acquire 40 per cent equity stake in the profitable capital goods business (in large part because of Lord Weinstock's reputation for 'ruthless' personnel policy). The pressing need to provide breathing space for restructuring was reflected in new trade union pressure on the federal government to take an equity stake in AEG, a proposal that was rejected by Social Democratic Chancellor Schmidt in favour of a 'private-sector' solution. Senior management drew the federal Economics Minister, the federal Finance Minister and the Chancellor into negotiations that led in July 1982 to an export credit guarantee of DM600 million (£140 million) on condition that the banks provided new loans of DM275 million (£64 million).

As a result of continuing losses and of the collapse of AEG-83, the parent company, AEG-Telefunken, was forced to fight off bankruptcy in the autumn of 1982 by invoking the West German legal procedure known as 'composition' (*Vergleich*). The *Vergleich* is a court-supervised settlement with a company's creditors. Its objective is to relieve the external debt burden so that the company can gain financial room to restructure its loss-making operations. Unlike in Britain, a company is able to apply to court for protection against its creditors. An administrator is appointed by the court to supervise the proceedings, which involve the attempt to persuade creditors to write off up to 60 per cent of the company's unsecured debts. Eventually the creditors are assembled to vote on a settlement. Insolvency is not a necessary condition for *Vergleich* proceedings: it is enough to show that debts exceed assets. By August 1982, the date of commencement of *Vergleich* proceedings, AEG had debts of at least DM5 billion; banks and other creditors faced prospective losses of at least DM2.6 billion. The protection that the banks gained from the *Vergleich* was the provision that any new credits would then become prior claims in any ensuing bankruptcy.

The impact of the AEG crisis on the German economy was considerable, particularly because the autumn of 1982 was also associated with threats of steeply rising unemployment, continuing economic stagnation, deteriorating export performance (notably in the steel industry), and the end of 13 years of the socialist–liberal coalition. The major impact was on business confidence. AEG had 95,000 employees in West Germany, and it was estimated that 300,000 other jobs were at risk if the firm collapsed. The psychological damage was all the greater because the AEG crisis cast doubt on the resilience of the German banking system. The Dresdner Bank faced losses of DM300 million on its unsecured loans of about DM500 million. A new centre–right coalition under Chancellor Kohl came to power on the defensive. AEG's crisis and the deepening difficulties of the steel industry in the Saar and the Ruhr indicated more clearly than before the limits of the ability of West Germany's system of self-organized capitalism to manage industrial crises.

Management of Growth

In its annual report 1981–82 West Germany's Council of Economic Experts concluded 'that the range of domestic exports, both its emphasis on finished goods and its high technological standard, is compatible with the requirements of contemporary processes of international adjustment'. This judgement reflected two factors. First, the international economic crisis after 1973 generated new economic opportunities for profit that were particularly suited to the specialized character of West Germany's industrial structure. Second, the vitality of German industry and of its supportive banks was apparent in the priority that was given to an offensive adaptation in areas like energy technology and computers.

The exploitation of innovation in the field of energy technology is characteristic of the 'export-oriented' modernization policy, of the concern to exploit major export opportunities, to reduce dependence on oil with its cost to the balance of payments and to improve the competitiveness of German goods on the domestic market. High oil prices have encouraged industry to exploit alternative energy sources, both old (such as coal) and new (such as nuclear energy). West Germany achieved a leading position in the production of nuclear reactors, gaining two of the four contracts that were internationally tendered in 1980 and participating in the construction of France's fast-breeder reactor. German firms were also able to sell their 'know-how' in coal liquidification, oil extraction and solar energy to a range of countries. Energy-saving technology was recognized as crucial not just to the balance of payments but also to the competitiveness of German products in the engineering, electronics, automobile and construction industries.

Another field of considerable success was computers. German banks and government had long been aware of the crucial importance of the computer industry, which in 1977 became the world's third-largest industry (after petroleum and motor cars). The government's high level of support for the industry was coordinated from 1967 onwards in the electronic data processing programmes. These programmes offered general measures of support for the industry in the form of loans and grants for research and development and for computer research by public bodies. In part reflecting the unfortunate experience of Siemens in the large computer market, support was increasingly concentrated on small computers and the development of peripherals. German small computers were a great commercial success: Nixdorf, which is closely linked to the Deutsche Bank, had achieved 35 per cent of this market by 1978. Special programmes for integrated circuits date back to 1969 and helped West Germany capture 37.2 per cent of the West European market for integrated circuits by 1978. Whereas the British computer industry experienced a slow growth of sales between 1971 and 1977, the West German industry underwent a rapid growth and from 1974 had a strongly favourable balance of trade in computers (Peacock *et al.*, 1980). While government supplied general industry-wide support, the banks were central to the performance of particular firms like Nixdorf.

In both energy technology and computers, banks and government left the initiative to firms. At the same time, their priorities were clearly focused on modernization. Both altered their structures to reflect these priorities. The banks' interest in research and development policy found its expression in their collaboration to found a risk-finance company that was to help innovation in medium-sized and small firms. In 1972 the federal government established the Federal Ministry of Research and Technology and supported its continuing and rapid expansion as a funding agency for the strategy of 'export-oriented' modernization. An elaborate research planning system gave a systematic character to the Ministry's activities. More generally, the development of total financial aid for industry (grants, loans and tax allowances) reflected the dominance of 'Model Germany'. This aid is divided into three categories by the federal government's annual subsidy reports: maintenance (safeguarding jobs and income), adjustment (encouraging a smooth adaptation of industry), and productivity (increasing growth potential and innovation). The respective proportions of maintenance, adjustment and productivity aid were 55.4, 38.1 and 6.5 per cent in 1970; 50.7, 41.3 and 8 per cent in 1973; and 34.5, 56.1 and 9.4 per cent in 1978. In fact, grants and loans to the coal industry and tax allowances as a regional policy measure accounted for most maintenance aid. Otherwise, in the 1970s maintenance aid was not typical of West German industry.

The problems of managing growth led to a new corporatist device at the federal level. From 1979 the Ministry of Research and Technology organized a technology policy dialogue that brought together some 20 representatives of employers, trade unions and scientists to consider in particular the application of microelectronics and the social problems associated with that application. The focus of discussion was two-fold: the need for urgent action in order to keep pace with Japan and the USA and the problem that microelectronics were estimated to threaten a net job loss of 1.65 million by 1985 and of another 1.2 million by 1990. This dialogue represented the kind of institutional framework through which SPD intellectuals like Volker Hauff and Fritz Scharpf sought to stabilize 'Model Germany'.

The Political Limits of Modernization

Despite the remarkably smooth adaptation of the West German economy in the face of a new challenge of industrial crises, the modernization strategy reflected in the political slogan 'Model Germany' was seriously challenged during the 1970s. Its political limits were revealed in the conflicts about nuclear energy and the consequent emergence of the 'Greens' or 'Alternatives' as a phenomenon of political protest against materialist values and conventional parliamentary politics; in the variety of citizen action groups (*Bürgerinitiativen*) that were particularly active over environmental matters and were able to block large investment projects; in the occupation of property, which revealed a serious housing shortage in the large cities and reflected a rejection of conventional values; and in the emergence of the peace movement, which contained within it values hostile to industrial society and which gained political expression in the new Green party of 1980. This complex body of protest was in part a reaction to the social consequences of modernization (exclusion of the unskilled and the old) and in part an intellectual rejection by many young people of the values of a strongly 'achievement-oriented' society that was pledged to competition and growth. The Social Democratic Party as the traditional party of the left was faced with internal conflicts about whether and how to assimilate the so-called *Aussteiger* ('drop-outs'). Although the protest against industrial society took the spectacular extra-parliamentary form of 'sit-ins', occupations and large demonstrations, the new concern for a humanistic politics that emphasized self-realization, 'natural simplicity' and participation was not confined to the margins of politics. 'Post-industrial' values appeared to enjoy considerable public support, according to opinion polls: they found their expression within the traditional parties, especially the SPD, and generated conflicts that proved difficult to resolve and that threatened to block the policy process.

Nuclear energy became a major political issue in the 1970s and had a great impact on the consciousness of policy-makers (the nuclear issue is discussed in detail by Dyson, 1982b). Here the traditional power and values of industrial groups was directly and decisively challenged from the 'grass roots'. Chancellor Schmidt, successive FDP economics ministers (Friederichs and Lamsdorff) and successive SPD research and technology ministers (Ehmke, Matthöfer and Hauff) viewed the nuclear energy industry as central to the modernization of the economy. Trade union leaders were also agreed on the importance of the peaceful exploitation of nuclear energy, not just in order to reduce dependence on expensive imports of oil and to meet future energy needs, but also because it would generate employment in the electrical engineering and chemical industries. However, the attempt to construct reactors at Brokdorf and Wyhl and a huge disposal site at Gorleben led to mass demonstrations, occupations and repressive police measures in 1976 and 1977. In addition, 'alternative lists' that emphasized the nuclear and related environmental issues began to have successes in local and state elections (for example in Berlin, Bremen and Baden-Würtemberg). Conflict about nuclear energy developed within the political system: within the FDP parliamentary party in Bonn, between the SPD–FDP governments in North-Rhine Westphalia and Bonn, and especially within the SPD. Regional party leaders in the Saar, Schleswig-Holstein and Baden-Würtemberg began to express the values associated with the protest movement. The SPD took refuge in general formulas that, in effect, kept options open with respect to nuclear power while accepting that the strength of protest made it difficult to carry through the nuclear energy programme. According to the trade unions, the blockage of the nuclear energy programme meant a loss of over 20,000 jobs by the end of 1977. The SPD faced the threat of a divide between trade union and environmentalist camps. Characteristically, the federal government's response was to establish a series of corporatist devices. However, it proved impossible to co-opt dissent into the modernization strategy. Faced by the alternatives of pushing through its policy or of compromise, the federal government opted for the latter. It regarded the political costs of the 'hard' option as prohibitive. The blockage of the nuclear programme remained a monument to the limits of the modernization strategy and, moreover, suggested that these limits were set not just by the scale of protest but also — in contrast to France — by the unwillingness of the federal government and most state governments to impose modernization policies in an overt manner.

CONCLUSION

West Germany's experience of industrial crises displays the continuing viability and influence of the doctrine of the social market economy. In 1966 the new SPD Economics Minister Schiller published the 'Principles of Sectoral Policy'. The five general principles have remained the basis for government's role in crisis management and seem to have found a concrete expression in the cases of crisis that have occurred. Structural intervention was justifiable only when the difficulties concerned the whole sector and were based on lasting economic changes; the entrepreneurs and managers were to be primarily responsible for the necessary structural adaptation; the government's role was to support measures of self-help, provided these measures promised to strengthen on some lasting basis the competitiveness of the enterprises concerned; special governmental aids or other interventions could be considered only if the individual sectors were undergoing major changes at a rapid rate, and if the changes would generate undesirable economic and social consequences; the aids should be temporary, should be gradually withdrawn and should not cripple the competitive process. Emphasis on the subsidiary role of government has been characteristic of West German crisis management, as in the Krupp and Saar steel rescues; alternatively, as in the case of AEG, government has preferred to rely on the self-organization of capitalism. Another characteristic of government's role in crisis management has been a reliance on general measures of support for a sector rather than on intervention at the level of the firm (for example, with regard to the shipbuilding and computer industries). Detailed intervention and monitoring of rescues has been primarily the function of the banks. It is, however, clear that the character of German crisis management owed more to the structure of German capitalism than to the doctrine of the social market economy *per se*. Put another way, the viability of the doctrine of the social market economy rested on a highly organized and efficiently functioning capitalist system in which finance and industrial capital were mutually supportive. Industrial policy is, nevertheless, likely to evolve as the subsidy and policy competition of other governments put this highly organized and self-reliant capitalist system under greater pressure. By 1981 the term 'workable competition' had already begun to characterize industrial policy debate and was used to justify the shipbuilding programme of 1979 and the steel programme of 1981.

Another important feature of German crisis management has been the preference for corporatist devices, for 'crisis cartels'. They have been a particular feature of crisis management in the heavy industries like coal and steel. Companies in these industries are heavily dependent on external financing through the banks and are also characterized by parity co-determination. They are, in other words, locked into a structure of interests that need to be accommodated. The presence of bankers and trade union leaders on supervisory boards means that crisis management is typically a slow process and lacks the instant drama of Britain, where the existence of crises and crisis measures are often announced simultaneously.

There is, of course, no guarantee that 'Model Germany' will function effectively for ever. West Germany faces the same dangers as other national economies with a comparable position in the world market, notably, institutional rigidity. It is, above all, uncertain whether the adopted path of modernization, the specific 'mix' of modern industries, will prove successful within the sphere of international competition (with Japan and the USA as the main competitors). On the other hand, it is clear that any modernization strategy has to be paid for by massive losses of employment and a greater insecurity within the workforce. Meanwhile, as the number of unemployed approached a record level of 2 million in 1982, criticism of the so-called 'state fixation' of the trade unions (Zeuner, 1976) mounted and provoked calls for alternatives to trade union compliance with the constraints of economic modernization.

Despite these general risks, West Germany continued to perform well by international standards. The specific threat to 'Model Germany' arose from evidence — for instance, the rise of the 'Greens' — that the process of modernization as such was no longer beyond controversy. More than in France, economic modernization was obstructed by political counter-pressures. The impact of a growing 'Green' movement was heightened by the hesitancy of the established political parties, especially the Social Democrats. Such turbulences were not likely to stop the process of modernization. Nevertheless, they suggested a reduction in the flexibility and adaptability of the German economy.

REFERENCES

Altvater, E. (1980), 'Deutschland — eine Modelskizze', in H. Gremliza and H. Hannover (eds), *Die Linke*, Hamburg, VSA-Verlag.
Altvater, E., Hoffman, J. and Semmler, W. (1979), *Vom Wirtschaftswunder zur Wirtschaftskrise*, Berlin, Olle und Wolter.

Arndt, H. (1977), *Wirtschaftliche Macht — Tatsachen und Theorien* (2nd edn), Munich.

Dyson, K. (1981), 'The Politics of Economic Management in West Germany', in W. Paterson and G. Smith (eds), *The West German Model*, London, Frank Cass.

Dyson, K. (1982a), 'The Politics of Economic Recession in West Germany', in A. Cox (ed.), *Politics, Policy and Recession in Western Europe*, London, Macmillan.

Dyson, K. (1982b), 'West Germany: The Search for a Rationalist Consensus', in J. Richardson (ed.), *Policy Styles in Western Europe*, London, Allen and Unwin.

Esser, J. (1982), *Gewerkschaften in der Krise*, Frankfurt, Suhrkamp.

Esser, J. *et al.* (1978), 'Die sozialen Kosten einer modernisierten Volkswirtschaft', *Politische Vierteljahresschrift*, no. 9, 140–68.

Esser, J. *et al.* (1979), 'Das Modell Deutschland und seine Konstruktionsschwächen', *Leviathan*, no. 1, 1–11.

Hack, L. and Hack, I. (1979), *Bewirtschaftung der Zukunftsperspective*, Frankfurt, Suhrkamp.

Hauff, V. and Scharpf, F. (1975), *Modernisierung der Volkswirtschaft: Technologiepolitik als Strukturpolitik*, Frankfurt, Europäische Verlagsanstalt.

Hirsch, J. (1980), *Der Sicherheitsstaat: Das Modelldeutschland, seine Krise und die neuen sozialen Bewegungen*, Frankfurt, Europäische Verlagsanstalt.

Kohl, W. and Basevi, G. (1980), *West Germany: A European and Global Power*, Lexington Massachusetts, D. C. Heath.

Kommission für den Wirtschaftlichen und Sozialen Wandel (1977), *Wirtschaftlicher und sozialer Wandel in der BRD*, Göttingen, KWSW.

Kreile, M. (1978a), 'West Germany: The Dynamics of Expansion', in P. Katzenstein (ed.), *Between Power and Plenty*, Cambridge Massachusetts, Harvard University Press.

Kreile, M. (1978b), 'Die Bundesrepublik Deutschland — eine 'Economie Dominante' in Westeuropa?' *Politische Vierteljahresschrift*, no. 9, 236–56.

Kuster, G. (1974), 'Germany', in R. Vernon (ed.), *Big Business and the State*, Cambridge Massachusetts, Harvard University Press.

Markovits, A. (1982) (ed.), *The Political Economy of West Germany: Modell Deutschland*, New York, Praeger.

Monopolkommission (1978), *Fortschreitende Konzentration bei Grossunternehmen*, Baden-Baden, Monopolkommission.

Peacock, A. *et al.* (1980), *Structural Economic Policies in West Germany and the United Kingdom*, London, Anglo-German Foundation for the Study of Industrial Society.

Smith, G. (1979), *Democracy in West Germany*, London, Heinemann.

Vogt, W. (1964), *Makroökonomische Bestimmungsgründe des wirtschaftlichen wachtsum der BRD von 1950–60*, Tübingen.

Zeuner, B. (1976), 'Solidarität mit der SPD oder Solidarität der Klasse?' *Prokla*, no. 26, 3.

5

Liberal State and Party Competition: Britain

Stephen Wilks

For Britain, industrial crises are a far more salient policy issue than for most of the other countries examined in this collection. The regularity with which important elements of British industry are reported to be facing crisis is a testament to the progress of the 'British disease' as well as to the powers of journalistic hyperbole. Crisis as an organizing concept in analysing industrial policy might therefore be said to be a rather self-indulgently British hallmark, were it not for the post-1979 world recession, which has obliged all industrial states to confront this phenomenon.

In relation to contemporary economic developments, 'crisis' is typically used in two senses. In broad terms it is employed to describe the structural evolution of the British economy as evidenced in productivity trends, share of world trade and per capita GNP. More specifically, 'crisis' is used to capture the pressures that arise from the failure of industrial sectors or large industrial undertakings. In this second sense failure relates to large loss of market share, abrupt reductions in employment or outright bankruptcy. This chapter concentrates on crisis in the second, and more rigorous, sense. Such failures can properly be regarded as crises in that they represent a turning point, a rapid and qualitative change, which invites collective action (by public or private authorities).

Three recent examples of industrial crises give the flavour of the problem and illustrate some of the issues discussed later in greater depth. During the winter of 1981–82 the Conservative government found itself making decisions about the closure of British Aluminium's Invergordon smelter with a loss of 900 jobs (December); the receivership of Laker Airways, with 2600 employees; and the receivership of the De Lorean car company, with a residual workforce of 1500 (both in February). The fact that exceptional action was contemplated but did not materialize in these three cases suggests that the reasons why some companies are not 'rescued' are at times as interesting as the criteria for rescue. Nevertheless, they displayed some typical characteristics of the state's dealings with industrial crises.

First, in none of these cases could failure be attributed solely to pure market forces. In each case, government's influence over production costs, financing and markets was a contributory factor. Laker operated in a highly regulated market in competition with state-subsidized British Airways. Although its collapse was attributed to Sir Freddie's failures of financial judgement, the five-year battle with the Civil Aviation Authority (CAA), US Civil Aeronautics Board (CAB) and the IATA price-fixing cartel to operate Skytrain and secure remunerative routes were important contributory factors (Monkton and Fallon, 1982).

The Invergordon closure in Scotland was even more closely linked to state intervention. In 1968 the Labour government encouraged the creation of an aluminium smelting industry through investment grants and cheap power contracts for three smelters (the two others were Alcan at Lynmouth and RTZ/Kaiser at Anglesey). For a long time this policy was seen as a model of anticipatory intervention (Dell, 1973). Its major weakness was, however, its inflexibility in the face of an increasingly uneconomic energy source. By contrast, De Lorean has always been a high-risk state investment with a large subsidy content. It was negotiated in 1978 by the Northern Ireland Office under Roy Mason and the Northern Ireland Development Agency (NIDA) with minimal involvement from the Department of Industry (DoI). In return for the creation of 2600 jobs in Belfast, the company had received nearly £80 million by January 1982, when an application for £35 million from the Export Credit Guarantee Department provoked a governmental review of the project and a decision to withhold further aid.

Second, in each case individual public agencies had assessed the problem and evaluated the social, economic and political implications from their particular departmental viewpoint; then, after inter-departmental consultation, decisions to allow closure were taken by Cabinet ministers and approved in Cabinet Committee. This fragmented structure is important: in the three cases different administrative actors were involved; each case was treated on an *ad hoc* basis and argued apparently from first principles; and each decision was unpredictable and taken ultimately on 'political' criteria. Thus, Laker involved the Prime Minister, who personally decided against intervention (*The Guardian*, 6 February 1982) as well as the

Department of Trade and the Bank of England, which had chaired
bankers meetings and 'guided' the banking consortium that kept
Laker afloat. Invergordon was handled by the Scottish Secretary
with the involvement of the Highlands and Islands Development
Board (HIDB). The decision not to intervene was reportedly taken
in a Cabinet Committee chaired by the Prime Minister in December
1981 after negotiation with the DoI, the Treasury and the Department of Energy (*Daily Telegraph*, 31 December 1981). The HIDB
was granted an additional £10 million to help cushion the blow of
closure. De Lorean was also treated as a regional problem. It was
handled primarily by James Prior as Northern Ireland Secretary with
the aid of the NIDA and with relatively little contact with the DoI.

These three cases illustrate the futility of attempting to compart-
mentalize government and the economy and underline the unrealistic
view of industrial affairs that a 'free market' analytic framework and
vocabulary imply. Government action plays a constitutive role in
industrial affairs. However, as we shall see, although government is in
part responsible for industrial success, it has no adequate intellectual
framework or administrative machinery with which to discharge that
responsibility.

Initially, the problem of crisis management should be set in its
context. Economic change can be characterized at three levels. At
the most general level, and as with all advanced economies, there has
been a shift of employment and share of GNP from primary (agriculture and extraction) and secondary (industrial) towards tertiary
(service) activities. Thus, in 1959 manufacturing accounted for 38 per
cent of total employees in employment and for 34 per cent of GNP;
by 1977 the proportions had fallen to 32 and 29 per cent respectively. An even more remarkable contraction occurred between 1979
and 1981, when manufacturing employment fell by 16 per cent
(Clare Group, 1982, p. 9). Based on such trends, a concern has arisen
about 'de-industrialization'.

In fact, de-industrialization is a remarkably vague concept, metho-
dologically problematic and describing so general a phenomenon
that one is tempted to dismiss it as a misleading orthodoxy (Grant,
1982b, p. 9). It is, however, useful in characterizing an aspect of the
perceptions of economic policy-makers. To borrow Geoffrey Vickers'
term, it forms a significant aspect of the 'appreciative system' (the
way in which they conceptualize reality) of politicians (Vickers,
1965). From 1975 onwards, when the term was first coined by Tony
Benn (*Trade and Industry*, 4 April 1975), it began to appear prominently in Budget speeches and major economic pronouncements. In a

somewhat amended form it has been popularized by the economists Bacon and Eltis, who talk less of manufacturing/service or even public/private, but rather of market and non-market activities (Bacon and Eltis, 1978). They hypothesize that the growth in the non-market sector pre-empts resources, imposes a burden on the market sector and inhibits growth. These lines of argument have unquestionably been most influential and have been manifested in policy terms in the shape of the attempts to give preference to manufacturing industry in the Labour government's 1975 Industrial Strategy, and in the prominence given to the 'crowding out' thesis under the Thatcher government (Cross, 1982, p. 141).

The second level at which the environment of British industrial crisis can be characterized is that of the industry sector. Policy is increasingly operating in sectoral terms, yet the concept of the industrial sector is far from unambiguous, since one can classify by input, market served, process used or technical substitutability (the last is used in Britain) (Johnson, 1980, p. 2). Since the 1974 recession, policy recommendations, especially at the international level, have stressed the need for 'positive adjustment' policy as opposed to formal protectionism (through trade restraint) or hidden protectionism (through domestic industrial subsidy) (see chapter 1, p. 20). Adjustment implies an ability to identify and support growing sectors but, more important, a willingness to countenance, and perhaps to manage the contraction of, declining sectors. Sectoral policies in Britain have embraced both sides of the adaptation equation. The Thatcher government is belatedly financing microelectronics, information technology and robotics on the one hand; and successive governments have facilitated planned rationalization in textiles, steel and other declining sectors on the other. Various microeconomic exercises, especially the National Economic Development Council sector working parties and the DoI sectoral investment schemes have contributed to a constructive rationalization of declining sectors (such as wool textiles and footwear). These initiatives suffer in that they are highly voluntaristic, relatively under-financed, and vulnerable to political redefinition. They do, however, offer a flexible and forward-looking policy instrument which Patrick Jenkin, as Industry Secretary, began once again to employ at the end of 1981 in the form of a £22 million scheme to assist private-sector steel firms.

The third level of characterizing decline is that of the individual enterprise. Government willingness to intervene at the level of the firm and therefore to discriminate between firms is the acid test of an active industrial policy, and was the rock on which Labour's

Industrial Strategy finally foundered (Wilks, 1981). When it comes to decisions about firms, rather than sentiments about sectors, economic arguments and market judgements begin to break down in the face of social and political priorities.

Decline at the level of the enterprise has clearly become a more pressing and pervasive problem as the recession deepened after 1979. The factors that prompt state involvement in some firms rather than others are exceedingly difficult to classify. Furthermore, a huge volume of routine economic adjustment escapes governmental attention. The job loss experienced in many large firms often exceeds figures that, if attached to a bankruptcy or closure, would be regarded as a crisis. The 1977–81 figures are particularly dramatic, as table 5.1 demonstrates.

In the face of such large changes, a number of questions are raised by the unpredictability of government's response to crises. For instance, why do governments intervene in some potential bankruptcies and not in others? How is it that enterprises of obvious national importance are allowed to degenerate to crisis point? What prompts intervention? Can unions prompt action, or will government intervene only when other cherished policy objectives are threatened? Why are governments so reluctant to follow through interventions? Why is the commitment of public money so weakly monitored? Why do rescue plans fail consistently in implementation? The next two sections discuss such questions in relation to the framework of industrial policy and the political and administrative structures of the British state.

CRISES AND INDUSTRIAL POLICY

One of the most glaring inconsistencies in economic policy during the past 15 years has been the propensity for governments to develop and declare principles of industrial policy, and then to act, under the pressure of events, in a diametrically opposed fashion. Perhaps politicians have been foolish to enunciate industrial policies that must always be very vulnerable hostages to economic fortune. Yet industrial policies are of course designed to appeal to far larger audiences than industry or economic interests. They embody appeals to ideological values such as planning and freedom, and comprise such potent appeals that politicians are loath to take a lower key and perhaps a more sensible approach of regarding industrial policy, in Dell's words, simply as 'case work in the public interest' (Dell, 1973, p. 222).

Table 5.1   *The 20 largest UK employers among the top 50 exporters, 1981*

	Number employed in the UK ('000)			Percentage change in employment		
	1973	1977	1981	1973–77	1977–81	1973–81
				%	%	%
GEC	170	156	157	−8.2	+0.6	−7.6
British Steel	229	209	110	−8.7	−47.6	−52.1
BL (British Leyland)	171	172	104	+0.4	−39.5	−39.3
Thorn–EMI[1]	79	75	91	−5.0	+21.7	+15.7
British Aerospace	71	66	79	−7.0	+19.7	+11.3
Unilever	89	92	79	+3.8	−13.9	−10.6
Courtaulds	125	112	77	−10.4	−30.9	−38.1
ICI[2]	104	95	74	−8.7	−22.0	−28.8
Ford	70	73	70	+4.5	−4.5	−0.2
British Shipbuilders[3]	−	−	67	−	−22.1	−
Hawker Siddeley[4]	82	51	55	−38.2	+8.0	−33.3
Lucas	71	67	55	−3.6	−20.0	−22.9
GKN	78	73	51	−6.6	−30.0	−34.9
Rolls Royce	61	57	55	−7.8	−2.9	−10.5
Tube Investments	54	51	50	−4.3	−2.3	−6.5
BAT	37	36	47	−1.1	+30.4	+29.0
BP	26	34	39	+29.3	+15.7	+49.6
Northern Engineering[5]	−	34	36	−	+6.9	−
BICC	36	32	32	−11.0	0	−11.0
Dunlop	52	48	32	−7.7	−33.3	−38.5
Overall	1605	1533	1360	−4.5	−11.3	−15.3

[1] Merger EMI 1980.
[2] 1973 excludes IMI.
[3] Post-nationalization figures, 1978–81.
[4] From 1975 excludes BAe subsidiary.
[5] New group 1977.

Source: *Financial Times*, 1 December 1981.

Questions of intervention have featured prominently in declarations of industrial policy. The pattern has been for each government during the 1970s to bring into office an ideological industrial policy that is highly pro- or anti-intervention in the market. After a period, consensual pressures and industrial circumstances have obliged a return to a more pragmatic and so-called 'mixed-economy' approach. Individual crises have played a considerable role in this regular return

to the middle ground. Each government has had its crises — UCS and
Rolls Royce for Mr Heath and his Industry Secretary John Davies;
BL and the cooperatives for Mr Wilson and Mr Benn; steel, ICL and
BL again for Mrs Thatcher and Sir Keith Joseph. Each crisis has
prompted a reappraisal of the practical utility of the enunciated
policy. During 1981 the Conservative government executed a more
sedate and less personalized 'U-turn' than those of its predecessors in
1972 and 1975. This different style could not conceal the fact that,
by December 1981, industry policy and the DoI, under its new
Secretary of State Patrick Jenkin, had a more pragmatic and interventionist approach than under Sir Keith Joseph during 1979–81.

Michael Stewart has characterized these reversals in policy as the
'Jekyll and Hyde Years', during which, especially in the industrial
and incomes policy areas, governments have abandoned their more
ideological pretensions and have been obliged to revert to 'sane'
pragmatic policies (Stewart, 1978). The explanation for the policy
roller-coaster has been couched in terms of 'adversarial politics',
where, under the whip of ideological purity and the demands of
the two-party adversarial system, governments have come to power
equipped with a manifesto that demands impractically idealistic
policies (Finer, 1980). As far as industrial policy is concerned, it is
difficult to reject the broad accuracy of this insight as history repeats
itself under Mrs Thatcher. But while rhetorical policy shifts have
certainly taken place, both when governments change and during the
life of individual governments, it should be noted that the adversary
politics thesis is far from universally accepted, either as a description
or as an explanation for the course of industrial or economic policy
(Grant, 1982b, p. 13; Rose, 1980). Party competition has had a significant impact on the course of industrial policy, but it is not the
fact of competition that is important so much as the historical nature
of the two main protagonists, and the conventions of government
that define the rules of the battle. The former has produced a sterile
class-ridden debate and the latter has consolidated traditional liberal
practices of state passivity. Rhetorical and actual policy reversals
should be regarded as symptoms of a deeper malaise (Grant and
Wilks, 1983), some of the dimensions of which are explored below.
One of the most persistent problems is the degree to which institutions as well as policies reflect a failure to cater for the requirements
of a modern, concentrated and highly interdependent industrial
economy.

The immaturity of industrial policy formulation has thus been
accentuated by the rapidity of change in relevant institutions.

The more closely an institution has become involved directly with selective intervention, the more vulnerable it has become to destabilizing change or even the threat of abolition. Responsibility for industry has been the subject of numerous reorganizations, from the Board of Trade through the Department of Economic Affairs and various incarnations of the Ministry of Technology to the Department of Trade and Industry (1970–74) and now the DoI (although even that was under threat of merger during 1980). The advantage of continuity of personnel has been lost as roles have been radically redefined, and morale has suffered. Among the non-departmental agencies, the Industrial Reorganization Corporation (IRC), the National Enterprise Board (NEB) and now the British Technology Group (BTG) have existed under the sword of Damocles. Likewise, the National Economic Development Council (NEDC) has felt vulnerable, and its senior officials are apt to express incredulity at their continued survival. This instability is frequently underemphasized, although Blank gives prominence to 'the remarkable failure of government of both parties to comprehend the necessary foundation of institutional development' (Blank, 1978, p. 129), which, he says, has contributed to the inability to build consensus and effectively to coordinate policy. In a recent reform-orientated study Coombes examines the issues of consensus generation and 'industrial representation'. He argues for fundamental constitutional change and gives pride of place to parliamentary reform as preferable to corporatist devices of functional representation (Coombes, 1982, p. 188).

A further consequence of institutional instability and inadequate mechanisms for expressing industrial priorities within government is the lack of a base for industrial leadership. Other than the Industry Minister, frequently a highly politicized appointment, neither director-generals of NEDO nor chairmen of the NEB have spoken with sufficient authority to promote bipartisan policies — although they have tried (McIntosh, 1976; Murphy, 1980). The problem of weak ministerial leadership is of long standing and is not, of course, peculiar to industrial policy. The former head of Mrs Thatcher's policy unit, Sir John Hoskyns, recently reaffirmed its importance, talking in general terms of 'a sort of leadership vacuum' and 'a small policy-making monopoly' within Whitehall (Hoskyns, 1982, pp. 168–9). The outcome of an institutional base that, although fluid, has constantly been operated along conventional Whitehall lines, is an insular, precedent-bound policy-making process which adapts slowly to changing industrial problems; British industrial policy follows rather than leads.

Amidst this institutional fluidity, the role of the Treasury has remained paramount. It would be difficult to exaggerate the Treasury's
predominately constraining role in relation to industrial policy or the
criticism its role has aroused (Pollard, 1982). Its more pressing concerns with expenditure control and short-term macroeconomic policy
make it institutionally uncommitted and intellectually sceptical
about any form of 'positive' industrial policy. The Treasury's view on
'rescues' is clear. It dislikes them intensely. Any attempt to manage
industrial crises faces, therefore, a vigorous free-market argument
and an uncompromising parsimony from a Treasury machine that
has been strengthened rather than weakened under the Thatcher
government. The Conservative attachment to monetarism and the
free market, allied to Mrs Thatcher's consistent support for Sir
Geoffrey Howe and her decision in November 1981 to abolish the
Civil Service Department rather than split the Treasury, has enhanced
the tendency towards a minimalist industrial policy. There is no
counter-balance comparable to the French inter-ministerial committees that are concerned with industrial issues (see chapter 6 below).
As Middlemas points out in his argument for a Cabinet 'Committee
for Industry', 'the structural problem is that industry as a whole has
no thematic focus in Cabinet to match the economic directorate'
(Middlemas, 1981).

Attempts at implementation of ideological industrial policies have
varied in their sincerity, especially under Harold Wilson during 1974–
76. None the less, serious attempts to implement such policies have
been made, stimulated not only by electoral commitment but also
by the appointment of ideologically motivated individuals to the
industry portfolio. Implementation of pure forms of a 'market' or
a 'managed' model of industrial politics has confronted two acute
obstacles; absence of consensus and economic failure.

The absence of consensus manifests itself in splits within the industrial policy community. These differences between ministers and
officials, between departments, between the two sides of industry
and the divisions of capital (financial/manufacturing, large/small,
owners/managers, nationalized and the Treasury), have at times been
so marked that the expression 'community' is positively misleading.
The divisions between unions and the CBI are familiar enough, but
disagreements between business and the Conservatives (Grant, 1980),
between the unions and the Labour Party or between pragmatic officials and ideological ministers deserve emphasis. Running throughout
is a form of 'institutional isolation' whose most important manifesta-

tion is the insularity, independence and rejection of collective action exhibited by large and small industrial undertakings in the name of firm autonomy. The entrenched and substantial disagreements over the objectives and mechanisms of industrial policy make any one model of industrial politics impossible to introduce in the short term. Only economic success could legitimize any given model, but success in this field is inherently long-term and requires many other supportive factors. Consensus-building is thus a distinctive problem faced (or avoided) by British industrial policy-makers. Consequently, governments in practice have been reluctant to abolish the 'talking shop' of the NEDC, which supplies one of the few arenas for consensus generation.

The second obstacle to implementation of an ideological model is economic failure. In practice, the rhetoric of the symbolic policies introduced after each election in the name of 'disengagement', 'socialist planning' or 'incentives and market forces' has been tested by crises. Under each of the Conservative governments the collapse of major undertakings has led to a redefinition of policy. Under Labour from 1974 to 1976 an inclination to engage in rescue and subsidy was inhibited by a collapse of business investment. In other words, crises have provided the experimental conditions under which industry can ascertain the essence of policy and separate the rhetoric from the actuality (the economic term 'revealed preferences' sums up the process). Further, one suspects that it is only in reaction to crises that operational principles of policy have been defined. Policy-makers do not fully appreciate the constraints under which industrial policy operates until faced by the imperative for decision as a result of crisis.

CHARACTERISTICS OF BRITISH CRISIS MANAGEMENT

Although the rhetoric of British industrial policy has exhibited startling fluctuations, there is a strong evidence of basic consistency and continuity in administrative practices and attitudes. Such continuity has been facilitated by the impermanence of political initiatives. Thus, the classic regulatory and supportive functions of government have been maintained. Routine processes such as 'sponsorship' of industries, monopolies and company legislation, export promotion by the British Overseas Trade Board and the Export Credit Guarantee Department (ECGD), government-sponsored research and dissemination of results — all constitute contemporary expressions of the classic functions of the *laissez-faire* state, in other words, 'holding the ring'. In line with the increasing priority given to industrial policy, state activity has gone beyond that classic role. In areas such as regional policy, tax concessions (such as stock relief or small business schemes), sectoral assistance schemes and pollution control, government is doing more than maintaining the market. Yet even in these cases policy has followed rather than led. As ideas have, in Schon's phrase, come into 'good currency' (Schon, 1973, p. 116), policy has been formulated and legislation enacted in a gradualist and non-assertive process.

Shonfield (1965, pp. 88, 386) has argued that the British style of government, with its emphasis on a passive liberal state, makes 'active government' difficult to achieve. Government is seen, and sees itself, as a more or less equal group within a pluralist society. Certainly any idea that the state is 'above' society with a national purpose and unique competence is anathema to British policy-makers (Dyson, 1980).

In the industrial policy field this ideological inclination is translated into an abdication of responsibility. The traditional response of the British liberal state has been to define industrial problems as, prima facie, the problems of industry, to be resolved by the market and with a presumption against government action. This philosophy of government, which reflects and was reinforced by the *laissez-faire* economic tradition, is very influential in a British civil service that remains remarkably immune from reform and whose structure, recruitment and behaviour has clear unbroken links with the nineteenth century. The increasing concern with industrial policy and industrial crises evident over the past 20 years has yet to be translated into fundamental changes in the machinery of government. In comparison with countries like France and Japan, government remains aloof from industry so that one can speak of a form of 'elite isolation' (Blank, 1978, p. 91). Although the need for closer working relationships is clearly recognized by both industry and senior officials, the formula to legitimize and inspire such integration remains elusive (Coombes, 1982, p. 182).

Operationally, industrial policy is permeated by a norm of 'commercial freedom'. The market is seen as independent of the state rather than as dependent on state regulation and support. The same set of assumptions shapes the expectations of industry, so that defence of the norm of commercial freedom must be seen as embedded deeply in the value system of British capitalism. The historical process of British industrialization, led and fuelled by the entrepreneurship and accumulative talents of small businessmen, operating independently of the state and of investment banks, produced an almost moralistic antagonism to state help or 'subsidy' (Gamble, 1981; Checkland, 1971, p. 204). For British industrial management the state was external, irrelevant, most usually encountered as a regulator and to be fended off wherever possible. Reticence and suspicion on the part of industrialists has been reinforced in the postwar era by two further factors. First, macroeconomic policy has been perceived as consistently biased towards the requirements of financial and international capital. Second, industry's experience of industrial policy and indicative planning has been one of unfulfilled promises and what is seen as a disturbing willingness to subsidize market failure. Business distrust of government has been reinforced by the lack of industrial policy successes.

Thus, a major operational value of British industrial policy is not maintenance of market principles (as in West Germany), the national interest (as in France) or the productivity of enterprise (as in Japan), but rather a concern to sustain the autonomy of the firm. This concern might be regarded as the purest of market principles or, more correctly, as the ultimate market ethic, since it really presupposes that national economic benefit (the good of all) is derived only from the individual's (in this case the individual firm's) interpretation and unfettered pursuit of personal benefit.

The combination of an inability to take unilateral initiatives, with desirable objectives, and some capability for action means that industrial policy is largely reactive. The management of industrial crises in Britain tends, therefore, to comprise a set of negatives. On government's side, there are no regional programmes for industrial adaptation, no anticipatory loan financing — only rudimentary anticipatory sectoral reconstruction — and no lame duck rescue agency (the IRC and the NEB were both formally concerned with 'viable' enterprises).

This vacuum is deepened by the nature of the British banking system. The big British clearing banks have defined their roles in the financial and commercial terms of deposit banking and feel little obligation to encourage or participate in industrial restructuring, although this attitude is becoming increasingly controversial. The contrast with Germany is especially marked. Furthermore, there is no well established social or informal network that links industry and the civil service via the banking system. The absence of some such network is a serious shortcoming, because industrial crises will be anticipated most often by bankers, who are guided by the routine yardsticks of borrowing limits. The Midland Bank, for instance, provided unequivocal confirmation of the central importance of the banks when in July 1982 it revealed that it had a danger list of 70 firms, employing around 70,000, which were in an 'intensive care unit' receiving special advice, monitoring and, by implication, special assistance (*The Guardian*, 31 July 1982). The surprise that the announcement created underlined the novelty of the Midland's commitment to some of its corporate customers, although it became clear that the other clearing banks had adopted similar, if less extensive, practices. The Midland's suggestion that special government assistance in the form of loan guarantees be made available was not taken up, but it indicated a very belated recognition by the clearing banks of the dangers of relying on traditional banking criteria. While inter-agency consultation is becoming more usual it is still true that, as in the BL and ICL cases, crises are frequently precipitated by a bank's unilateral refusal to extend lines of credit.

During 1980 the Bank of England became increasingly concerned by the impact of high interest rates and low liquidity levels on intrinsically healthy concerns and adopted a new leadership role, encouraging banks to hang on rather than liquidate. Bank staff, especially the ex-merchant banking Governor, Gordon Richardson, have developed this rather uncharacteristically positive attitude to crisis management. Towards the end of 1981 Richardson spoke of the development of a closer relationship between bankers and industry, remarking that 'the comforting feature of recent British experience is the extent to which companies have weathered the storm, through a combination of self-help and constructive help from their bankers' (Richardson, 1982). The Bank's discreet intervention becomes most evident when things go wrong, as with the Laker collapse and again in March 1982, when the mixed engineering firm Stone Platt Industries went into receivership. The Bank of England had orchestrated support for the latter company during 1981 and organized last-minute crisis talks before the Midland Bank put in a receiver (*The Guardian*, 19 March 1982). The Bank's launch of its so-called 'industrial lifeboat' is thus an important but rather limited development. It is *ad hoc*, involves no public expenditure, and apparently works on the basis of informal criteria (Smith, 1981).

When industrial crises do occur, the first inclination of the government is to define the problem as the concern of the enterprise. At this point a set of pluralistic negotiations takes place within and outside the central administration, focused on whether or not government should act. Ahead of these negotiations, it would be foolhardy even for a senior official to predict whether action will be taken and its likely character. Hence senior officials are in the absurd position of being acutely aware of a potential crisis in a major undertaking (be it steel, motors or electronics), perhaps as the result of confidential discussions, and yet being unable to act until the crisis 'breaks'. This frustrating 'confidential *immobilisme*' is based upon the presumption against government action. In practical terms it is necessitated, first, by the absence of a social network in which the discussion of restructuring and anticipatory action between businessmen, bankers and officials is possible and, second, by a lack of administrative discretion that makes major selective interventions subject to approval only at ministerial or Cabinet subcommittee level.

Once crisis has been triggered by public pronouncement, the likelihood of governmental reaction depends on the scale of the crisis, its location, the articulation of the various interests, the economic situation, previous government involvement and even timing. Government reactions are fickle and can appear cynical. The decision to rescue Chrysler (UK) Ltd in December 1975 was widely interpreted as an opportunist device to win Scottish Labour votes. Subsequently government has applied market principles more strictly or perhaps been more circumspect. Certainly the civil service has attempted to avoid *ad hoc*, even perverse, reaction to crises and to introduce logic and predictability through an emphasis on commercial viability. The DoI and the Treasury accordingly produced a document entitled 'Criteria for Assistance to Industry' late in 1975 (DoI, 1976). The Criteria admit the problem of defining cases, other than those linked to regional policy, where rescue of 'non-viable' enterprises is justifiable, and attempt to limit intervention to cases where viability is present or attainable. The civil service were attempting to limit ministerial choice. As Sir Peter Carey, DoI's Permanent Secretary, noted, 'ministers must always retain discretion . . . but criteria have been drawn up in such a way as to emphasise that such a decision . . . [to rescue a non-viable concern] . . . would be the extreme exception rather than the rule' (Public Accounts Committee, 1976, p. 308). The attempt was successful. The proportion of rescues to possible candidates, impressionistically at least, declined as the 1970s progressed. In the battle to avoid subsidy a major part has been played by the statutory Industrial Development Advisory Boards at national and regional level. They have based their influential recommendations on the criteria and have acted, therefore, to institutionalize an expression of market and business values within the interventionary process.

Government reaction to crises has, however, frequently appeared to be motivated by non-economic criteria. *Ad hoc* reactions allow relatively random policy linkages to become influential. An active response to crisis is more likely if the bankruptcy or closure threatens other cherished goals, which may even be seen as more legitimate than industrial policy goals and may be argued for powerfully by non-industrial departments. Potential crises that threaten goals concerned with devolution (Chrysler), defence (Rolls Royce, British Shipbuilders), trade (BL), technology (ICL, Herbert, Rolls Royce) and Northern Ireland's stability (De Lorean, Harland and Wolff), have produced an active response. Curiously, linkages with labour market policy have been very weak. Thus one finds that large sums are devoted to job creation or youth employment at the same time as massive redundancies are announced and apprenticeship schemes are cut back.

Because of the inability of successive administrations to routinize intervention on a consensual base, every industrial crisis has tended to produce a unique response. Hence generalization is a risky business. More over, the rate of crisis and, to a lesser extent, of intervention has escalated since 1974, and the analyst is faced with an embarrassment of variegated riches that range from ships to newspapers. There follows an examination of crises within two industries, which are selected for their intrinsic importance and interest rather than on the basis of any claim to representation.

THE MOTOR INDUSTRY: BL AND CHRYSLER (UK)

Government's involvement with the motor industry has not always been involuntary. Although the pattern from 1974 on has been for governments to be sucked ever deeper into involvement, ownership and massive subsidy, the industry had formerly been an instrument rather than an objective of policy. From 1946 to approximately 1966 the industry was exploited by governments as they pursued non-industrial economy policy goals. As a dollar earner for the first postwar decade, as an agency for regional expansion from 1959 to 1964, and as a convenient demand management 'regulator' for most of this period, the industry was used with relatively little consideration for its economic health or growth potential (Dunnett, 1980). From 1967 to 1973 one can discern a period of less destructive intervention, marked by the encouragement of the merger of BMC and Leyland in 1968 on the part of Harold Wilson and the IRC. The subsequent 'hands off' approach of the Conservatives continued from 1970 to 1974, when the combination of falling demand, escalating imports, long-standing structural deficiencies resulting from low investment and poor labour relations precipitated the continuing and unresolved crisis in the industry. Government's response to this major industrial crisis can be considered under four headings.

Anticipation

The Conservative 'disengagement' experiment of 1970-72 has disrupted the links developed between MinTech, the IRC and the major assemblers. It was not until Tony Benn became Industry Secretary in March 1974 that the DoI resumed active discussions with British Leyland Motor Corporation (BLMC) and Chrysler (UK) (CUK). In both cases the possibilities of receiving regional aid for investment provided the opportunity for detailed examination of the companies' operations. In the case of BLMC, it was too late to avoid rescue as the company could no longer finance capital investment. The government's response involved the close personal interest of Wilson and Benn, the holding operation of an overdraft guarantee given in December 1974, and the appointment of the Ryder team. These measures constituted a judicious and reasonable response to the problem. It was later argued (Expenditure Committee, 1975; Wilks, 1983), that Benn had always intended to take BLMC into public ownership, and that the brief for the Ryder team was simply to produce a justification. While Ryder was producing his grandiose and controversial plant he was in fact pre-empting the Central Policy Review Staff (CPRS), which had been asked to produce a report on the motor car industry as a whole. With the publication of the CPRS Report in December 1975, and its recommendations on cutting capacity, increasing productivity and improving attitudes, the government came very close to giving substance to the mirage of a coherent long-term strategy for the motor industry. That strategy, which was based on support for British Leyland and a programme of behavioural reforms and rationalizations, suffered a decisive setback with the Chrysler rescue, which evolved, with high drama, during November and December 1975 when Mr Riccardo, Chairman of the American parent corporation, suddenly threatened to close its UK plants (Expenditure Committee, 1976).

Failure to anticipate the Chrysler crisis is far less easy to explain. For at least a year before Mr Wilson put his head to Mr Riccardo's infamous pistol the government had been well aware of CUK's problems. Meetings had been held and letters exchanged between senior executives of the Chrysler Corporation, Mr Benn and Mr Wilson. From July 1975 the DoI had been investigating the company's finances in connection with an application for regional aid. It was suggested (Economic Intelligence Unit, 1976) that the strategy evolved by the DoI called for a reduction in capacity and also a cathartic shock to the industry. A bankruptcy of CUK, unaided by the government, would fulfil both objectives admirably. In the event, the implications of Mr Riccardo's threats to close CUK proved too serious for ministers to tolerate and a rescue took place. The obvious question is why no steps were taken to avoid or ameliorate the threatened closure. The government maintained that surprise over the timing and content of the closure threat was important, but more fundamental than a shortage of information was a shortage of political will and administrative discretion. In the tradition of liberal government outlined above, civil servants are not expected to plan encroachment into the autonomy of the firm unless invited to do so by the firm or instructed to do so by ministers. This denies them the network of necessary contacts outside government and administrative resources within government, neither of which will be available unless ministers decide to act. But ministerial commitment cannot be secured ahead of a crisis decision. Thus, in the CUK case, despite the clearest warnings of impending crisis, politicians collectively did not have the stimulus or time, and civil servants did not have the resources or nerve, to engage in concrete contingency planning.

Interventionary Pressures

Although Labour politicians used to talk of 'unacceptable' levels of vehicle imports, and unions used to threaten total opposition to major plant closures, crisis was operationally defined as insolvency and liquidation of a major manufacturer. In the BLMC case British banks, and in the CUK case American banks, affected the timing of crisis by refusing further credit. In the Chrysler case the industrial departments and agencies were wholly antagonistic to intervention. The government's eventual decision to define the problem as a crisis and to take action was influenced by the nature and timing of the negotiations. The requirements of engaging in almost diplomatic talks with the Chrysler Corporation, together with the collective decision-making process, allowed William Ross (Scottish Secretary) and Harold Lever (Chancellor of the Duchy of Lancaster) to inject other policy objectives into the discussion. The deciding factor was the credibility of Labour's devolution strategy. Halfway through the negotiations a devolution White Paper (*Our Changing Democracy: Devolution to Scotland and Wales*, Cmnd 6348) was published which argued that devolution of economic powers was unnecessary and harmful. It was felt that the argument would be destroyed if the Cabinet allowed the closure of Chrysler's Scottish plant at Linwood. The devolution case, backed by Ross's threatened resignation, proved more persuasive than an ephemeral industrial policy.

By contrast, in the case of BLMC, and now of BL, the economic arguments were more influential. The shock to the manufacturing sector of a complete liquidation of BL's activities would be too large and unpredictable for any responsible government to contemplate. Overlying this calculation is the 'national champion' argument. There has always been a reluctance to countenance the dominance of the major British industries by foreign corporations. In the 1960s this reluctance was articulated in clear if general terms by Labour ministers (Wilson's 'industrial helotry'), but was never consolidated into a coherent policy (Hodges, 1974). In the 1970s the same sentiments existed as even vaguer values incorporated into the mix of Whitehall presumptions. Thus there has never been any explicit rationale for the 'national champion' motive in supporting BL, although at times, like Concorde, it is difficult to understand continued subventions as anything other than applied xenophobia. Only with the appointment of Sir Michael Edwardes at the end of 1977 did national independence and employment begin to be sacrificed to the perceived imperatives of international competitiveness.

Rescue Packages

The BL and CUK interventions resulted in government's commitment of large sums of money in order to cover operating losses and new capital expenditure. In both cases rescue was justified by reference to a corporate plan and was tied to evidence of progress in achieving the plan. In the Chrysler case the fact that government involvement went no further suggested that its rescue was opportunistic. In the BL case the reaction to crisis was altogether more systematic and sophisticated. BL's adherence to its corporate plan was initially enforced by linking funding to benchmarks in its progress. In practice, this system proved destructive and was superseded by a more flexible, continuing dialogue between the company, the NEB and the DoI through which BL justified changes in its plan to officials in a process that culminated in an annual approval of aid.

The other distinctive feature was the willingness of government to consider the calibre of management. A new team of Lord Ryder and company executives was brought in after the rescue and was replaced by Michael Edwardes and his appointees in 1977–78. For the period 1977–79 government oversight was exercised through the mediation of the NEB; after 1979 BL dealt directly, but still in considerable detail, with the DoI. The funds committed over the period, especially to BL, are immense and indeed warrant detailed accountability, as table 5.2 demonstrates.

Table 5.2   Government support for BL and CUK/Talbot, 1975–82 (£ million)

		BL	CUK/Talbot
Grants	1976–79		64
Equity	1975–81	1942	
	committed 1982–83	370	
Loans	repayable 1985–86 onwards		50
		2312	114

Note. Compiled from diverse sources. The BL figures include £25 million NEB finance for vehicle sales and the £46 million cost of buying out the BLMC shareholders in 1975. A further £150 million has been requested for 1983–85. A useful summary is provided by Economist Intelligence Unit (1981). The CUK/Talbot figures are the sums drawn rather than those approved.

Continuity in industrial policy and a bipartisan approach to crisis management forced on governments by the pressure of circumstances is illustrated by the Conservative's continued support for BL. In December 1979 Sir Keith Joseph agreed further aid, but in a conditional fashion that did not promise a firm commitment. In January 1981, however, the Conservatives fully backed Sir Michael and his corporate plan by approving an equity injection of a massive £990 million over two years. This subsidy was clearly in total contravention of Conservative ideology, and Sir Keith argued against further aid in Cabinet, to be defeated, paradoxically, by a coalition that included the Treasury; to close the company would have cost more in the short term than to maintain subsidy. The lack of any possible pretence that BL was 'viable' can be judged by the crude indicator of pre-tax profits, which from 1979, the first year of the Conservative government, declined catastrophically from slim profits to a loss of £112 million in 1979, £387 million in 1980 and £333 million in 1981. When Sir Michael left the company in September 1982 he could only promise an 'aim to break-even at the trading level [before interest] in 1983' (*Financial Times*, 16 September 1982).

Implementation and Evaluation

British government faces a dilemma in implementing rescue schemes. If it is rigorous and committed to the objectives of rescue, the logical approach would be to establish formal control through equity, directors or a formal contract so that the company could be monitored until success is achieved or additional action is required. This approach was adopted in the case of BL. While success is more probable, the government finds itself 'over-exposed'. It has institutionalized encroachment into the autonomy of the firm and may be engaged in continuing subsidy. The 'BL option' carries penalties in the shape of high political salience and media attention, and a presumption is formed of further action should plans go awry. For the company there may also be penalties in the shape of poor financial discipline (a lender of last resort always in the background) and of the danger that strategic decisions may become attuned to a political rather than a commercial market.

The other horn of the dilemma, the 'Chrysler option', also carries penalties. In this case the government hands over the money and monitors at a distance, largely to ensure that funds are not misused (Hogwood, 1979, pp. 226–31). The lack of control over management and strategic decisions carries the welcome corollary of lack or responsibility, so that if things do go wrong, government may well be able to disclaim commitment. The overwhelming problem with this deference to the autonomy of the firm is simply that things do tend to go wrong again (Young, 1974, p. 205). A single rescue intervention is far from guaranteed to resolve the problems that precipitated the crisis, and, if a fresh crisis should occur, government may again be called upon to intervene in an *ad hoc* unproductive manner. This predominant mode of implementation prompts sporadic, spasmodic intervention; the government treats each involvement as the final one. In the Chrysler case such an approach produced some shabby episodes. The Talbot UK Linwood plant (near Glasgow), which closed eventually in June 1981 with the loss of nearly 5000 jobs, is the prime victim of the 'Chrysler option'. The plant was built at Board of Trade insistence from 1960–62; was taken over from Rootes by

Chrysler in 1967 after MinTech encouragement; and, with DoI involvement, was rescued in 1975, taken over by Peugeot/Citroen in 1978 and closed in 1981. The original hopes of producing a 'growth pole' were unfulfilled and appeared positively disastrous.

The 'BL option' has appeared rather more successful, owing in large part to Sir Michael Edwardes's ability to sustain confidence within the government and conviction within the company. It has also, of course, proved vastly more expensive, and since 1978 has allowed huge job losses. BL's UK employment fell from 176,000 in 1977 to 96,000 in 1981 and was projected to fall gradually during 1982 (Industry and Trade Committee, 1982, p. 12). Sir Michael departed at the end of 1982 leaving a company far more vulnerable to closure or break-up than the concern he took over in 1977.

THE COMPUTER INDUSTRY:
INTERNATIONAL COMPUTERS LTD (ICL)

Since the early 1970s the international computer industry has been dominated by the five big American companies, with IBM really in a league on its own. In Britain ICL makes a sixth competitor, and has about one-third of the UK market (Stoneman, 1980, p. 160).

A long-standing aspect of industrial policy has been creation and encouragement of ICL as an indigenous computer manufacturer (Hodges, 1974, chapter 6). ICL was a product of the merger enthusiasm of the 1964–70 Labour government. Its formation was sponsored by the IRC, which contributed equity finance of £3.5 million. The company also received substantial public research and development funding in 1968 (£13.5 million) and again in 1972–73 (£40 million). It therefore received the great bulk of the British government's rather meagre aid to the computer industry. Further encouragement was provided by the preferential purchasing policy introduced in 1968. The policy has been to acquire large computers from ICL whenever possible on a 'single-tender' basis. As important as the value of the sales gained in this way has been ICL's opportunity to develop, design and install large, complex, and to some extent experimental, computer systems in government departments. It has thus been able to perfect the operation of its new machines in government before selling them as proven products to private customers. The Treasury and the Ministry of Defence have been long-standing critics of the hidden delays and costs involved (Committee of Public Accounts, 1981, p. 2).

From 1976 to 1979 the government's 25 per cent share in ICL was held by the NEB, and the company was sufficiently successful to enable the state holding company to allow ICL almost complete autonomy (Willott, 1981, p. 206). ICL seemed a worthy 'national champion', well able to fulfil one of the original aims of policy by competing in the home market against the transnational American manufacturers (especially IBM), and thus guaranteeing British technological independence and security of supply. By 1979 the government and the company itself were confident that the policy had reached maturity, the time was ripe for the public shareholding to be sold. There were more overtly political reasons for the sale. Mrs Thatcher's government had an ideological distaste for state ownership, especially of profitable concerns. The complete 'privatization' of ICL would also raise cash to contribute to lower public borrowing targets. In addition, aid to ICL was seen as becoming less relevant. Mainframe computers are only one, and a relatively stagnant, sector of the increasingly integrated 'information technology' market (*Business Week*, 1982). It was argued that ICL had absorbed more than its share of attention and money, that government should be supporting micro-chip and micro-processor production and be turning its attention to smaller firms producing peripherals, office equipment and software (Hills, 1982, p. 78).

In December 1979 the government 'placed' its shares in ICL with eager City institutions. The shares were priced at the equivalent of 114p and yielded £38 million, a £25 million profit for the NEB, which was able to use the money to pay a substantial part of the £100 million asset realization that the Conservatives had demanded for 1979–80. The sale was later the subject of acute controversy and recrimination. It subsequently became clear that, just as the shares were being placed, the company was reaching its peak of profitability, and within 12 months it was making losses, as table 5.3 illustrates. In December 1980, when ICL announced the onset of losses, the City institutions were astonished and angry. There was talk of a breakdown in communications between managers, shareholders and bankers; there was certainly a collapse of confidence. The shares, which had approached 200p during 1980, sank to 38p in March 1981. Banks were reluctant to extend credit and the company declared itself to be 'a prisoner of the Stock Exchange' (*Sunday Times*, 11 January 1981), by which it meant that its deteriorating relations with the City were producing an unjustified breakdown in confidence. ICL's transformation from a 'high flyer' at the beginning of 1980 to a 'lame duck' at the end of the year underlines the speed with which crises can develop. It also raises once again the issue of the short-term and instrumental approach of City institutions and banks.

Table 5.3   ICL pre-tax profits, 1976–82

Year to September		£ million
1976–77		30.3
1977–78		37.5
1978–79		45.7
1979–80		
First half	20.5	
Second half	4.6	
		25.1
1980–81		
First half	(50.6)	
Second half	(82.5)	
		(133.1)*
1981–82		
First half	(13.5)	
Second half	37.2	
		23.7

*Includes £78.1 million costs of closures and redundancies.

Anticipation

The DoI were as unprepared as the City for the revelation of ICL's problems. Its response to ICL's appeal for help was therefore typically reactive and constrained by time. In conjunction with the company, the DoI frantically pursued a merger either with cash-rich British companies such as BP and GEC, or with foreign computer companies. Almost every company except IBM, but including the Japanese, was apparently approached (*Financial Times*, 20 March 1981). No satisfactory saviour emerged, and in March 1981 Sir Keith Joseph announced that the government was providing bank loan guarantees of £200 million, effective for two years. Confidence was restored, banks resumed lending, and a breathing space was gained to open the way for a more fundamental reappraisal.

ICL's crisis can therefore be seen as primarily financial. Although there are valid criticisms to be made of the company's product strategy, it can be depicted as 'technologically healthy' but 'financially ill'. The strategy of technological and commercial independence has, however, brought penalties. First, the research and development programme has been seriously under-capitalized. The often remarked fact that IBM's R and D budget is almost twice as large as ICL's turnover emphasizes the size difference (Peacock *et al.*, 1980, p. 67). Other competitors are able to match IBM through government R and D support, provided either directly or through defence contracts; through specializing in one sector of the market, such as Burroughs with financial applications; or through riding on IBM's success by producing 'plug-compatible' equipment which can run on IBM software. ICL had taken advantage of none of these devices. Second, it has been argued that the sale by the NEB of its ICL equity was a mistake. One commentator went so far as to assert that, 'had the Board not been instructed to dispose of its holding in ICL, the present crisis would probably not have arisen' (K. Owen, *The Times*, 20 March 1981). He argued that the NEB would have had early warning and would have been able to sustain confidence and mobilize credit.

Interventionary Pressure

In justifying the loan guarantees, Sir Keith Joseph emphasised the government's reliance on ICL machines. The cost of adapting to a new technology would have been considerable and, as he pointed out, ICL machines 'supported vital operations' in 20 government departments, so that the government had a 'special interest' (*Hansard*, 19 March 1981). But this was only part of the story; there were three additional lines of justification. At the nationalistic level, ICL can still be regarded as a national champion to be supported for reasons of national prestige and economic autonomy. It is still thought sensible not to be entirely dependent on Japanese and American multinationals. Sir Peter Carey, the top civil servant at the Department of Industry, recently remarked on 'the desirability of having a capability which was truly indigenous, because one does observe with multinationals that they shift the balance of their resources around the world . . . so that there is some long-term diminution of control in this' (Committee of Public Accounts, 1981, p. 13). More pragmatically, the government was developing a new information technology policy. It therefore appeared logical to maintain computer manufacturing capability in a form open to government influence so that a major base for future initiatives could be secured. The third line of justification was more cynical. Reports of the rescue alleged that the only company willing to take over ICL had been Sperry Univac.

The terms on which it would have been willing to take on ICL were regarded as unacceptable; it would probably have abandoned production and the ICL technology, as it was really interested in the customer base. The loan guarantee was therefore seen simply as a short-term expedient to bring ICL back into sufficient health, in an improved economic climate, when it might appear more attractive to a wider range of foreign bidders (Stothard, 1981). This sort of holding operation, which postpones definite but unpalatable decisions, is characteristic of British crisis management.

The extent to which these three lines of argument were deployed in Whitehall is, of course, unknown. Institutionally, however, the bargaining within government would have ranged the DoI civil servants and the Civil Service Department's Central Computer and Telecommunications Agency (CCTA) against ministers, the Treasury, the Central Policy Review Staff and possibly the Ministry of Defence. The CCTA was established in 1973 to coordinate central government computer procurement, and although wound up later in 1981 it was seen as ICL's spokesman within central government. Consistent with the familiar pattern of crisis intervention, the decision was taken finally in Cabinet subcommittee and was identified personally with Mrs Thatcher (Stothard, 1981).

Rescue Package

The government's reaction to the ICL crisis was very much an interim measure. Certain conditions were attached to the loan guarantees, which were initially valid for only two years. The only condition so far made public has been the government's right to change senior management. Accordingly, in May 1981 the Chairman and Managing Director were replaced by Christopher Laidlow and Robb Wilmot, respectively. This is characteristic of the Thatcher government's preference for selecting high-calibre management, paying them generously, and leaving them to operate independently. Wilmot had established a high reputation while Managing Director of Texas Instruments' British subsidiary. He is reputedly being paid in excess of £150,000 (*The Economist*, 12 June 1982) and was only 36 when appointed. He has moved quickly to alter ICL's product strategy. Merger talks have been broken off with major competitors and instead a series of 'collaborative agreements' have been negotiated. The most important agreement is with Fujitsu, which will give ICL access to their chip technology and allow it to market large Fujitsu IBM-compatible machines in Europe in 1984. In addition, the workforce has been cut from 33,100 to 23,500 and ICL is moving aggressively into integrated small-scale telecommunications and data processing systems.

The interesting aspect of the package was that the government was simply guaranteeing bank loans, with no immediate expenditure (or impact on the public sector borrowing requirement!). It was thus mobilizing bank support, a process that involved consultants' reports and detailed discussions with the four banks involved; and selecting a new management team. The government therefore facilitated a bank rescue of the sort that in countries such as West Germany might have happened voluntarily.

Implementation and Evaluation

The government has indicated strong approval of ICL's strategy and of its progress in reducing the scale of losses. In November 1981 Patrick Jenkin, the new Industry Secretary, announced that the two-year loan guarantee would be extended, on a reducing basis, to five years. This enabled the company to make its peace with the City and to raise £32 million in a rights issue in December. 1981–82 saw a return to profit; the share price performed well and a further rights issue of £103.7 million was made in December 1982. Support is due to end in 1986, and, as usual, government declarations are adamant that no further aid will be forthcoming. One additional factor is that the EEC/GATT rules on public purchasing, which came into effect on 1 January 1981, require competitive tendering. ICL's preferential access to the public market has thus in theory ended. There are, however, wide exemption clauses in the rules that relate to machine compatability and to security, and it would be surprising if ICL did not continue to be a major government supplier. For instance, the huge £40 million project to computerize Britain's income tax system was awarded to ICL in 1980 just before single-tendering contracting ceased. This was followed in August 1982 by ICL winning the £20 million competitive contract for desk terminals to complete the system. Overall, the government's reluctant support for ICL appears spectacularly successful. The company is profitable, its management and technological strategy are receiving wide approval, and as yet the government has had to make no financial contribution.

It is still too early to be sure whether the 'BL option' will be adopted for implementation with lasting responsibility and continuing intervention; or whether the 'Chrysler option' of a 'hands-off' approach is envisaged. From the historical record and the steps taken to change management, the BL option appears more likely. When government adopts some variant of the BL option with a continuing commitment to the company, three basic implementation strategies are available. They can be presented as the 'three P's' — support based on Plans, on Products or on People. For both BL and ICL the emphasis has increasingly been placed on people in the form of management teams. This emphasis has been supplemented in the BL case by approval of the corporate plan and in the ICL case by some attention to products, historically the 2900 series and currently more modest support for specific new products. But detailed objectives of intervention, such as import substitution and technological independence, are in practice supplanted during implementation by a free market emphasis which stresses the simple survival (and profitability) of the company. For instance, the logic of the ICL intervention was to use the resources of the company to further the government's information technology policy. There is, however, little indication that the priorities of Kenneth Baker, the information technology minister at the DoI, are having an influence on corporate decisions.

Evaluation of the rescue in relation to the development of Conservative industrial policy underlines the importance of the ICL crisis. The short-term ill effects of a collapse of ICL would have been far from intolerable. Unlike BL, the employment, trade and negative multiplier effects of closure were not the decisive factors in prompting rescue. In its concern with future technological development and independence, the rescue was 'strategic' and particularly objectionable to a new conservatism that prizes market judgement. Moreover, ICL, unlike BL or BSC, was not a problem inherited from Labour. The rescue was, therefore, ideologically incomprehensible. As John Elliott rather sweepingly remarked, 'there is now virtually nothing credible left in Sir Keith's avowed policy of non-intervention in industry' (*Financial Times*, 20 March 1981).

The ICL rescue is thus an important element in the Conservatives' new era of 'constructive intervention'. The government has reverted to a pragmatic industrial policy which, for want of a better term, takes a 'mixed-economy' approach. The signposts along that path include the ministerial reshuffle that brought Kenneth Baker into the Industry Department in January 1981; and the £990 million aid to BL announced in the same month. Influenced also by increasingly voluble back-bench criticism of lack of direction, and by the ICL rescue itself, Sir Keith was pushed in April 1981 into making his first comprehensive statement on industrial policy. He outlined unanticipated problems, from oil prices to the inertia of government expenditure, but summed up the variation from expressed policy as 'occasional detours', maintaining that 'We have not changed our diagnosis or our aim. Some unpredictable factors have made the transitional stage more difficult. We have already taken many of the critical steps to pave the way to a more competitive economy' (*The Times*, 3 April 1981). The rhetoric and the practice continued to co-exist on separate planes until Sir Keith's replacement by Patrick Jenkin in September 1981. Jenkin's review of industrial policy commenced in January 1982 and confirmed a return to the traditional middle ground of qualified support and arms-length intervention (Elliott, 1981). By November 1982, when the results of the review were revealed, the DoI had even begun to boast of its strategic aspirations. Patrick Jenkin unveiled a management framework which defined strategic aims, one of which was to improve efficiency through 'selective aid to raise UK output' (*Financial Times*, 16 November 1982).

CONCLUSION

Examination of the British record of dealing with industrial crises suggests a series of conclusions that are critical in tone. Britain has faced intense problems of adaptation, and it is difficult to generalize about the range of responses. Nevertheless, one can argue that the following characteristics of crisis management tend to be displayed.

First, there is a low capability for adaptation in the sense of anticipating and forestalling crises. This shortcoming reflects under-developed mechanisms for predicting crises and an administrative inability to prepare contingency plans or take action ahead of political decision. Second, there is a reluctance, or, more correctly, an inability, to define crises that is related to the lack of explicit and consensual policy. Hence, crisis definition involves a pluralist process of bargaining within as well as outside government. Third, policy style, and to some extent policy content, is 'reactive'. Objectives tend to be redefined by reference to current crises. Fourth, the factors that encourage rescue are complex and distinctive in each case. However, influential elements appear to be: the level of previous involvement and whether government has implicitly taken responsibility (the 'BL option'); tacit norms, in particular the quasi-nationalistic commitment to 'national champions' in strategic sectors; and policy linkages. Important current policy preoccupations are injected into the political decision-making process. For instance, devolution under Labour and the public sector borrowing requirement (PBSR) under the Conservatives were major extraneous, non-industrial, criteria of decision.

The fifth characteristic is that private sector solutions are vastly preferred. Preference is always for takeover or merger. However, this outcome is inhibited by the very characteristics of crisis and by the absence of private sector mediators or initiators, such as investment banks. Sixth, implementation is typically company-led and emphasizes the autonomy of the firm and the initiative of the managers. There is, in other words, a tendency to back management teams. The implementation process of monitoring and adjustment involves distant relations between government and industry and is therefore *post hoc* and sporadic. Attempts to routinize the process, as in the case of planning agreements, have been strongly resisted. Finally, policy fluctuations and institutional instability have inhibited the development of a body of administrative techniques and experienced personnel. The 'learning process' has been constantly disrupted. The range of policy instruments has been broadened but their choice and use is highly constrained by precedent.

The surprising feature of the British scene has been the circumscribed nature of the debate about restructuring. The primary reference points continue to be a set of judgements and assumptions based on a liberal theory of the state and on classical free market economics. In other words, the private–public barrier remains as impermeable as ever, with the issue of industrial success, failure and crisis still located firmly in the private sector. The obstinate persistence of these traditional attitudes has been the subject of much recent comment (Gamble, 1981; Pollard, 1982). The combination of the liberal state and the sovereign market helps to explain the characteristics of crisis management outlined above, and in relation to crises is damaging in two more general senses.

First, Britain's industrial decline makes the problem of crisis management more urgent and also more familiar. Since the problems associated with commercial failure are so frequently encountered, one might have expected the development of some more systematic and longer-term doctrines of restructuring analogous to the rationalization enthusiasm of the 1964–70 period. Both BL and ICL, for instance, were formed with government encouragement in 1968 in moves that had a certain logic and could be regarded as reasonable adaptation strategies. When the doctrine itself was abandoned, the companies were left to their own devices until acute problems were encountered which produced fresh government 'intervention'.

Attempts to develop a fresh doctrine, as with Labour's 1975 'Industrial Strategy' (Grant, 1982a, p. 62) were abandoned in favour of the more traditional arm's-length approach which continues to predominate. The government's arm's-length approach originates in a fear of interfering with commercial judgements and of limiting the discipline of the market, but it has produced equally harmful effects in the form of unhelpful (because uninformed) government policies, and inadequate warnings of problems. The emphasis on the market encourages the government to implement crisis interventions through changes in management by appointing executives who are hoped to be better judges of the market or better imposers of commercial discipline. In the same vein, the monitoring of government support stresses increasingly the requirements of international competitiveness as an operating principle, without any direct commitment from government to assist.

A second consequence of the lack of any consistent rationale for crisis intervention is a growing resistance to subsidy and subvention. The resistance within the civil service and the business community has been fuelled by some of the more controversial interventions, such as the Chrysler 'rescue' and the large subsidies given to Polish ships built by British Shipbuilders (Committee of Public Accounts, 1979, p. xxxii). Consequently, although crisis intervention may be justifiable in political and even economic terms, hostility to rescue has hardened and discussion of crisis management has become even more dramatized and politicized.

This stress on the absence of any remotely technocratic dialogue serves to emphasize one final theme of the chapter. A striking feature of government and industry in Britain is the relative isolation of what Wright calls 'the "three cultures" of government, bureaucracy and enterprise' (1982, p. 4). Isolation is evident in the form of different sets of ideas and assumptions, and also in the relatively low level of informal and institutional contact. In the comparative analysis of industrial crises much can be explained by the degree to which large manufacturing enterprises are integrated into the social, political and administrative structures of the state. In Britain integration is low. Enterprises are substantially isolated from the civil service and the major parties and have only a conditional loyalty to peak organizations. Firms are not extensively penetrated by 'activist' banks or coordinated through cartels or joint shareholdings. In their various ways, the other states examined in this collection have far higher levels of firm integration and firm interpenetration. Such integration appears to facilitate their relative success in managing crises.

REFERENCES

Bacon, R. and Eltis, W. (1978), *Britain's Economic Problem: Too Few Producers* (2nd edn), London, Macmillan.

Blank, S. (1978), 'The Politics of Foreign Economic Policy: the Domestic Economy and the Problem of Pluralist Stagnation', in P. Katzenstein (ed.), *Between Power and Plenty*, Madison, University of Wisconsin Press.

Business Week (1982), 'Moving Away from Mainframes', 15 February.

Checkland, S. (1971), *The Rise of Industrial Society in England 1815–1855*, London, Longman.

Clare Group (1982), 'Problems of Industrial Recovery', *Midland Bank Review*, spring.

Committee of Public Accounts (1979), *First Report from the Committee of Public Accounts*, HC 173, London, HMSO.

Committee of Public Accounts (1981), *Government Financial Assistance for International Computers Ltd*, HC 17, London, HMSO.

Coombes, D. (1982), *Representative Government and Economic Power*, London, PSI/Heinemann.

Cross, R. (1982), *Economic Theory and Policy in the UK*, Oxford, Martin Robertson.

Dell, E. (1973), *Political Responsibility and Industry*, London, Allen and Unwin.

DoI (Department of Industry) (1976), *Industry Act 1972: Annual Report for the Year Ended 31 March 1976*, HC 619, London, HMSO.

Dunnett, P. (1980), *The Decline of the British Motor Industry*, London, Croom Helm.

Dyson, K. (1980), *The State Tradition in Western Europe*, Oxford, Martin Robertson.

Economist Intelligence Unit (1976), 'The Multinational That Wanted to be Nationalised: A Case History of the Chrysler Rescue', *Multinational Business*, 1.

Economist Intelligence Unit (1981), 'A Financial Profile of BL', *Motor Business*, 2.

Elliott, J. (1981), 'Department of Industry: The Search for a *Raison d'Etre*', *Financial Times*, 21 December 1981.

Expenditure Committee (1975), Fourteenth Report from the Expenditure Committee, *The Motor Vehicle Industry*, HC 617, London, HMSO.

Expenditure Committee (1976), Eighth Report from the Expenditure Committee, *Public Expenditure on Chrysler UK Ltd*, HC 596, London, HMSO.

Finer, S. (1980), *The Changing British Party System 1945–1979*, Washington DC, AEI.

Gamble, A. (1981), *Britain in Decline: Economic Policy, Political Strategy and the British State*, London, Macmillan.

Grant, W. (1980), 'Business Interests and the British Conservative Party', *Government and Opposition*, spring.

Grant, W. (1982a), *The Political Economy of Industrial Policy*, London, Butterworths.

Grant, W. (1982b), 'The Political Analysis of Industrial Policy', *Public Administration Bulletin*, April.

Grant, W. and Wilks, S. (1983), 'British Industrial Policy: Structural Change and Policy Inertia', *Journal of Public Policy*, February.

Hills, J. (1982), 'Political Responses to Growth Markets: A Comparative Analysis of the Information Technology Market', *Public Administration Bulletin*, April.

Hodges, M. (1974), *Multinational Corporations and National Government: A Case Study of the United Kingdom's Experience 1964-1970*, Farnborough, Hampshire, Saxon House.

Hogwood, B. (1979), *Government and Shipbuilding: The Politics of Industrial Change*, Farnborough, Hampshire, Saxon House.

Hoskyns, Sir John (1982), 'Whitehall and Westminster: An Outsider's View', *Fiscal Studies*, November.

Industry and Trade Committee (1982), *BL Limited*, HC 194, London, HMSO.

Johnson, P. (1980), 'The Changing Structure of British Industry', in P. Johnson (ed.), *The Structure of British Industry*, London, Granada.

McIntosh, Sir Ronald (1976), *Future British Industrial Policy*, Mercantile Credit Lecture, Reading University.

Middlemas, K. (1981), 'The Chamberlain touch in Government?' *Daily Telegraph*, 16 March.

Monkton, C. and Fallon, I. (1982), *The Laker Story*, London, Christenson.

Murphy, Sir Leslie (1980), 'Government and Industry: Is there a Way Forward?' *Policy Studies*, July.

Peacock, A. *et al.* (1980), *Structural Economic Policies in West Germany and the United Kingdom*, London, Anglo-German Foundation for the Study of Industrial Society.

Pollard, S. (1982), *The Wasting of the British Economy*, London, Croom Helm.

Public Accounts Committee (1976), *Sixth Report from the Public Accounts Committee*, HC 584, London, HMSO.

Richardson, Sir Gordon (1982), 'The Tasks of the Banks in a Time of Recession', speech in Bonn, 14 December 1981, *Bank of England Quarterly Bulletin*, 1st quarter.

Rose, R. (1980), *Do Parties Make a Difference?* London, Macmillan.

Schon, D. (1973), *Beyond the Stable State*, Harmondsworth, Penguin.

Shonfield, A. (1965), *Modern Capitalism*, Oxford University Press.

Smith, M. (1981), 'The Silence of the Teller', *The Guardian*, 9 February 1981.

Stewart, M. (1978), *Politics and Economic Policy in the UK since 1964: The Jekyll and Hyde Years*, Oxford, Pergamon.

Stoneman, P. L. (1980), 'Computers', in P. S. Johnson (ed.), *The Structure of British Industry*, London, Granada.

Stothard, P. (1981), 'Battle to Save Britain's Computer Industry', *Sunday Times*, 3 May 1981.

Vickers, Sir Geoffrey (1965), *The Art of Judgement*, London, Chapman and Hall.

Wilks, S. (1981), 'Planning Agreements: The Making of a Paper Tiger', *Public Administration*, winter.

Wilks, S. R. M. (1983), *Industrial Policy and the British Motor Industry*, Manchester University Press.

Willott, W. B. (1981), 'The NEB Involvement in Electronics and Information Technology', in C. Carter (ed.), *Industrial Policy and Innovation*, London, Heinemann.

Wright, M. (1982), 'Government–Industry Relations', *Public Administration Bulletin*, April.

Young, S. with Lowe, A. V. (1974), *Intervention in the Mixed Economy*, London, Croom Helm.

6

Strategic Management and the State: France

Diana Green*

> there is . . . an ingrained mistrust of the natural play of forces
> of a free economy, and a profound conviction that it is better
> to produce synthetically, as in a laboratory, the theoretical
> conditions of a competitive market than to risk the shocks
> and hazards of real competition.
>
> *Herbert Luthy (1955, p. 455)*

French industrial development has not only taken place at a different pace,[1] but has also differed radically in nature from the British model. France opted for a brand of 'state-sponsored' capitalism, totally at odds with the *laissez-faire* ethos of the British capitalist tradition. Although state intervention in industry is a long-standing tradition in France, it is not ideologically motivated. Until the 1981 elections brought a Socialist regime to power, there had been no *systematic* attempt to increase the scale of public ownership. Governments have tended to 'guide' the pace and direction of industrial change. This predilection for 'administered industrialization' can be explained partly by the deep-rooted belief that market forces are blunt and ineffective as a tool of resource allocation. Only the technocrats within the state machine are judged to possess the skills that are needed to guide industrial development along the chosen path. In addition to this entrepreneurial role, the state has traditionally provided protection for French industry both at home and as it expanded overseas, in the captive markets provided by the Empire.

This chapter examines the French approach to crisis management. It focuses primarily on the policies and policy instruments that were applied both generally and in specific sectors after 1973. It shows

*The author thanks the Nuffield Foundation who provided a research grant to assist in the preparation of this chapter.

161

that the traditional *étatist* mode of economic and industrial management was not displaced or eliminated by the neo-liberal Giscardian regime of 1974–81. Similarly, the arrival of the Socialist government of President Mitterand in 1981 did not appear to have resulted in a radically different approach to crisis management. Crisis management in France reveals how changes at the level of political rhetoric have served to hide continuity of policies.

During the postwar period, France has been transformed from an inefficient and predominantly agricultural economy into a prosperous, modern industrial state, one of the leaders in the 'league table' of economic and industrial powers. The process of transformation has been remarkable. The so-called 'economic miracle' of the 1960s was marked by faster rates of growth of GDP and productivity than in most other European countries.[2] Incomes, and expenditure on public services and social security benefits, all rose substantially, in real terms, throughout the 1970s. By 1980 French per capita income was higher than in the USA and Japan. Although no single economic, social or political explanation adequately explains this rapid 'takeoff', the French state has clearly played a considerable part in the process of transformation. Indeed, if we had to look for key words to sum up the characteristic features of French economic development, they would be *dirigisme* and the concomitant reduction (or suppression) of the power of market forces.

State intervention is traditional in France. Nationalization dates back to Louis XIV (who nationalized the tobacco industry), and the extensive state regulation of trade and commerce introduced at the time of Colbert is legendary. The twentieth century has been marked by increasing intervention in the economic life of the nation. The bulk of today's public sector emerged under the 1936 Popular Front regime and the postwar governments of 1945–46. The immediate postwar period also saw the imposition of an extensive system of price regulation and the introduction of national economic planning. State intervention has, in addition, been exerted through influence over, if not control of, finance. Investment finance (for both public and private investment) has always been in short supply, partly because French savers have a preference for liquidity. Consequently, the banks and other credit institutions have been important as a source of longer-term finance. Close relations between the state and the banking sector[3] were strengthened after the Second World War by the nationalization of the major banks (as well as some of the insurance and credit institutions). These close relations provided the state with a means of reorganizing specific industrial sectors and of 'guiding' industrial development. Indeed, it could be argued that the dominant role of the state-controlled financial institutions explains the failure of development of the domestic capital market.

Intervention in industrial affairs has been more extensive and direct than in the other countries considered in this volume. The French have always been rather sceptical about the effectiveness of market mechanisms (Friedberg, 1971). Since the market is, on occasion, 'blind', the state is needed to supplement market forces, such as they are, and replace them altogether if necessary. When this argument is translated into industrial policy, it becomes an apology for protection and subsidy. Firms should be insulated as far as possible from market forces, from 'unfair' competition, especially from overseas countries. At the same time, those industries that for nationalistic as well as economic reasons are considered important should be protected and/or promoted. Broadly speaking, French economic and industrial policies have been motivated by two main and related objectives: to promote economic and industrial development in order that France can rapidly ascend the 'league table' of economic growth and industrial power; and at the same time to carve out for French firms a path protected from the wilderness of international competition.

State intervention has not followed any coherent pattern. It is widely believed that, since the French are 'planners', industrial policy must be rational, integrated and coherent. In reality, interventions have been motivated by widely diverging (and often conflicting) aims and pursued by a variety of different means. This lack of coherence is partly an institutional problem. Industrial policy functions have tended to be dispersed among a number of political and administrative agencies so that the Ministry of Industry's responsibility has been essentially nominal. At the same time, despite the emphasis on coordination of economic and industrial policies within the framework of the medium-term National Plan, industrial interventions have been haphazard and *ad hoc*. They are more akin to 'fire fighting' than to industrial planning.

There has been a significant divergence between theory and practice in the area of industrial policy, especially in recent years. One analyst suggests that governments have pursued parallel industrial policies: an explicit policy that generally bears a resounding and purposeful label (for example, the 'Industrial Imperative', which was launched at the end of the 1960s), and an implicit policy, whose characteristics are much more difficult to determine (Stoffaes, 1977, p. 247). This predilection for inspiring myths is not simply a product of economic constraints; it is also explained by the nature of the French political system. The Right have dominated French politics for most of the postwar period. This domination means that 'industrial policy', in the sense of planned and coordinated intervention at the microeconomic level (in the sphere of decision-making normally left to the price mechanism), did not officially exist. 'Industrial policy' was therefore, in theory, limited to procuring a general framework within which industrial development could take place. In practice, the nature of economic and industrial problems, coupled with a predisposition to meddle in industrial affairs, has meant that governments have continuously monitored the pace and direction of industrial development.

MODERNIZATION OF THE INDUSTRIAL STRUCTURE

Analysis of France's postwar economic and industrial performance suggests that its success was assisted by a number of factors other than just state intervention. Structural weaknesses were an important prerequisite of, and justification for, intervention. The industrial 'take-off' got under way relatively slowly and then accelerated after the end of the Second World War. As late as 1936, about 35 per cent of the total workforce was still employed in agriculture, while industry remained largely composed of small family-owned firms. French trade was similarly relatively underdeveloped. The share of French manufactures in world trade at this time was half that of West Germany or Britain. The trade balance was secured by income from overseas investments and by high trade barriers. An acceleration of industrial development was assisted at least partly by the availability of a large pool of cheap and unskilled labour (initially from agriculture and, after de-colonization, from immigration). Hence, the low degree of specialization that took place tended to be in labour-intensive, consumer goods industries with a low skill requirement (such as textiles and clothing) — in addition to those with a higher capital content (such as volume cars). Rapid growth was also facilitated, during this phase of industrial development, by two contradictory trends. The cost of energy and raw materials had been falling continuously in real terms, while the price of manufactured goods was increasing. The former advantage was, of course, eliminated by the 1973 'oil shock'. Rising oil prices meant that balance of payments considerations dominated French economic policy during the late 1970s (Green, 1981a).

The structural weakness and technological backwardness of France became increasingly apparent, particularly as the economy was slowly opened up to international trade after France signed the Treaty of Rome in 1957. French industrial policy-makers became worried by what they saw as France's vulnerability in the face of the traditional strength of Germany in capital and intermediate goods and by the rapid expansion of American capital in Europe in the shape of multinationals. The exposure to international competition prompted some attempt at specialization, while concern about company size resulted in a massive restructuring throughout the 1960s. The aim was to produce new and larger groupings, oligopolies on an international scale, in the capital goods and some 'key' intermediate goods industries. Examples include Pechiney Ugine Kuhlmann (PUK) and IMETAL in non-ferrous metals, Rhône-Poulenc and PUK in chemicals, and Saint Gobain-Pont à Mousson in glass and materials.

The extent of the state's involvement in the creation of these 'national champions' is difficult to determine. Certainly, restructuring was the cornerstone of what passed for industrial policy at the time. In some cases where intervention did take place, it appeared to have been dictated by political rather than economic motives, especially in the advanced technology sectors. In many cases, the state drew up 'contracts' with designated firms: the state traded favours such as public purchasing and price de-control for merger agreements that included a commitment to increase investment and improve productivity. The industrial logic behind the creation of some of the largest conglomerates was far from clear. The theory was that these conglomerates would act as the 'motor' of industrial development. There was certainly an assumption, based on American experience, that big was not just beautiful, but also, by definition, efficient. In practice, the success of this strategy was uneven. It took time for the industrial groups to absorb new partners, and in the eagerness to pursue *gigantisme* the importance of the medium-sized firm was overlooked. Indeed, it was not until relatively recently (as a result of the severe adjustment problems caused by the post-1973 recession) that the costs of this strategy were appreciated.[4] At the same time, the 'national champions' strategy forced governments to stretch the definition of a 'French' presence in key sectors to quite remarkable lengths. Thus the preservation of a French computer company (under the banner of the *plan calcul*) meant promotion of a merger between French and American capital. Similarly, the restructuring of the nuclear industry, and the foundation-stone of the ambitious nuclear energy programme, was based on the Westinghouse process (in other words, on a dependence on American technology).

The keynote of the industrial strategy pursued after 1957 and baptized (rather belatedly towards the end of the 1960s) the 'Industrial Imperative', was the desire to preserve 'national independence'. This notion was used to justify almost all the important decisions made in industrial policy and related areas. 'National independence' was used, for example, to justify an increase of the national capacity for producing crude steel, with disastrous results, as is shown below (p. 170). The same logic underlay the so-called *grands programmes*, the prestige projects such as Concorde. For De Gaulle, 'national independence' meant also turning France into a military power with an independent nuclear capability. It provided the rationale for the state's decision to back a number of militarily strategic industries. Individual firms such as the computer firm CII-HB, Dassault and Thompson were chosen in advanced technology sectors and built into 'national champions' by the provision of substantial assistance for research and development and by public purchasing programmes.

The accession to power of Giscard d'Estaing in 1974 marked a critical economic watershed for the Fifth Republic. The assumption that the 'economic miracle' would continue in an uninterrupted fashion within the framework of a stable international system received a rude awakening in the mid-1970s. Under the combined impact of the collapse of the international monetary system, the muscle-flexing of the OPEC cartel and the rapid industrialization of a number of countries in the Third World, inflation accelerated, the growth rate halved, and unemployment rose alarmingly. There was no significant immediate change in the government's approach to economic and industrial problems, although the scale of intervention increased sharply as the 1973 oil price rise plunged the economy into a recession. The reaction of the (Gaullist) government was essentially defensive. A plethora of 'support' plans was launched, covering almost all industrial sectors. A special agency (the CIASI) was set up to bail out 'lame ducks' (see below, p. 176); and companies were asked to postpone redundancies for as long as possible. Typically, the government's response was launched under the banner of a new 'offensive' that promised a coherent approach to the problems of industrial development, the 'Industrial Redevelopment Strategy'. In reality it differed little from the crisis management of the past.

GISCARDIAN INDUSTRIAL POLICY

The 'real' brand of Giscardian policy did not emerge until Raymond

Barre became Prime Minister in 1976. Even then it was not possible to detect the main and distinctive features of that policy until 1979. This problem of identification arose in part because, at the level of rhetoric, industrial policy ceased to exist. Barre was an economic liberal and, as such, was convinced that French industry would become competitive in world markets only if it were released from the burden of state intervention. He asserted, right from the outset, his belief in the pre-eminence of market forces and his conviction that industrial choices were the prerogative of the *firm*, not of civil servants.

Initially the plan was to cut back selective intervention. State assistance to industry should be restricted to general measures (that is, non-selective measures such as tax relief, soft loans, regional development grants, grants for research and development). At the same time, an attempt was made to remove the constraints on, and provide incentives for, the operation of the market. Controls on prices were abolished. These controls had been in force for most of the postwar period and were seen as one of the most obvious symbols of the heavy hand of the state, since they were effectively a means of controlling the investment and trading activities of the individual private firm.[5] Competition policy was strengthened by the establishment of a Competition Commission; economic pricing was introduced for the nationalized industries; restrictions on overseas investments were removed; and there was a partial relaxation of the controls on inward investment. Similarly, an attempt was made to reduce the state's virtual monopoly over investment finance (directly and through its control over the financial sector) by encouraging the development of the private capital market. The 'Loi Monory' of July 1978, for instance, introduced a package of measures to encourage small savers and small-to-medium-sized companies to use the stock exchange. These specific measures were supplemented by a constant stress on the virtues of efficiency and competitiveness. The government pointed out that French firms should not expect the state to act as a lifeboat or to bear the costs of essential structural adjustment.

Changes did take place. The combination of the 1973 oil shock and the government's uncompromising rhetoric appears to have induced a gradual change in both the attitudes and the strategies of the French business community after 1976. Whereas the traditional emphasis had been on increasing capacity and overall growth, firms now started to diversify and to undertake rationalization and disinvestment even when the consequence was plant closures and manpower reductions. Thus Saint Gobain, the industrial conglomerate, moved

out of construction and into electronics; BSN stopped glass production and concentrated on food processing; and Rhône-Poulenc,
the chemical group, closed down its loss-making synthetic fibre
production and sold its petrochemicals interest to the state-owned
oil company Elf-Aquitaine in order to concentrate on fine chemicals.
Many firms began to look overseas. Some relocated part of their
production process in low-wage cost countries. Others entered joint
ventures with foreign firms as a means of finding new markets
and extended their interests beyond the traditional domestic and
European markets (Green, 1981a).

The extent to which the state 'guided' these corporate strategies
is difficult to determine, although the number of cases in which
financial assistance was provided suggests that they were in line with
the government's *de facto* industrial strategy. Prima facie, the scale
of state intervention was not reduced, despite the neo-liberal rhetoric.
The necessity for restructuring in order to increase international competitiveness produced a more refined ranking of industrial sectors.
Internationally competitive industries continued to benefit from
dirigiste assistance, while the liberal ideology was used to justify a
more permissive approach to the contraction of declining sectors.
After the collapse of the Left in the March 1978 legislative elections,
the government was able to hasten the process of rationalization in
declining sectors (Cohen *et al.*, 1982, p. 65), as the textile and steel
cases discussed below illustrate. Paradoxically, therefore, Giscardian
industrial policy reinforced the hold of the state. The main change
was in the *style* of crisis management: the style became more selec-
ive and more deliberate once it accepted the need for an orderly
contraction in the more internationally vulnerable industries.

After 1979 industrial policy focused increasingly on stimulating
technological advance. The 1973 energy crisis had underlined, once
again, the weakness of the French industrial structure. This time
structural weakness was the product not so much of the fragmentation and the size of the production units as of the product structure.
Rather belatedly, the French realized that the Japanese had begun
the process of anticipating and accommodating demand in world
markets in the 1950s. The relatively underdeveloped pattern of
French specialization was evident in the fact that, in addition to
the increasing difficulties being experienced by the more mature
industries (such as textiles, leather and shipbuilding) in the face
of competition from the Third World, some of the newer industries
(for example chemicals and France's most successful industry,
volume cars) clearly faced adjustment pressures in the medium term.

These newer industries appeared not to constitute a firm foundation for the longer-term development of the French economy. Related to this weakness of product structure was a realization that France was still lagging behind her main competitors (Germany, the USA and Japan) in the race towards the new technologies. The need to focus on, and support, 'technology-intensive' products was, therefore, increasingly stressed. This emphasis on 'technology-intensive' products was the rationale of the 'Strategic Reinforcement' approach to industrial development that was launched in the summer of 1980 (see p. 172 below).

Although the policy of restructuring industries around 'national champions' continued, the more selective nature of government interventions was evident in the shift of emphasis to the *firm*. Acting rather like a bank manager, the state considered the commercial and financial record of each client before distributing its largesse. Paradoxically, the application of a pragmatic, market-orientated attitude to finance supply resulted in a more detailed and direct involvement of the state in the pace and direction of industrial development. *Dirigisme* was not abandoned but simply transformed into 'liberal direction'.

POLICY TOWARDS THE DECLINING INDUSTRIES

Despite its relatively recent industrialization, France has its share of declining industries. The problem has been handled by a combination of different types of measures, sometimes within the framework of a sectoral support 'plan' and sometimes as part of a programme for industrial reconversion of the depressed and 'mono-industrial' regions. At the level of the sector, the state tied financial assistance to rationalization and re-equipment. In some cases, this assistance was backed by temporary measures to protect the industry during the process of adjustment from 'unfair' competition, whether that competition came from the newly industrializing countries or from France's main competitors in the industrialized world. For example, quotas and tariffs were used to support the ailing textiles and clothing industry, a 'voluntary' import restraint agreement with Japan protected the car industry, and the government quite systematically blocked takeover bids by foreign companies or engineered 'French solutions' to secure a French presence in 'key' industrial sectors. At the regional level, state assistance was provided to assist the modernization of the infrastructure. At the same time, the battery of regional aids, designed to attract new investment, was extended.

Steel

Steel is an example of an industry that has been tackled within the framework of a sectoral plan. It was technically in private ownership until 1978, when the major steel producers found themselves unable to meet the debts accumulated as a result of continuous government-sponsored restructuring operations and were forced to ask the government to bail them out. Indeed, steel provides a classic illustration of an industry where government policies have exacerbated rather than assisted the problem of industrial change (Green, 1981a, chapter 4).

French governments have regarded steel as a 'strategic' industry for most of the postwar period. It was one of the six priority sectors of the First National Plan, which was introduced to reconstruct the economy after the Second World War. As such, it received a larger share of investment finance than any other private industry. Exposure to international competition, first when the European Coal and Steel Community was created and second when France joined the Common Market, drew attention to its structural weaknesses. During the 1960s the emphasis was, therefore, on modernization and increased cost competitiveness. The Fifth National Plan, which spelt out the 'national champions' approach to industrial policy, explicitly singled out steel. Unfortunately, the merger strategy adopted was only partly successful. Concentration was often achieved by horizontal rather than vertical integration. The consequence was larger holding companies rather than bigger production units.

Government intervention in the industry's investment plans was detailed and specific. It took the form of a bargaining process with the trade association, the Chambre Syndicale de la Sidérurgie Francaise (CSSF), which resulted for instance in the 'Steel Agreement' of 1966. This agreement was important in two main respects. First, by providing substantial financial assistance, the government signalled its commitment to the process of rationalizing and modernizing the industry. Second, this commitment was formalized in a *'programme d'action concertée'*, a semi-contractual agreement that was used first for steel and subsequently for other industries such as data processing (the *plan calcul*) and industrial electronics, in order in these cases to plan systematic rationalization and reorganization (Hough, 1979, p. 205). The steel agreement can thus be seen as the forerunner of the various 'state-to-firm' contracts that have become such a prominent feature of French industrial policy (Green, 1982).

During the 1970s it became increasingly difficult for governments to square their industrial policy aims with other economic and social policy objectives. The 'national champions' strategy necessitated further rationalization, which involved the modernization and closure of existing plants as well as the creation of new and more efficient capacity. In the case of the steel industry, two ultra-modern integrated plants were constructed on seaboard sites — at Dunkirk in the north and on a greenfield site at Fos, near Marseilles, in the south. While they initially complemented older steel-producing plants in regions such as the Nord and Lorraine, they were designed eventually to replace them (Green, 1979). The decision to increase capacity was partly dictated (although this was not officially admitted) by the desire to match the industrial performance of France's traditional rival, West Germany. It proved to be a costly decision when demand slumped with the post-1974 recession. Furthermore, the government was at least partly to blame for the industry's continuing lack of competitiveness (especially in relation to Japan and newly industrializing countries in the Third World). For example, the state controlled steel prices as part of its short-term stabilization policy. This decision was clearly a constraint on corporate competitiveness. Similarly, since the older steelworks tended to be located in 'mono-industrial' regions, governments were reluctant to encourage the shedding of labour, especially when the number of those unemployed started to escalate.

After an abortive intervention by the government in 1977, the industry hovered on the edge of crisis until 1978, when the threat of bankruptcy forced the Barre government, which had been strengthened by the Assembly elections in March, to produce another rescue plan. A major financial reconstruction (in which the government and the banks took over the industry's outstanding debts) gave the government *de facto* control over the industry.[6] At the same time, a radical reorganization plan cut capacity from 32 million to 24 million tonnes. Production was to be concentrated in the modern plants at Fos-Marseilles and Dunkirk and in the newly rationalized installations of Sacilor in Lorraine. The workforce was also pruned (although at a slower rate than initially planned, after the steel riots in Paris early in 1979). About 16,000 jobs were lost between 1978 and 1981. This process was cushioned by generous redundancy terms, state-sponsored retraining schemes and the promise of new jobs.

Textiles

In the case of the textile industry, the policy response was a mixture of 'defensive' and 'offensive' measures. This industry has retained its fragmented and mainly family-owned structure despite measures by the government to promote concentration during the 1960s. In the face of 'unfair' competition from Third World countries and more efficient textile producers in the industrialized world such as Italy, the Barre government acted in two directions. The traditional resort to overtly protectionist measures was pursued, including a successful application through the EEC Commission in 1975 to invoke safeguard clauses under the Multi-fibre Agreement. At the same time, restructuring schemes were organized, principally through the CIASI. Restructuring, which involved loans and mergers, was aimed at shoring up selected firms and encouraging them to be efficient. In the case of one of the regions most severely affected by the crisis, Alsace, state assistance was provided under the guise of a regional assistance package. The so-called 'Vosges Plan' was launched in 1978 and provided funds for individual firms to promote investment, research and, at the limit, conversion. At the regional level state assistance was made available for improvements in the infrastructure in a bid to attract new investment.

In the case of the declining and labour-intensive industries, the examples of steel and textiles illustrate the overall concern to separate the efficient from the inefficient and, more generally, to distinguish between the social and industrial aspects of adjustment. The aim was to reduce the sector to a 'defensible segment', to encourage the modernization of the efficient firms within that segment, and to redeploy surplus labour (by means of generous redundancy payments and retraining schemes) into the growing areas of the economy. Yet this 'offensive' strategy was paralleled and supported by a 'defensive' strategy (including the use of temporary import controls and quotas) that was designed to ease the problem of adjustment in the case of 'sensitive' industries or products.

Giscardian industrial policy also differed from that pursued under previous regimes to the extent that, after 1979, there was an attempt to adopt a more *strategic* approach to interventions. This change was signalled by the launch of the 'Strategic Reinforcement' approach in the summer of 1980. The main aim of this approach was to promote certain 'key' technologies that were regarded as crucial to the future development of the French economy. Firms within the six priority areas initially chosen[7] were to benefit from state assistance (mainly, but not exclusively, financial assistance) in their bid to become competitive in (if not leaders of) world markets. The new strategy was based on accelerating the development of *French* technology and particular *French* products. It underlined the extent to which the

Barre government was attempting to emulate the Japanese model of industrial development.

THE MECHANISM OF 'LIBERAL DIRECTION'

As international competition became increasingly intense, and the rate of economic growth in France slowed down after 1974, French firms found it increasingly difficult to come to grips with the recession. Despite its 'liberal' stance, the French government responded to crises by creating a number of new forms of financial assistance (mainly subventions and loans). Typically, many of these measures were designed to deal with specific problems or to achieve specific aims. At the same time, a clutch of new inter-ministerial committees was created to promote, and eventually to coordinate, these actions. The first of these was the Inter-ministerial Committee for the Adaptation of Industrial Structures (CIASI), which was set up in 1974 to bail out 'lame ducks'. Since then three other new committees have been created: the Special Fund for Industrial Adaptation (FSAI), established in 1978 to assist the conversion of those regions most severely affected by the recession; the Inter-ministerial Committee for Industrial Development and Support of Employment (CIDISE), designed to support expanding firms (in other words, proven 'winners') in the small business sector; and the Inter-ministerial Committee for the Development of Strategic Industries (CODIS), established in 1979 and designed to promote winners in the six strategic 'industries of the future'. All of these committees are served by and geographically located in the Trésor (Treasury), one of the most powerful divisions of the Finance Ministry.

In addition to their intrinsic interest as new and powerful mechanisms for industrial crisis management, the inter-ministerial committees were important for two further reasons. First, they epitomized the dilemma at the heart of the Giscardian industrial policy: the desire to disengage pitted against the pressures for intervention. The government had taken a hard line against the featherbedding of industry. The emphasis had been on efficiency, which was seen as a prerequisite of competitiveness in international markets. Radical rationalization might be painful, but it would produce a slimmer, healthier industry. This attitude was made quite explicit by the Prime Minister, Raymond Barre: 'we must not hesitate to cut out the dead wood, that is, sectors where we cannot hope to compete. The future of France does not depend on the number of ships we build at a loss, nor on the production of steel which we cannot sell' (*L'Expansion*, April 1978). The Industry Minister, André Giraud, argued similarly that industrial interventions should not be motivated by social and political considerations, such as the need to save jobs: 'You cannot ask the State to guarantee the present number of jobs in every one of France's 42,000 enterprises' (*Financial Times*, 19 May 1978). Yet, as we have seen, this uncompromising attitude towards uncompetitive firms was, in reality, offset by an increase in the state's involvement in the adjustment process. These new mechanisms can, therefore, be seen as symptomatic of the schizophrenia of the French government's industrial tactics: they were 'liberal' mechanisms invented to implement an 'active' industrial policy. Nevertheless, they did underline the Barre government's determination to point the apparatus of state intervention in a new direction — promoting, rather than preventing, industrial change.

Second, these new committees were important because their interministerial character made it possible for the first time to introduce some coordination into industrial policy decisions. Previously, industrial policy functions had been dispersed through a number of different agencies. Broadly speaking, policy was initiated at the centre while implementation of policy decisions was decentralized, via the involvement, *inter alia*, of the banks and financial institutions and para-public agencies such as the Institute of Industrial Development (IDI),[8] the Regional Development Agencies (SDRs),[9] and the regional offshoots of agencies providing funds for innovating firms. However, in the case of industrial policy, as of other aspects of French administration, generalizations about the centralization of policy misrepresent greatly the complexity and fragmentation of relations with industry (and investment). At the centre, the division of labour had never been clear.

Although the Ministry of Industry had a nominal responsibility for industrial policy, in fact a number of other ministerial departments intervened. For example, the Planning Commission, which was responsible for drawing up the National Plan, was concerned with moderating the government's short-term time horizon. Its role was to argue that the government should not simply react to the short-term concerns of its more vociferous constituents but should consider the longer-term interests of the wider industrial policy community. Empirical evidence suggests, however, that the Plan has had less of an influence over industrial policy than is generally believed. Similarly, DATAR, the regional development agency, intervened to ensure that the employment consequences of industrial policy decisions were respected.

The Ministry of Finance was also intimately involved in the industrial policy process. For example, the Trésor sanctions the investment programmes of the nationalized industries, presides over the allocation of capital and soft loans from the Economic and Social Development Fund (FDES) to firms in both the public and private sector, authorizes borrowings from abroad, and controls the flow of inward investment. Indeed, the Trésor has some claim to be the most important agent, as well as coordinator of industrial policy. In addition to exercising overall control of credit, it supervises the specialized financial intermediaries, such as the Caisse de Depots et de Consignations (CDC) and the Credit National (CN), which give French industrial policy its peculiar effectiveness, and which have taken on an increasingly important entrepreneurial and rescue function (Cohen *et al.*, 1982, p. 61).

The Industry Ministry has very little discretion over the allocation of real resources. Its role has virtually been limited to one of filter and channel. It screens demands from the industries and firms that it sponsors and, after some kind of selection, channels these demands to the Trésor. Indeed, the structure of the Industry Ministry has arguably reinforced the tendency to develop clientelistic relationships with the industries that it sponsors. Moreover, there is considerable evidence that industrial decisions are arrived at as a result of collusion between the Ministry and specific firms.[10] The Trésor sees itself, and has become, the *de facto* interpreter and guardian of the government's industrial policy intentions.

The multiplicity of agencies in the industrial policy process and a concomitant compartmentalization of the machinery of government militated against any real coordination of policy. The creation of powerful inter-ministerial committees made it possible to short-circuit cumbersome administrative procedures and squabbles over competencies. A further advantage is that, broadly speaking, there is a common membership of the main committees that furthers informal communication and understanding. Coordination did not, however, become a reality until industrial problems were accorded political importance with the creation of the last of these committees, the CODIS, which is chaired by the Prime Minister. The inter-ministerial committees are at the heart of French efforts to manage industrial crises. Ostensibly, they constitute an imaginative and highly appropriate innovation within a tradition of state responsibility for industrial success.

The willingness of the French state to devise and implement

industrial strategies has its roots in a tradition of the centralized administrative state that goes back to Napoleon and indeed beyond to the *ancien régime*. Central to the functioning of this 'administrative state' are the elite *grands corps* of senior and specialized civil servants. The self-confidence, cohesiveness and sense of mission of the *grands corps* rests on a close identification with the French state and on a sophisticated system of elite education whose aim is to train public servants (Suleiman, 1974). In particular, the *grands corps* networks link together different parts of the state apparatus and provide a distinctive mechanism that facilitates crisis management. An especially important role is played by the elite finance inspectorate, whose members are scattered across French administration, industry and finance, and which sustains the close and informal links that have been so important for the coordinating role of the Trésor. The inter-ministerial committees must be evaluated within this distinctive administrative environment and, although evaluation must at this stage be tentative, an analysis of the more significant committees illustrates the willingness of the French state to devise and implement far-reaching strategies of adaptation.

The CIASI: Financing Rescue

The Inter-ministerial Committee for the Adaptation of Industrial Structure (CIASI) was the first of the committees set up to 'manage the crisis' and was the model for the later committees. It was set up when, in the wake of the 1973 oil price rises, a sudden escalation in the number of bankruptcies threatened to turn France into 'the biggest graveyard for companies in Europe'.[11] The French government looked for a means of rescuing ailing firms that would use scarce public resources in the most efficient way possible and avoid the allegation of 'back-door' nationalization. The consequence was a procedure that was both ingenious and administratively revolutionary. Officially, rescues were to be limited to firms that were basically efficient but were experiencing temporary difficulties. The theory was that a frequent cause of firms' difficulties, which had been exposed by the 1974 recession, was the lack of capital. This lack of capital was partly a function of the industrial structure and was exacerbated by the national pattern of saving and investment. The aim, therefore, was to remedy a particular form of market failure. In order to ensure that rescues were limited to efficient firms, the government insisted that rescues should be *joint* operations, involving public and private capital and the minimum of hard cash from the state. Although there was no specific ceiling on the amount of state funding available in each rescue operation, in practice this ceiling tended to be in the order of 10–15 per cent of the total cost. Moreover, the stipulation that private capital must be made available ensured that the banks and (where they existed) the shareholders demonstrated their faith in the company's longer-term viability. Where the firm's difficulties were caused by poor management or 'problems of succession', the CIASI's remedy was either to seek out a 'healthy' firm in the same business and persuade it to take over its ailing competitor, or, at the limit, to replace the existing management and shut down the least efficient parts of the business.

The CIASI procedure also broke new ground in its administrative practices, which were fast, flexible and straightforward. The committee brought together ministers and the most senior officials from the key economic ministries and financial institutions (including the Governor of the Bank of France) once a week. The seniority of its members meant the decision-making delays were minimized, a critical consideration in the case of rescue operations. A *rapporteur* from the Trésor was responsible for coordinating the administration of the procedure, which involved a rapid but detailed appraisal of the firm.[12] As a general rule, decisions would be taken within a week of referral. As the economic crisis worsened, the number of firms that sought assistance from the CIASI increased. Whereas about 90 cases a year were handled by the committee in the first two years of its operation, in 1980 (the last full year of its operation before the elections) the number rose to 649. Similarly, whereas 431 firms received financial support in the first three years of the scheme's operation, approximately the same number was bailed out in 1980 alone.[13]

Any attempt to judge the success of this procedure depends on criteria by which success is measured. In the case of industrial rescue, the definition of meaningful and objective criteria is particularly difficult. Rescues were motivated not simply by the need to save jobs, as was illustrated by the government's uncompromising attitude towards the collapse of the Boussac textile empire in 1978; the bankruptcy of Terrin, France's largest ship-repairer, in the same year; and, more recently, the collapse of Manufrance. Nevertheless, according to the committee, one indicator of its success is the fact that it has 'saved' 300,000 jobs since 1974 (with 4000 of these being saved in 1980). The proportion of rescues by arranged takeovers has increased; 50 per cent of the rescues in 1980 were engineered by this mechanism. The committee regards this evidence as a measure of its success. Yet, in a number of cases, the acquisition of an ailing firm proved ultimately the undoing of the rescuer, so that 'the healthy firm, instead of curing the ailing one, caught the disease itself' (Curzon Price, 1981). The plight of the Boussac–St-Frères group (discussed below) demonstrates this process. Timing is a major difficulty in any judgment about success of rescues. To what extent an ultimate failure reflects the inadequacy of the rescue mechanisms used or, more generally, questions the very principle of undertaking rescue in a market economy is a moot point. In any event, the Socialists were sufficiently impressed with the potential of the mechanism to retain this committee, although it has been renamed the 'Inter-ministerial Committee for Industrial Restructuring'. The new CIRI replaced officially the CIASI on 8 July 1982. Six regional commit-tees (called CORRI – Regional Committees for Industrial Restruc-turing) have been established on an experimental basis in line with the government's desire to decentralize decision-making.

The FSAI: A New Regional Policy Tool

In September 1978, the government set up a Fr.3 billion (£750 mil-lion) Special Adaptation Fund (FSAI) to assist the conversion of those geographical areas that were dominated by the declining industries and that had been severely affected by the economic crisis. The Fund was administered by a committee modelled on the CIASI. It broke new ground by abandoning the principle of tying subsidies to specific job-creation targets, until then a central feature of French regional development aids. The pattern was to finance capital invest-ment by loans and grants of up to 50 per cent of total cost.

The FSAI scheme introduced a new form of subsidy, the 'partici-patory loan' (*prêt participatif*), a long-term loan at low rate of interest, with repayment geared to profits, which becomes part of the company's capital for its duration. This subsidy subsequently became a key funding mechanism for other forms of selective assist-ance; it was used by the CIASI and the other committees that had been set up to 'manage the crisis'. Its importance as an industrial policy tool cannot be overstated. In addition to strengthening the financial structure of the business sector, the participatory loan provided the state with (nominally temporary) holdings in private sector companies. The long-term nature of the loans, which are typi-cally for 17 to 20 years, provided the authorities with a further means of controlling the pace and direction of industrial development.

The usefulness of the FSAI scheme in comparison with other industrial and regional policy tools is debatable. It proved a more expensive means of securing jobs than conventional regional aids. Because the scheme was introduced at a time of escalating unemployment as a result of the deepening recession, the decision to break the traditional link with job creation was also untimely. Indeed, prima facie, the scheme seems to have been an inappropriate method of dealing with the problem of conversion.

The CIDISE: Picking (Small) Winners

Enthusiasm for the new committee model was confirmed in March 1979 with the creation of the Inter-ministerial Committee for Industrial Development and Support of Employment (CIDISE), the third of the committees set up to deal with industrial adaptation. It differed from the two committees previously discussed to the extent that its approach was more 'offensive' and its target more specific. The CIDISE concentrated exclusively on firms in the small business sector; it underwrote their expansion by providing risk capital. Its guiding philosophy was 'help for the strong', and it restricted its support to 'exceptional' firms that were well-structured and financially sound, that stood out from other firms in their sector by the size of their profits, the quality of their products and so on, and that were producing internationally competitive products. Financial assistance under this scheme was limited to firms that wished to undertake investment programmes in order to increase their exports and share of the domestic market at the expense of an imported product; to develop new products and attack new markets; or to develop new techniques in an advanced technology sector. The CIDISE was modelled on the CIASI procedure, and therefore involved a joint venture between public and private capital with the state taking a share of the risk and the eventual rewards.[14]

Despite the French government's desire to play down its active role, it is quite clear that the CIDISE was yet another mechanism for picking and promoting actual and potential 'winners' in both the domestic and overseas markets. How successful it has been in this respect is rather difficult to determine. Figures produced by the committee show that, in the first 21 months of its operation, CIDISE contributed to the financing of 431 investment projects with a total value of Fr.4.3 billion (£358 million), at a cost to the state of Fr.626 million (£52 million). In 1980 investment programmes undertaken to the tune of Fr.3.3 billion (£275 million) produced 10,400 jobs at a cost to the state estimated as equivalent to a subsidy of Fr.5500 (£458) per job, considerably below that of other job support schemes.[15] Officially CIDISE is felt to be highly productive. It is relatively cheap, is investing in success, and, despite the fact that job creation was not the primary aim, it is proving unexpectedly efficient at creating jobs.

The CODIS: Strategic Commitment

The genesis and operation of this committee reflects a concern that the longer-term evolution of industrial structure should be coherently evaluated and influenced by government. The committee format gives the exercise the highest political priority and ensures effective administrative coordination. It is the most ambitious and arguably the most important of the inter-ministerial committees and as such has been discussed at greater length elsewhere (Green, 1983b).

The Inter-ministerial Committee for the Development of Strategic Industries (CODIS) was established in October 1979. Its aim was much wider than that of the other committees discussed here: to steer the development of strategic industries during the 1980s. CODIS grew out of, and was set up to underpin, administratively, the Barre government's decision to assist the rapid development of French technology and the particular French products that had been spelt out in the 'Strategic Reinforcement' policy, discussed above (p. 172). The role of the committee was to select a limited number of 'strategic areas', define a strategy, find a suitable firm to spearhead the strategy, and coordinate state action in order to assist the selected firm to pursue that strategy. The rationale of the state's interventions and the measuring rod of its success was 'international competitiveness'. The firm was expected to increase its share of world markets as well as of the domestic market.

After much consultation, it was decided to limit the number of 'priority areas' (initially six, although a seventh — textiles — was added later, at the insistence of the Prime Minister). This delimitation underlined the government's selective approach to industrial policy. At the same time, limitation of the number of areas made it possible to keep the administrative machinery to a reasonable size, thus increasing its efficiency and avoiding allegations of excessive interventionism.[16] The CODIS grouped together the key economic ministers (the Ministers of the Budget, the Economy, Industry and Trade) and was chaired by the Prime Minister. The inter-ministerial nature of the committee made it possible to mobilize and coordinate different modes of state intervention. Coordination and direction are the keynote, for CODIS has no separate budget.

The precise nature and the scale of the state's involvement with leading firms was specified in a 'development contract'. These contracts are bilateral agreements between the state and the firm which spell out a number of performance targets, for instance export targets, to be achieved over the period of the contract (generally three to four years). In return, the state provides different forms of assistance such as export subsidies, government orders and, where necessary, import controls. These 'development contracts' were modelled on the 'growth contract' formula that had been used to accelerate the growth of selected firms in the electronics sector. They provided another example of the way in which the Barre government 'guided' industrial development by direct intervention in the investment decisions of private sector firms. Indeed, despite the limitation of its jurisdiction, the launch of the CODIS procedure gave the government the possibility of pursuing systematic and detailed industrial planning of a type never before seen in France. Whether, in time, the committee's remit would have been extended to cover all the state's actions in the industrial policy area is a matter for speculation. The attitude of the Socialists under Pierre Mauroy (Prime Minister) and Pierre Dreyfus (the first Industry Ministry) to the CODIS machinery was, at least up to the end of 1982, ambiguous. By January 1981 about ten projects had been selected for aid under this scheme at a cost of about Fr.1.5 million (£125,000). Despite the Socialist government's dislike of 'picking winners' and doubts about the effectiveness of bilateral contracts in the light of a number of failures,[17] it honoured these and even signed new contracts. Significantly, as the contract signed with Intertechnique shows, the Socialist government used them to achieve *job-creation* rather than specifically industrial targets.[18]

AGACHE-WILLOT-BSF:
A CASE STUDY OF RESCUE IN THE TEXTILE INDUSTRY

At the end of June 1981 Boussac–Saint Frères (BSF), the manufacturing arm of the Agache-Willot textile and retail group, collapsed with long- and medium-term debts of the order of Fr.2 billion and with losses of Fr.10–15 million a month. Three months later the holding company (Société Foncière et Financière Agache-Willot — see figure 6.1) was put into the hands of a receiver. The empire that had been built by the controversial Willot brothers over the previous 30 years collapsed.

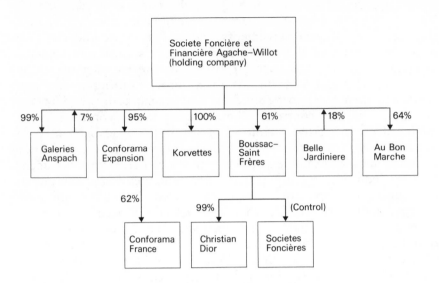

Figure 6.1   The Agache–Willot Empire.
(*Source: Nord-Eclair*, 2 July 1981)

The collapse of the Willot empire happened just three years after Agache-Willot took over the Boussac textile group in order to save it from liquidation, with the backing of the government. Willot provides a particularly interesting case study of the problems that confront a government that attempts to manage industrial change. First, it highlights the adjustment problems that are faced by declining and labour-intensive industries. Second, it illustrates some of the policy responses that are available to an active government and their consequences. Third, it highlights the social and regional repercussions of industrial crises. Finally, the timing of the collapse, and the controversial nature of the Willot brothers' activities, add an interesting political dimension to the crisis.

The collapse of the BSF and later of the Willot empire presented the new Socialist government with a particularly difficult economic and political problem. Measured by the number of jobs at stake, it was France's biggest postwar bankruptcy. The Agache–Willot group employed 33,000 people, and its annual turnover of about Fr.12 billion made it one of the top 20 French businesses. The industrial subsidiary, BSF, accounted for nearly half of the turnover and employed 20,000 in 80 factories. Over half of these people were employed in two regions, the Nord and the Somme; 6200 worked in the area around Lille. A further 5200 people were employed by BSF in the east of France, mainly in the Vosges, one of the areas most severely affected by the textile crisis (see above, p. 172). The collapse of the group also had an indirect impact on employment in these regions to the extent that it affected a number of sub-contractors, some of whom were subsequently forced to make workers redundant.[19]

The Agache–Willot empire was from start to finish family-owned. Its origins, sudden growth and final collapse are virtually a potted history of the evolution of the French textiles industry and of its problems of adjustment in a changing economic and political world. The empire was founded by the grandfather of the Willot brothers, who started making bandages near Lille at the turn of the century. When the brothers inherited the business at the death of their father in 1954, they expanded into textiles and took over more than 100 firms in the space of ten years. In 1967 they merged with another textile group, Agache, and, two years later with Saint Frères, the French market leader in jute. A second phase of expansion took place during the 1970s, when the brothers decided to diversify into distribution and purchased two famous Paris stores, Au Bon Marché and La Belle Jardinière, a Belgian store, Galeries Anspach, and in 1976 the furniture chain Conforama. By 1978 the group was one of the biggest textile groups in France. However, this rapid growth had been achieved at some cost. In 1974 all four brothers were prosecuted for offences, including fraud and forgery, committed during the process of acquiring Saint Frères and the Paris stores. Although charges were dropped under the traditional amnesty when Giscard acceded to the presidency, they failed to regain respecta-bility until 1978, when they entered into a takeover battle with Maurice Biderman for the remains of the Boussac textile group, which included the illustrious Christian Dior fashion house.

The Boussac acquisition marked the beginning of the end for Agache–Willot. The Boussac group, which was owned by the so-called 'Cotton-King', Marcel Boussac, had been in difficulty for some time and was finally put into the hands of a receiver when the government refused to bail it out. With the acquisition of Boussac, Agache–Willot's annual turnover doubled (from Fr.6 billion to Fr.12 billion), and its workforce increased from 20,000 to 35,000. It became not just a national textiles champion but also the leading European group. At the same time, however, it took over the prob-lems, and the outstanding debts (reputed to be about Fr.900 million), of the Boussac group. A second mistake was made the following year when the Willot brothers decided to break into the US market with the purchase of Korvettes, a chain of cut-price stores. Within a year this operation was in difficulty and had to be closed. Meanwhile, the position of the BSF group had deteriorated. Despite a rationalization that involved 2000 redundancies in the autumn of 1980, monthly losses continued to grow and reached a peak of Fr.25 million in January 1981. Although the group managed to cut losses back to Fr.10 million a month, high interest rates and the continuing crisis in the industry exacerbated BSF's problems. In June, when suppliers started to refuse to deliver and BSF could no longer pay the wages bill, it asked the court at Lille to wind up its affairs.

Whether the collapse of BSF was the result of bad management or was due primarily to the depressed state of the textile industry is difficult to determine. Nor is it clear how far government should take the blame. The problems of the French textile industry are not new and go back to France's entry into the EEC in 1958, when the protective barriers that the industry had previously enjoyed were removed. The opening of France's frontiers, and the loss, some time later, of her traditional markets as a result of de-colonization, presented the industry with a major adjustment problem. Despite the modernization and some restructuring that had occurred after the Second World War, the industry remained fragmented, with a predominance of craft-based, family-owned firms.

During the 1960s a massive restructuring of the industry took place, partly as a result of increased competition and partly encouraged by the state. Mergers produced a few big groups (such as La Lainière de Roubaix, Agache–Willot, Groupe Mulliez), and a large number of firms disappeared. Between 1963 and 1969 the number of textile firms fell from 7400 to 4800 (Mytelka, 1982, p. 135). The scale of the industry's contraction can also be measured by the number of jobs lost. The cotton industry lost 50 per cent of its labour force between 1955 and 1971, and employment in the wool industry fell by a similar magnitude (from 100,700 to 60,000 in the same period). Because of the geographical location of the industry, the impact on some regions, especially those where textiles was the only industry, or where the only other industries were also in structural decline, was particularly severe. Thus, in the Nord-Pas de Calais region, 80,000 textile jobs were lost in 20 years, and in a single *arrondissement* at Lille 28,000 jobs disappeared in five years.

The crisis worsened during the 1970s as the industry felt the repercussions of increased competition from aggressive Third World producers and industrialized countries like Italy and the USA. At the same time demand fell continuously: the annual rate of growth of textile and clothing consumption fell from 5 per cent between 1959 and 1973 to 0.8 per cent between 1973 and 1981. An increasing share of domestic demand was met by imports: import penetration increased from 7 per cent in 1962 to 50 per cent in 1980. The French government reacted with a mixture of offensive and defensive measures. 'Unfair' competition triggered both multilateral action (the Multi Fibre Agreements (MFA) of 1973 and 1978) and unilateral actions (for example, the introduction of quotas on T-shirts, in July 1977, as part of a last-minute attempt to save the Boussac textile group, and more recently controls on sweaters imported from Italy). At the same time, government continued to encourage restructuring in a bid to produce powerful groups that would be capable of competing in international markets. Indeed, the collapse of the Boussac empire has to be seen in this context. The takeover by Agache–Willot was not only preferable to a state-financed rescue; it provided also an opportunity to create a 'national champion' in this sector. Moreover, the Willot brothers' bid was retained against that of Biderman largely because it required no direct financial involvement by the state, and because they promised to keep redundancies to the minimum.[20]

With hindsight, it is difficult to see how Agache–Willot could have been expected to absorb Boussac and rescue it without some rationalization (given the company's problems and the state of the market). As far as the Willot brothers were concerned, this may simply have been a question of inadequate management. As far as the government was concerned, it seems to have been a case of political expediency outweighing industrial judgement. The collapse of BSF and the Agache–Willot empire is arguably not just a case of the 'national champion' strategy going wrong: it casts doubt also on the assumption that bigger firms are necessarily more efficient and hence more profitable. The whole episode emphasizes a basic dilemma of the 'national champion' strategy. The failure of a 'champion' is liable to bring the collapse of an industry already recognized as significant by the state. Government must either over-commit funds or accept exit from the market. More generally, the textile example illustrates that the French state is no exception to the rule that 'picking winners' is a chancy business.

In this particular case, given its size in relation to the textile and clothing sectors, the collapse of the Agache–Willot group presented the Socialist government with an embarrassing political, as well as an economic and social, problem. Further, it constituted the first real test of its attitude to industrial crises. Whereas the rescue of sectors like steel could be defended as being in the national interest, the rescue of the Willot brothers' empire was more difficult to justify, despite its importance in this troubled sector. The problem was exacerbated by the fact that, as a result of their unsavoury business dealings, the Willot brothers had become symbolic to French Socialists of the 'unacceptable face of capitalism'.[21]

The task of devising some compromise was entrusted to M. Anatole Temkine, Chairman of the Industrial Development Institute (IDI). As expected, the Willot brothers were abandoned. However, the crisis in the textile sector, combined with the regional concentration of employment and the political importance attached to reducing unemployment, meant that a rescue of BSF, the manufacturing part of the conglomerate, was inevitable. The rescue plan was constructed within the framework of the wider textiles plan on which work had already begun by the Barre government. A new company was set up in March 1982 to run the group's affairs on a leasing basis. The government took an indirect interest in the company, to the extent that its Fr.200 million starting capital was to be split between the IDI (51 per cent) and the creditor banks (49 per cent). A cut of 1300 jobs was scheduled, and the group's activities were rationalized so that it could concentrate on its more profitable lines. A Fr.1 billion (£83 million) investment programme was drawn up, partly subsidized by the government but largely to be financed out of future profits.

The BSF rescue plan is interesting for a number of reasons. First, government was clearly not prepared to foot the bill; it expected the plan to be largely self-financed. If this intention was serious, it implied that, despite the rhetoric about the dire consequences of a policy based on helping only the strong, the Socialists recognized that some selectivity was essential in order to husband scarce resources. Second, such a plan was more efficient than using such resources as artificial respiration for dead ducks, although, as noted above, CIASI was retained under a new title (p. 178), indicating a continuing willingness to rescue. Third, the decision to intervene in the rescue operation *indirectly* suggested that the Socialists were no less reluctant than their predecessors to use industrial rescue as a means of extending state ownership. Prima facie, this type of rescue was incompatible with the importance attached to the nationalization programme, which was presented as the central feature of their industrial strategy. One possible interpretation was that the Socialists too had a preference for *managing* the process of industrial development, rather than *directing* it (in line with the preference for 'indicative planning).

CONCLUSIONS

The Socialist Party's victory at the polls in the summer of 1981 was expected to usher in a new approach to industrial policy. They had argued that the Giscardian strategy of picking and backing industrial winners was producing a dual economy that was characterized by the privatization of profits and the socialization of losses. Hence the Socialists promised to return to a more diversified industrial base that would embrace both 'mature' and 'growth' industries. An ambitious nationalization programme and the pledge to 'revive' national planning symbolized the break with the past. Five major industrial groups were nationalized (Saint Gobain, CGE, Rhône-Poulenc, Thomson-Brandt, PUK), and the state's holding in Matra and Dassault was increased. The state gained control also over shares in a number of other companies via its acquisition of two holding companies, Paribas and Indosuez. As a result of the decision by Honeywell to reduce its shares in the mainframe computer company CII-HB, the government was left holding these additional shares. Private sector banks with deposits of more than Fr.1 billion were also nationalized in a bid to channel more funds into industrial investment.

The impact of these changes of ownership is not yet, of course, fully clear. The new management of the companies was announced in February 1982, when President Mitterand declared that the nationalized undertakings would retain full autonomy. Continuity with past practice was also confirmed by the choice of new managers who were seen as traditionalist. As one commentator observed, 'their nomination would not have caused surprise under the previous regime of President Giscard d'Estaing' (*Financial Times*, 18 February 1982). All the same, an active debate was being conducted during 1982 to redefine the social and industrial role of the old and new state industries and, in particular, to clarify the extent to which full managerial autonomy will actually be permitted. It can be concluded, however, that the state's obligation to manage industrial crises has not been reduced. State holdings in manufacturing industry have risen from 18 to 32 per cent (by turnover) and have greatly increased in actual or potential crisis sectors such as steel, basic chemicals, synthetic textiles and aircraft production. As far as planning was concerned, the Eighth National Plan (or rather, the draft prepared by the Barre government) was jettisoned. An 'Interim Plan', covering the period 1981–83, was hurriedly drawn up while the next (Ninth) Plan was prepared.

The substantive changes in the content of industrial policy did not materialize under the Socialists. In practice, their strategy appeared to be broadly in line with previous policy; changes were limited to emphasis rather than content. A number of weaknesses — structural and technological — remained untackled. Indeed, the magnitude of the problems that were faced both by individual firms and by whole sectors meant that the government's priority was a massive 'fire-fighting' operation.[22] Support plans were formulated for a long list of ailing sectors, including textiles, wood and furniture, and machine tools; while the steel industry continued to hover on the brink of crisis despite further state intervention.[23] Government's actions had the hallmarks of previous policy measures: shot-gun marriages and sectoral restructuring, backed by an impressive range of protectionist devices (baptized, in traditional fashion, with a purposive label: 'reconquering the domestic market'). The longer-term problem of accelerating France's technological advance has been tackled in yet another electronics plan, which provides Fr.140 billion for research into, and the application of, developments in this sector over the next five years.[24] Moreover, despite the Socialists' dislike of 'winner-picking', the state has continued to intervene in a highly selective fashion. It has not only deployed the traditional instruments of crisis management (such as soft loans, loan guarantees and public purchasing), but has also extended the contractual approach that was used so extensively under the previous government.

The initial character of crisis management under the Socialists was one of continuity rather than change. French industrial policy has traditionally been, and is likely to continue to be, a series of *ad hoc* responses to unexpected crises combined with the purposive language of forward planning. There has, however, been a shift in the focus of this planning, and to some extent in the level at which interventions took place. Greater emphasis was placed on microeconomic planning, as the protective barriers have been progressively removed and as French industry has had to come to grips with competitive pressures in the wider international environment. Their ideological predispositions and the priority that they have given to halting the apparently inexorable rise of unemployment have led the Socialists to adopt a more 'defensive' posture in the industrial policy area. They have attempted to slow down the pace of industrial change. There were, however, powerful economic as well as political constraints on their ability to change direction. For example, balance of payments problems continued to exert pressure for specialization in those areas where France has a comparative advantage. At the same time, the lack of indigenous resources, especially of energy, and relative technological backwardness moderated protectionist pressures, at least in the medium term. In addition, the powerful tradition of the administrative state as well as the centralized control of the Trésor over credit policies and its ability to manipulate industrial policy decisions suggested that French crisis management was likely to continue to be the same curious mixture. In other words, while the positive and forward-looking features of government industrial policy are posted in the traditional flag-waving fashion, the implicit and unstated policy will be the same mélange of protectionism and selective entrepreneurship that has always typified the state's involvement with industry.

NOTES

1   Reference is often made to the 'stagnant' nature of the French economy during the nineteenth century and the relatively slow rate of industrial growth compared with that of Britain. Studies have shown that the problem was rather one of *uneven* performance. (See for example Marczewski and Markovitch, 1967.)

2   GDP in France grew at an average annual rate of 5.8 per cent in the late 1960s and early 1970s, while productivity in the industrial sector grew at an average rate of 7.5 per cent per year during the 1960s and 5.4 per cent during the early 1970s.

3   There seems to be some disagreement about the extent to which the French banks were involved in the process of industrialization in the period preceding the Second World War. According to Landes (1972), the industrial banks played a more important role in the process of industrialization in Germany than in France, although the model was drawn from France. Bouvier (1970) suggests, however, that the role of the French banks was passive rather than active — that is, that they followed rather than led industrial growth (Zysman, 1977).

4   A Senate committee set up to look at the problem of French overseas trade found that medium-sized firms had made a much greater contribution (in terms of output, employment and exports) to the West German economy than to that of France (for example, medium-sized firms were responsible for only 20 per cent of French exports, compared with 50 per cent in West Germany in 1978) (Green, 1981a).

5   They also provided the government with a means of implementing an 'informal' incomes policy. Prices would be allowed to rise to some agreed level, as

a result of bargaining between the state (that is, the Finance Ministry) and the firm, *provided that* the firm had adhered to the government's specified 'norm' for wage increases. In other words, although formally no incomes policy existed (except in the public sector), in fact it was operated by putting pressure on employers.

6 The industry's outstanding debts were something in excess of Fr.30 billion. Most of the Fr.9.4 billion owed to the commercial banks (private and state owned) and the Fr.9 billion owed to the government was converted into subordinated loans. A special fund, managed by the Caisse des Depots et des Consignations (CDC) took over the responsibility for repaying the Fr.14 billion owed to small investors. It was calculated that, as a result of these arrangements, about two-thirds of the industry's equity was in the hands of the state or the financial institutions it controlled.

7 Under-water exploration ('off-shore'), automation of office procedures ('the office of the future'), consumer electronics, robots, bio-industry and energy-saving equipment (Green, 1981b).

8 Technically a private sector investment company, although in reality state-influenced if not state-controlled. The IDI was set up in 1970 to strengthen the financial structure of the corporate sector by taking temporary holdings in the capital of small firms. It has also been involved in a number of restructuring exercises (Green, 1983a).

9 Regional Development Agencies (Sociétés de Développement Régionales) were set up in 1955 to provide loan capital for small firms in the regions.

10 The priority areas that formed the backbone of the Barre government's 'Strategic Reinforcement' approach were drawn up largely in consultation with those industrialists who would have to cooperate in carrying it out. Similar evidence of bilateral collusion between the Ministry and the industries it sponsors is also found in the area of energy policy (Lucas, 1979).

11 Bankruptcies increased from about 10,000 a year between 1968 and 1973 to 13,000 a year between 1974 and 1977 (Mauras, 1979).

12 Independent studies were carried out simultaneously to assess the industrial and financial viability of the firms in the longer term. The industrial appraisal was carried out by the Ministry of Industry and the financial appraisal by one of the financial institutions, such as the Credit National (a number of people from this bank were drafted to the Trésor, on short-term contracts, to administer the CIASI procedure) or, at the local level, the CODEFI.

13 Figures supplied by an official attached to the committee.

14 Shareholders are expected to match the amount of capital applied for in the participatory loan during the period of the investment programme. A feature of these loans is that the state shares in any profits accruing as a result of the venture. There is a ceiling on the state's contribution of 25 per cent, although it is possible to combine the participatory loan with other forms of selective assistance up to a ceiling of 40 per cent of the cost of the investment.

15 About 60 per cent of the jobs created in France each year are subsidized directly by the state at a cost of about Fr.24,000 per job. (If the loans from the FSAI are included, the cost per job rises to Fr.37,000 per job.)

16 Analysis is carried out by sectoral working parties (one for each designated 'strategic area'), composed of private sector consultants and civil servants. These report to a steering committee composed of senior officials from the ministries concerned with economics, industry, trade and employment, which in turn puts its recommendations to the inter-ministerial committee.

17 One of the 'stars' of the computer industry, LOGABAX, collapsed at the end of 1981 after receiving financial assistance as a 'winner' picked under this scheme.

18 Intertechnique, the computer peripherals subsidiary of the Dassault group, signed a contract at the beginning of 1982, in which it was agreed to create 350–400 jobs at a new plant at Montpelier. In return, the government agreed to put Fr.61.5 million into the company in the form of direct subsidies and a further Fr.24 million in the shape of participatory loans. The company also pledged to increase its own capital by a rights issue and by ploughing back profits at a rate of Fr.26.5 million per year.

19 According to the *Nord-Eclair*, about 7000 firms (sub-contractors and suppliers) were affected by the collapse of BSF; 99 of these, in the greater Lille area, expected to make 340 workers redundant as a direct result of the crash (*Nord-Eclair*, 10 July 1981).

20 There have been hints that the Willots received indirect financial support ('Une lamentable affaire aux conséquence dramatiques', *Croix du Nord*, 6 July 1981). They also acquired the Boussac assets at the remarkably cheap price of Fr.700 million.

21 The Willot brothers have been investigated by the Stock Exchange Committee for misrepresenting company accounts and illegal share-trading. They are currently charged with the misuse of company assets, some of which have allegedly been illegally transferred into BSF.

22 When the Socialists took office, the CIASI presented them with a list of 15 firms needing immediate rescue; by the end of June 1981, one of the unions (the CFDT) had drawn up its own list comprising more than 170 firms.

23 Within a few months of full nationalization, one of the two main steel producers, Usinor, had announced losses of Fr.3.9 billion for 1981 with a deficit of at least Fr.1 billion expected for 1982. The government then produced another steel plan, involving further rationalization in return for financial assistance of up to Fr.9 billion for investment to the end of 1985.

24 The state has agreed to provide up to one-third of the cost of the investment programme, which includes nine 'national projects' which will bring together industrialists and publicly financed research laboratories (*Le Monde*, 30 July 1982).

192   *D. Green*

REFERENCES

Bouvier, J. (1970), 'The Banking Mechanism in France in the late 19th Century', in R. Cameron (ed.), *Essays in French Economic History*, Homewood, Illinois, Richard Irwin.

Cohen, S., Galbraith, J. and Zysman, J. (1982), 'Reshaping the Labyrinth: The Financial System and Industrial Policy in France', in S. Cohen and P. Gourevitch (eds), *France in the Troubled World Economy*, London, Butterworth.

Curzon Price, V. (1981), *Industrial Policies in the European Community*, London, Macmillan, for the Trade Policy Research Centre.

Friedberg, E. (1971), *Promoting Structural Change in the Industrial Sector: A New Role for the French State?* Cambridge, Massachusetts, Harvard University Press.

Green, D. (1979), *The Fos Maritime Zone: An Assessment*, London, HMSO.

Green, D. (1981a), *Managing Industrial Change? French Policies to Promote Industrial Adjustment*, London, HMSO.

Green, D. (1981b), 'Promoting the Industries of the Future: The Search for an Industrial Strategy in Britain and France', *Journal of Public Policy*, August.

Green, D. (1982), 'Government and Industry in France: A Contractual Approach', *Public Money*, September.

Green, D. (1983a), 'The French Institute of Industrial Development', in B. Hindley (ed.), *The Role and Performance of State Investment Companies in Market Economies*, London, Macmillan, for the Trade Policy Research Centre.

Green, D. (1983b), 'Giscardisme – Industrial Policy', in V. Wright (ed.), *Giscard, Giscardians and Giscardisme*, London, Allen and Unwin.

Hough, J. (1979), 'Government Intervention in the Economy of France', in P. Maunder (ed.), *Government Intervention in the Developed Economy*, London, Croom Helm.

Landes, D. (1972), *The Unbound Prometheus*, Cambridge University Press.

Lucas, N. (1979), *Energy Policy in France*, London, Europa.

Luthy, H. (1955), *The State of France* (trans. E. Mosbacher), New York, Praeger.

Marczewski, J. and Markovitch, T. (1967), *Histoire Quantitative de l'Economie Francaise*, Paris, Cahiers de l'ISEA (7 vols) vol. 7.

Mauras, V. (1979), 'SoS Canards Boiteux', *Le Monde*, 22 March 1979.

Mytelka, L. (1982), 'In Search of a Partner: The State and the Textile Industry in France', in S. Cohen and P. Gourevitch (eds), *France in the Troubled World Economy*, London, Butterworth.

Stoffaes, C. (1977), *La Grande Menace Industrielle*, Paris, Calmann-Levy.

Suleiman, E. (1974), *Politics, Power and Bureaucracy in France: The Administrative Elite*, Princeton, New Jersey, Princeton University Press.

Zysman, J. (1977), *Political Strategies for Industrial Order: State, Market and Industry in France*, Berkeley, California, University of California Press.

7

Public Enterprise and the Pursuit of Strategic Management: Italy

Michael Kreile

When the Italian economic magazine *Mondo Economico* (19 May 1982) is running a round table discussion on the theme, 'Is it possible to have an industrial policy in Italy?' one may safely assume that Italian industrial policy is less than a 'coherent, overall, homogeneous long-or-medium-term plan which seeks to stimulate a certain kind of quantitative, qualitative and territorial development of Italian industrial activities . . .' (Solustri, 1975, p. 144). Italian industrial policy during the 1970s confirms Diebold's (1980, p. 6) observation that '*ad hoc* unsystematic and sometimes inconsistent measures' account for the 'largest part of what governments do in the field of industrial policy'.

The context of Italian industrial policy is provided by the following factors: large-scale state intervention in the industrial sector, the fragmentation of economic policy-making, the importance of financial capital in the fortunes of industry, and a strong labour movement (Diebold, 1980, p. 10). State intervention to promote industrial development has a long tradition in Italy (Romeo, 1972, chapters 3 and 4). Instituto per la Ricostruzione Industriale (IRI), which was created in 1933 as a response to a banking crisis in order to salvage failing industrial companies, laid the foundations for the development of modern steel and heavy engineering industries in the postwar period. The establishment of Ente Nazionale Idrocarburi (ENI) in 1953 provided the country with a national energy and petrochemicals company which embarked on an aggressive strategy of expansion. In 1957 the state sector was also assigned the task of regional development. State companies were required by law to locate 40 per cent of their total investments (by 1964–65) and at least 60 per cent of new investments in the South. In 1971 these ratios were raised to 60 and 80 per cent, respectively. The strong presence of the state in industrial activities is complemented by large-scale public ownership of the banking sector. In 1977 public banks accounted for 67 per cent of total deposits and for 80 per cent of total loans (Schioppa, 1980, p. 260). The importance of the public credit institutions has been stressed by Romano Prodi (1974, pp. 52–3): 'Industrial credits have only come from public institutions; what is more, they have been directed chiefly to new investments, while practically disregarding all the other important financial needs of industry. Meanwhile, the private banks have confined their loans to short-run commitments in the safest and most conventional areas.' According to Prodi, 'Italian bankers have failed to develop much of the expertise needed to satisfy the necessities of a modern industrial structure.' Lending for industry comes mainly from the special credit institutes, that is, from medium- and long-term lending institutions that operate nationally (like Instituto Mobiliare Italiano — IMI) or on a regional basis (like Credito Industriale Sardo — CIS). These institutes are also the source of most subsidized credit, which — up to now — has been the main instrument of industrial policy (Templeman, 1981, p. 222). The importance of financial capital derives from the lack of a solid process of capital accumulation within the industrial sector and has been reinforced by the redistribution of income from profits to wages that occurred after 1969 under the pressure of a militant labour movement (Savona, 1980, p. 280).

Jurisdiction over industrial policy is exercised primarily by the Ministry of Industry and Commerce. There are close links between the ministerial bureaucracy and the private employers' association Confindustria (Confederazione Generale dell'Industria Italiana). La Palombara (1964, p. 262) has characterized these links as a *clientela* relationship.[1] The Ministry of State Holdings oversees the state holding companies. Typically, however, it proved to be too weak to exercise effective guidance and central control. The Ministry acted rather as a spokesman and chief lobbyist for public enterprise (Prodi, 1974, p. 61). The agency for special intervention in the South, the Cassa per il Mezzogiorno, is controlled by the Ministry for the South. Incentive schemes for commercial shipping and for shipyards are run by the Ministry of Commercial Shipping. Export promotion is the task of the Ministry of Foreign Trade. If one adds the trio of key economic departments (Treasury, Budget and Economic Planning, and Finance), and keeps in mind that portfolios are distributed according to the needs of coalition and faction arithmetic, one realizes that the formulation and implementation of a coherent industrial policy, integrated with macroeconomics, is made extremely difficult by the fragmentation of policy-making.

During the 1970s industrial policy was crucially affected by the strength of the labour movement. The losses of large private and public companies were often due — at least in part — to rapidly rising wage costs and low productivity growth, combined with an increasing rigidity in the use of the labour force. In large companies, which were the strongholds of the trade unions, the unions were able to exploit their organizational strength and the militancy of their rank and file to obtain a high degree of job security. As the report of an international consultancy firm (*Business International*, 1978, p. 107) put it bluntly, 'The biggest headache for companies operating in Italy is the difficulty of getting rid of unwanted workers — whether one man, a group or the entire work force.' Job preservation has become an imperative that acts as a constraint on all restructuring operations. In recent years, however, the burden of keeping excess labour has been increasingly shifted to the state budget.

A survey of industrial policy in the postwar period shows that, until the beginning of the 1960s, industrial policy relied essentially on the activities of the state companies and on a series of financial and credit incentives that were designed to promote the modernization and rationalization of Italian industry and to increase the international competitiveness of Italian firms. The industrial credit system that took shape at the end of the 1950s and remained substantially unchanged throughout the 1960s had three components (Solustri, 1975, p. 155):

(1) a low incentive system for industrial development in general and, above all, for export finance;
(2) a high incentive system for smaller firms and the industrialization of the South;
(3) a system for emergencies like natural disasters, the financial collapse of firms and the like.

The coalition between Christian Democrats and Socialists which came to power in 1962, moved to nationalize the electric power industry. The centre-left government had also the ambition to go beyond an industrial policy based on pragmatism and improvization and to develop an industrial policy within the framework of national economic planning (*programmazione*). However, the hopes of the planners were frustrated by the weaknesses of design and the formidable difficulties of implementation. As good treatments of the fate of economic planning are available elsewhere (Pasquino and Pecchini, 1975, pp. 70–92; Fraenkel, 1975, pp. 128–39), it will be sufficient to summarize the outcome of the First National Economic Plan for 1966–70. Support for research and development, which was to be one of the cornerstones of industrial policy, had materialized only in a single measure — the provision of subsidized loans for research. The development of infrastructure in order to improve the external economies of firms was realized only in the sectors that were controlled by the state enterprises. A reform of the social security system had been advocated by the employers' associations because of the heavy burden that was placed on firms by social security contributions. It did not take place. There were no new measures of export promotion. No progress was made towards the restoration of the financial balance of firms (Fraenkel, 1975, pp. 137–9; Solustri, 1975, pp. 174–5). The main obstacles that the planners had not been able to overcome were the fragmentation of policy-making, the political rivalries between ministers, the isolation of the planning bodies within the government bureaucracy, and the low level of cooperation among state enterprises, private business and labour unions.

When the Economic Plan for 1971–75 was drafted (it was never formally approved by Parliament, owing to an early dissolution of the fifth legislature in the winter of 1972), the planners demonstrated a greater awareness of the needs in industry. They recognized that the competitiveness of Italian industry had to be strengthened, that a higher degree of labour mobility was necessary to rationalize industrial structures, and that the self-financing capacity of firms had to be improved. Promotional programmes were to be developed for the following sectors: electricity, electrical engineering and metallurgical, nuclear, chemical, food and agriculture, textile and clothing industries (Solustri, 1975, pp. 176–7). Where industry-wide plans were put into effect, individual firms were required to obtain a 'declaration of conformity' from the Inter-ministerial Committee for Economic Planning (CIPE) when they applied for public loans at low interest rates to finance new investments (Prodi, 1974, p. 47). It should be mentioned, however, that CIPE itself sometimes failed to respect the national plan.

Even without the political crisis of 1972, the Second Economic Plan could hardly have been implemented as designed. The economic situation deteriorated dramatically as Italy was hit by the oil crisis of 1973. The OPEC shock caught the Italian economy at a time when it was recovering from a period of stagnation. The investment boom was accompanied by rising inflation and a deterioration of the current account, two trends that were both magnified by the oil price increase. The economy entered a period of instability. Economic performance reached its lowest point in the 1975 recession (when real GDP fell by 3.7 per cent), and recoveries ran up against the barriers of inflation and external disequilibrium (Lubitz, 1978, pp. 12–13). The Italian model of postwar economic development had been based on low wages, cheap energy and expanding foreign markets. Now the Italian model seemed to undergo a process of self-exhaustion as its constituent factors became victims of union strength, OPEC power and worldwide recession. As entire sectors of industry were faced with prospects of decline, industrial policy had to take up a double challenge: to prevent the financial collapse of many companies and industrial groups, and to promote a process of adaptation and structural change that would ensure the dynamism of Italian industry in the emerging new international division of labour.

INDUSTRIAL CRISIS AND THE STATE SECTOR

The crises of various sectors of Italian industry had complex origins. It is difficult, as Scognamiglio (1979, p. 79) pointed out, to establish a clear distinction between the *real* and the *financial* components of crisis, both of which are closely intertwined. For example, the growing burden of financial charges that had to be borne by companies resulted from the rise of interest rates owing to inflation. Inflation was in turn fuelled by rising labour costs and the growth of public sector deficits. The under-capitalization of Italian companies and the modernization efforts undertaken in the early 1970s reinforced the dependence of firms on external finance. Hence, firms became particularly vulnerable to the effects of inflation. The excessive reliance on external finance was caused by the decline in the self-financing capacity of firms and by the difficulty of raising equity because of the narrowness of the market for private shares and the troubled fortunes of large companies. In many cases the banking system did not set any limits to the indebtedness of large firms. This process encouraged the development of highly capital-intensive sectors, opened the possibility of covering operating losses through additional borrowing and, finally, led to the virtual abolition of the institute of bankruptcy in the case of large companies (Scognamiglio, 1979, pp. 28–9).

The financial plight of Italian industry is illustrated by table 7.1, based on the Mediobanca survey of 857 private and public companies in industry and services for the period 1968–78 (a sample representing about 74 per cent of total fixed assets of Italian joint stock companies. Debt–equity ratios mounted from 2.2 (1968) to 4 (1978). Total debt represented 45.9 per cent of total liabilities in 1968 (medium- and long-term debt, 20.2 per cent; short-term debt, 25.7 per cent) and 56.3 per cent in 1978 (medium- and long-term, 20.3 per cent; short-term, 36 per cent). Total debt increased from L.14 trillion (1968) to L.74.5 trillion (1978). The incidence of financing charges on sales climbed from 3.8 per cent in 1968 to 6.7 per cent in 1978 (Mediobanca, 1979, p. 26).

Table 7.1
Losses as a percentage of net sales of 856 Italian companies, 1974–78

1974	1975	1976	1977	1978
1	3.8	2.4	3.5	2.8

Source: Mediobanca (1979, pp. 38–9, Table III).

The contribution of internal sources of finance to investment is shown in table 7.2.

Table 7.2
Self-financing share of increase in gross fixed assets of Italian industry, 1968–78

1968	1969	1970	1971	1972	1973	1974	1975	1976	1977	1978
%	%	%	%	%	%	%	%	%	%	%
60.4	61.9	45.1	25.9	31.8	67.6	60.1	33.5	61.2	36.8	39.6

Source: Mediobanca (1979, p. 31).

If 115 medium-sized firms (out of the sample of 856) are considered separately, one finds that their financial situation was significantly brighter than that of the larger companies. Except in 1975, this group made profits. Their debt–equity ratio was 2.7 in 1978, and their debt represented 46.6 per cent of total liabilities. Financing charges came to 4.3 per cent of sales in 1978. The self-financing performance was consistently superior over the whole period. The better health of these firms is explained partly by the fact that they were under greater pressure to rationalize because it was more difficult for them to turn to the banks for funds (*Business International*, 1978, p. 120).

Disaggregation of the private and public companies in the Mediobanca sample indicates that industrial crisis is concentrated in the state holdings. In 1978 the 188 public companies accounted for 37.5 per cent of net sales, for 34.5 per cent of the workforce and for 52.8 per cent of fixed assets of the 856 companies. However, their losses amounted to 81.9 per cent, their debts to 53.3 per cent and their financing charges to 53.1 per cent of the total. In 1980 aggregate losses of 1078 companies (public and private) came to L.3 trillion, the sum of L.1.7 trillion of profits and L.4.7 trillion of losses. The share of the public companies was L.3.4 trillion in losses and L.0.4 trillion in profits. Thus, in aggregate, the private companies had balanced profit and loss accounts whereas the public companies had losses of L.3 trillion (*Mondo Economico*, 26 August 1981). These figures must not obscure the fact that there are private companies that are in deep trouble. Nevertheless, they provide some justification for turning the spotlight on the state sector.

Before probing more deeply into the crisis of state industry, it is necessary to outline the main features and the original philosophy of the state holdings. In 1979 the three big state holding companies employed around 700,000 people. IRI alone, the largest of the three, employed more than 500,000 people. Through six *finanziarie* (financial holding companies), IRI controls several hundred operating companies in the sectors of iron and steel (Finsider), engineering (Finmeccanica), shipbuilding (Fincantieri), shipping (Finmare), telecommunications (Stet) and infrastructure (Italstat). Some enterprises, like Alitalia and RAI (the national radio–TV company), are controlled directly by IRI. ENI operates in oil refining and distribution as well as in natural gas exploitation (AGIP), nuclear power (AGIP Nucleare), chemicals (ANIC), the construction of plants and pipelines (SNAM, Progetti, SAIPEM) and textiles (Lanerossi). Ente partecipazioni e Finanziamenti Industrie Manufatturiere (EFIM) controls about 120 medium-sized manufacturing enterprises, mostly in mechanical engineering. The fourth state holding company, Ente Gestione Aziende Minerarie e Metallurgiche (EGAM), which was created in 1971 to reorganize ailing state companies in the sectors of mining and non-ferrous metals, created a scandal when it diversified into shipping and insurance and was liquidated by law in June 1977 because of bad management and poor economic performance. The EGAM companies, with almost 30,000 employees, were distributed between ENI and IRI (*Business International*, 1978, pp. 32–7). Apart from conventional sources of finance (like bonds, loans and equity raised from private shareholders), the state holding companies have access to the state budget through increases of the endowment fund (*fondo di dotazione*). Increases in endowment funds must be voted

by Parliament and have been interpreted as capital grants from the
government that compensate the *enti* for activities in sectoral and
regional development that are unlikely to yield a profit in the short
run. Another view is that these funds represent a form of equity
investment by the government (Allen and Stevenson, 1974, p. 247).

The doctrinal justification for the activities of the state sector was
developed by the economist Saraceno, whose ideas became part of
an IRI philosophy. According to Saraceno, the Italian economy was
characterized by structural disequilibria that prevented it from
realizing its developmental potential. Keynesian policies of demand
stimulation were deemed inadequate to overcome the barriers to
growth. It was, therefore, the responsibility of the state sector
to take the lead in the country's industrial development. Public
enterprise was not expected to be devoted to profit maximization.
Nevertheless, it had to strive for financial self-sufficiency, in part as
a guarantee against policital interference with management (Prodi,
1974, pp. 56–7). During the years of Italy's economic miracle, the
performance of state enterprise corresponded closely to the IRI
philosophy. Allen and Stevenson have emphasized the state sector's
role in the development of southern Italy. They have also credited
the state holdings with 'leading the rest of the economy by example'
and injecting competition into parts of the Italian economy. The
state sector 'has tinged commerce with social considerations' by
maintaining employment in a labour-surplus economy (Allen and
Stevenson, 1974, pp. 255–9). The study by Stuart Holland (1972,
p. 1) celebrated IRI as an example of 'state enterprise as efficient and
dynamic, as leading private enterprise groups, yet still directly serving
the ends of government economic policy and the interests of society
as a whole'. And in the same volume (p. 55) Christopher Layton
praised the IRI leadership for not having fallen victim to the vices of
'nepotism, political placemanship, bureaucracy or corruption'.

Table 7.3   Profits and losses of state holdings (billion L.)

	1970	1971	1972	1973	1974	1975	1976	1977	1978
current L.	−33.8	−75.1	−85.4	+62.0	−100.0	−744.2	−664.2	−1316	−1407
1970 L.	−33.8	−69.0	−73.6	+47.8	−71.8	−404.4	−306.2	−518.1	−483

Source: Bognetti (1981, p. 20, table 3).

At the end of the 1970s these appraisals appear like a description
of paradise lost. Financial self-sufficiency belongs to the past. With
the sole exception of 1973, the state holding companies accumulated

growing losses over the 1970s, even if account is taken of the effects of inflation (see table 7.3). The major losses of IRI are concentrated in the steel and engineering sectors; for instance, the Alfa Romeo automobile company accounted for 80 per cent of Finmeccanica losses (Bognetti, 1981, p. 21). In the case of ENI, the sectors in crisis are chemicals, textiles and — not surprisingly — the former EGAM companies, which in 1978 accounted for more than half of total ENI losses (Bognetti, 1981). The cases of single companies are truly breathtaking. Two engineering companies of EFIM showed losses of L.99 million and L.63 million per employee in 1979. Finmeccanica's Aerimpianti showed a negative value added in 1978. The losses accumulated by AlfaSud came close to the entire labour costs paid out since it started operations. Italtel, the telecommunications equipment maker, lost L.268 billion on sales of L.704 billion in 1981 (Ragazzi, 1981, vol. 2, pp. 18, 45; *Financial Times*, 11 June 1982, p. 19). In some sectors the huge losses have practically destroyed the risk capital. At the end of 1980 Finsider's equity amounted to 7.5 per cent of debts, Fincantieri's to 1 per cent and Stet's to 10 per cent (*Mondo Economico*, 4 November 1981). No wonder that the participation of private minority shareholders has declined and that private shareholders are unwilling to bring in fresh capital (Cesarini, 1981, pp. 55–61). According to Scognamiglio (1979, vol. 1, p. 6), the system of state holdings ('historically the principal instrument of industrial policy used in our country') had reached a point where it was producing ever more modest results while costs for maintaining the system were increasing. In the three-year period 1977–79 the financial resources required by the state holdings corresponded to an average of 22 per cent of domestic credit to the private sector. At the same time, investments of the state holdings came to 9 per cent of total investment, and employment amounted to 8 per cent of the total workforce in industry and services.

There is no dearth of explanations of the differences in performance between the public and private sectors of Italian big industry. Although the explanations are not mutually exclusive, there are differences among the various authors and political actors about the emphasis to be put on individual factors. It may very well be, however, that in a context of multiple causality the weight of each factor can be assessed only by a detailed analysis of the individual operating companies, the financial holdings and the *enti* (Bognetti, 1981, pp. 23–4). The main factors held responsible for the crisis of state enterprise are the sectoral composition of state industry, the expansionary strategy of the early 1970s, the under-capitalization of the state holding companies, the subordination of management to political forces and the fulfilment of social obligations imposed by government and Parliament. These factors deserve individual examination.

There can be no doubt that some of the sectors of state industry are in crisis in other industrial countries as well — steel, basic chemicals and plastics, and shipbuilding for example. Some sectors, such as petrochemicals, cement and telephone services, operate under a regime of administered prices, and price rises normally lag behind cost increases (Scognamiglio, 1979, vol. 1, p. 7). For instance, the plight of Italtel derived partly from the fact that its sister firm and client, SIP, the main telephone company, had to reduce equipment orders because of huge losses, even though the demand for telephones is rising by at least 6 per cent a year (*The Economist*, 23 May 1981). The factor that is stressed by the top management of IRI is the under-capitalization of the group and consequent excessive indebtedness and high interest charges. They argue that, if IRI's capitalization had been equal to the average of medium and large private companies, its losses of L.1700 billion in 1979 would have been reduced by L.1150 billion to L.550 billion. They also emphasize the factor of administrated prices. If telephone charges had been raised earlier, SIP would have avoided losses of L.587 billion. These two factors are used to suggest the possibility of an operating profit of L.42 billion. In addition, the IRI managers build a third line of defence. The state holding companies have to bear so-called 'improper charges' (*oneri impropri*), linked to social functions and political decisions beyond the IRI's control. These services to the collectivity were estimated to amount to L.246 billion in 1979. If one subtracts the improper charges, and the L.54 billion of losses that resulted from the transfer of three EFIM companies to IRI ordered by the ministry, one arrives at a profit of L.342 billion for the industrial sector of the group.[2]

The under-capitalization argument and the 'improper charges' argument imply that the government has to be blamed for delaying the overdue increases in the endowment funds. Prodi (1981, pp. 34-7) has criticized the 'improper charges' argument as the latest attempt of the state holdings to get automatic access to sources of finance. It has also been argued that ENI tends to deny the existence of 'improper charges' and that private companies too are burdened by charges like those adduced by IRI — for example the impracticability of reducing employment in the course of restructuring operations, delays caused by urban planning and zoning restrictions, legislation on labour mobility (Scognamiglio, 1979, vol. 1, p. 35). The under-capitalization of the state holdings is not to be disputed. However, the high levels of debt and interest charges are a consequence and not a cause of losses accumulated in the past (Ragazzi, 1981, vol. 2, p. 5).

Table 7.4
Fixed investments by state holdings as a percentage of
total fixed investments, 1960–79

| | | | Mezzogiorno | |
Year	Fixed investments	Fixed investments in industrial sector	Fixed investments	Fixed investments in industrial sector
	%	%	%	%
1960–64	8.93	17.51	12.39	31.3
1965–69	8.83	16.77	11.74	30.6
1970–74	13.01	22.34	19.23	40.7
1975–79	10.01	16.24	–	–
1970	10.74	21.55	16.29	44.1
1971	13.92	28.01	22.21	50.1
1972	15.27	29.62	24.05	49.1
1973	13.99	22.37	21.08	40.4
1974	11.62	20.74	20.55	27.9
1975	12.00	20.90	15.40	31.3
1976	11.45	19.63	12.91	27.1
1977	10.27	15.82	11.17	21.3
1978	9.48	14.62	9.30	22.8
1979	8.32	13.23	n.a.	–

Source: Cassone (1981, p. 88, table 3).

A major factor in the crisis of the state sector has been the strategy of expansion conducted in the early 1970s. From 1968 onwards the investment behaviour of the private and the public sectors diverged substantially. Whereas private investment tended to stagnate, public enterprises launched new large-scale investments in steel, motor cars, chemicals, motorways and telecommunications. By 1972 investment by state holdings had reached 31 per cent of total investment in industry. In the South state holdings accounted for about 50 per cent of total industrial investment (see table 7.4). The anti-cyclical effects of this investment policy seem to have been accidental rather than planned. From 1974 onwards industrial investment of the state holdings decreased markedly: it fell from (1970 = 100) 117 in 1973 to around 60 in 1979. The retreat of the public sector occurred mainly at the expense of the Mezzogiorno, whose share of industrial investment dropped from 62 per cent in 1973 to 34 per cent in 1978. The strategy of expansion was also characterized by substantial increases of employment. Over the period 1960–69 the workforce of state holdings had increased by 76,000. In the five-year period after 1969 employment soared from 417,000 to 687,000 people, an increase of 65 per cent. The sectors with the highest growth of employment were engineering and electronics (from 83,000 to 168,000) and steel (from 75,000 to 138,000). After 1973 employment growth decelerated considerably. From 1974 to 1979 employment increased merely by 26,000 (Bognetti, 1981, pp. 18–20). Some of the additional employment created in the 1970s was due to the rescuing of private companies by the state sector or to the take-over of firms of which the owners wanted to rid themselves. The obligation to maintain employment made many salvage operations costly undertakings. The consequences have been aptly summarized by Padoa Schioppa:

> When transferred to an owner who never dies, the firms too become immortal. It follows that the sphere of publicly-owned concerns tends to expand. Even in those cases where it seems difficult to deny that the argument for public ownership is rather weak (e.g. the Christmas cake industry in Italy), the idea of a reversal to private ownership is rejected. [Schioppa, 1980, p. 251]

The process of disorderly expansion was accompanied and shaped by an increasing vulnerability of the state holdings' top management to political pressure and interference as the financial self-sufficiency of public enterprise waned. As a White Paper of the Ministry of State Holdings puts it,

> In the 1970s the dependence upon the 'public shareholder' has increased and — given the economic and social developments of those years — the demands of the shareholder have become more pressing. The state holdings have been used increasingly as an instrument of direct intervention and as a tool of short-term economic policy. This has contributed to the diffusion of a crisis mentality (among management) with the result that priority is given to tactical demands for help over the formulation of innovative designs. [De Michelis, 1981, p. 19; Grassini, 1981, pp. 71–6, 83–4; Martinelli, 1981, pp. 85–98]

Financial dependence made top management responsive to the wishes of political leaders and factions. The fragmentation of government and the extension of veto powers wielded by unions and parties produced the need for 'continuous diplomacy' (Prodi, 1981, p. 39) and sometimes a fair amount of demoralization. A prominent example is ENI, whose top management has been rocked first by factional strife within the Socialist Party and then by the power struggle between the Socialists and the Christian Democrats. Thus, two ENI presidents lost their jobs within roughly two years.

Remedies for curing the ills of state enterprise have been debated for years. Their enumeration provides a measure of the dimensions of the task. The Ministry of State Holdings — in its White Paper published in 1981 (*Rapporto sulle partecipazioni statali*) and in its programme for 1982 (*Relazione programmatica*) — formulated a list of objectives and proposed a series of sectoral interventions, financial measures and institutional reforms whose detailed analysis is beyond the scope of this chapter. The main objectives indicated by the ministry are:

(1) a return to profitability through the restoration of managerial autonomy and an efficient use of resources;
(2) the maintenance of the overall employment levels to the greatest possible extent without compromising the requirements of mobility;
(3) the sustained development of the South;
(4) a contribution to the development of those sectors that will acquire strategic importance in the 1980s: these include civilian electronics, telecommunications and telematics; large civilian and military systems, energy-related industry, aerospace, production of electrified mass transport systems; food processing, special steels, and so on;
(5) stimulus to the re-industrialization of strategically important sectors that are mature and do not offer real prospects of expansion, such as steel, basic chemicals, motor cars, shipbuilding and non-ferrous metallurgy;
(6) assistance to an improvement of the trade balance through increased competitiveness and a growing production of new import-substituting goods.

The necessary conditions for the economic recovery of the state holdings are considered to be as follows (De Michelis, 1981, pp. 21–6):

(1) a more organic, coherent and efficacious definition of industrial policy legislation;
(2) the identification of the specific financial requirements of state companies and of the methods of satisfying them;
(3) an increased contribution of private shareholders;
(4) the concentration of resources in clearly delimitated areas and an end to the instrumental use of the state holdings system for the purpose of rescue operations;
(5) the organization of a multinational presence of the state companies;
(6) the elimination of interferences by the 'hidden public shareholder' (for example, party factions, political leaders);
(7) an increase in the trade unions' share in the responsibilities for efficiency and productivity through adequate information and the development of industrial democracy;
(8) a reform of the institutional setting of the state holdings;
(9) a strengthening of the responsibilities and qualifications of management.

The main measures taken in 1981 were increases of the endowment funds (even though delayed by a Cabinet crisis and the slowness of the legislative process) and financial relief through the payment of interest on IRI bonds by the Treasury (Cesarini, 1981, p. 70). Some of the sectoral programmes that had been drawn up had to be revised owing to the deterioration of the economic situation in 1981. The attempts of the Ministry of State Holdings, which was headed by the Socialist De Michelis, to play a more dynamic role in the overall planning of the state sector met with resistance in the Christian Democratic camp, where the abolition of the Ministry was under discussion during the spring of 1982 (De Michelis, 1981, pp. 97–109). Gatti's (1981, p. 119) pessimistic observations may very well be justified: 'Too many rules of the game — institutional, political, cultural and those of industrial relations — would have to be changed simultaneously in order to achieve a revitalization of public entrepreneurship serving the development of our country.'

GEPI AND THE CONSORTIUM SOLUTION –
ALTERNATIVES TO SALVAGE BY THE STATE?

Probably one of the most original instruments of industrial crisis management in Italy is the Società di Gestioni e Partecipazioni Industriali (GEPI). This public financing agency was established by law in 1971 in order to avoid further indiscriminate rescue of ailing firms by the state sector. Its purpose was to restore aided firms to financial self-sufficiency. GEPI is organized as a private joint-stock company: and it is owned by the public credit institute IMI (50 per cent) and by the three state holdings ENI, IRI and EFIM (one-third of 50 per cent each). Its institutional mandate was broadly defined as 'contributing to the preservation and increase of employment levels, which are compromised by temporary difficulties of industrial firms, through interventions based on plans of reorganisation and reconversion. . .' (Ministero dell'Industria, del Commercio e dell'Artigianato, 1979, p. 274). Control was exercised by the shareholders. Political guidelines were issued by the Inter-ministerial Committee for Industrial Policy (CIPI), which was established in 1977. The interventions of GEPI could take one of the following forms:

(1) taking shares in industrial companies that suffer from financial or management problems considered temporary and surmountable, in order to realize the best conditions for the reorganization of the firms and the subsequent cession of the shares;
(2) setting up (or participating in setting up) companies for the management or the takeover of industrial firms in order to realize the best conditions for their reorganization and subsequent cession;
(3) the provision of finance — also at subsidized interest rates — to the companies mentioned under (1) and (2).

From its creation up to the end of October 1981, the capital grants provided by the state amounted to L.2.071 billion (*Mondo Economico*, 27 January 1982, p. 66).

According to a former director general of GEPI, the creation of this agency reflected the insight that the state has almost unlimited financial resources at its disposal but that the same is not true for its entrepreneurial capabilities. So GEPI went to look for entrepreneurial talents where they could be found, namely in the private sector. Hence the decision to conduct rescue operations by association with one or more private partners. GEPI insists also that firms go through bankruptcy proceedings if there is an imbalance between assets and liabilities (Grassini, 1981, p. 102). Initially GEPI remained true to its inspiration, although there were pressures from IMI, which was trying to rid itself of some troublesome exposures. Later in the 1970s the employment imperative tended to take priority over considerations of efficiency. Often GEPI did not find a private partner and assumed management and control alone. The Industrial Reconstruction Act of 1977 limited GEPI interventions to the Mezzogiorno and the under-developed areas of central Italy. As a consequence, the selection of firms became more difficult because closure of plants in the South was practically excluded (Grassini, 1981, pp. 103-6).

From its inception until the end of 1978, GEPI had intervened in 176 firms with a total of about 57,000 employees. Ninety firms were located in the North (with 39,483 employees), 27 in the centre (5265) and 59 in the South (12,434). In 82 companies there was a significant presence of private partners; out of those, 38 (with 9741 employees) had been sold to third parties (Ministero dell' Industria. . ., 1979, p. 275). At the end of 1981 GEPI was in charge of 169 companies with 37,128 employees. By then, 82 companies with 19,000 employees had been returned to the private sector. Those companies were probably the best in GEPI's portfolio. It has been pointed out, however, that the term 'cession' is misleading to the extent that many companies ceded owe large debts to GEPI (*Mondo Economico*, 27 January 1982, p. 63).

A decision that critically affected GEPI's mode of operation was taken by Parliament in November 1980. The Law no. 784 authorized GEPI to 'establish companies in order to promote productive initia-tives that allow for the re-employment of workers' of those firms for which GEPI is unable to find a private partner. In other words, GEPI could take charge of the workforce of companies in which its original mandate would counsel non-intervention. The workforce taken over by GEPI was to be employed in 'substitutive activities' that have to be defined within 18 months. During that period the employees were to be entitled to benefits from the wage compensation fund. It was very possible that real alternative employment opportunities would not materialize for the workers who were placed in the 'parking companies'. The unions attacked GEPI's policy of either association with a private partner or establishment of 'pseudo-companies'. They advocated a course of action comparable to that followed by the state holdings — namely, the direct takeover of crisis-ridden firms which would be run by GEPI on its own. This proposal seemed to envisage GEPI as the fourth state holding company, a prospect that, according to the critics of GEPI, was already taking shape (*Mondo Economico*, 27 January 1982, p. 63).

Another alternative to salvage by the state sector was the con-sortia of credit institutes, which was the subject of Law no. 787 of December 1978. The consortium formula was a reaction to the crises of large industrial groups in which the banks were heavily exposed. Chemical groups like Società Italiana Resine (SIR) and Liquichimica had received huge amounts of subsidized credits for investments in the South owing to their excellent political connections with key factions of the Christian Democratic Party. The credit institutes took increasing risks by assisting ventures in non-industrialized areas of the country. They saw 'their decisions as banks overshadowed by Government pressures and development programmes'. As Dr Baffi, then Governnor of the Bank of Italy, put it, 'The boards of the credit institutes were increasingly controlled by the authorities that effectively granted the credit facilities, and the decisions on the siting and the amounts of specific investment were therefore increasingly subject to sociopolitical considerations' (Banca d'Italia, 1979, p. 379; *Financial Times*, 19 November 1979, p. 11). When the difficulties of several big industrial groups brought them to the verge of financial collapse, a method of rescue was sought that would avoid further enlargement of the state sector or the more drastic solution of liquidation.

The Law no. 787 of 1978 authorized banks and special credit institutions to participate in the equity of industrial companies by investing in shares of rescue consortia in exchange for the debts owed to them by the failing enterprises. The banks that formed a consortium would ensure the financial survival of the company and would preside over a five-year recovery programme. If it proved impossible to create a consortium, a special commissioner would be appointed to take temporary control of a company. Liquidation proceedings would be suspended for 24 months in order to explore the possibilities of salvage (*Financial Times*, 19 November 1979, p. 2; 6 January 1981, p. 4).[3]

By the end of 1981, when the period of application of the law expired, only four consortia had been established: for Pirelli, Montefibre (a Montedison subsidiary), Tubi Italia and SIR (Banca d'Italia, 1982, p. 367). According to the Bank of Italy, the limited success of the consortium solution can be explained by the following factors. On the one hand, situations of structural crisis require interventions that amount to more than just financial relief operations; on the other hand, those companies whose problems were primarily of a financial nature benefited from an improved profit performance and were, therefore, able to raise equity in the capital market (Banca d'Italia, 1981, p. 331). Another factor was the difficulty of reaching agreement among creditors. A conflict of interest was bound to arise between (1) those banks that were heavily exposed in a given group and therefore interested in spreading the risk of a rescue operation among a larger number of credit institutes; and (2) those banks that were less heavily exposed and that might prefer writing off their outstanding loans rather than taking the risk of involving themselves in a salvage attempt with uncertain prospects. The efforts to refinance the chemical group SIR through a consortium established in December 1979 failed precisely for a lack of agreement among creditors. The government intervened to keep the company afloat, and finally authorized ENI to take over the lion's share of the group. A similar solution was adopted for Liquichimica (*Financial Times*, 6 January 1981, p. 4).

However, the takeover of SIR and Liquichimica by ENI did not lead simply to a further extension of the state sector through the absorption of inefficient firms. It became part of an overall restructuring of the Italian chemical industry, which was to be completed in the summer of 1982. In 1981 the government decided that IRI and ENI should sell to the private sector their 17 per cent stake in Montedison, a stake that had given them a majority in the controlling shareholders' syndicate. ENI set up a joint venture with the American group Occidental called Enoxy. Then ENI, Enoxy and Montedison negotiated an agreement on an exchange of chemical plants: Montedison, the 'private pole' of the chemical industry, was to concentrate on fine chemicals; ENI and Enoxy were to concentrate on bulk chemicals. The aim of the exchange was to exploit the advantages of specialization and to alleviate the problem of overcapacity. The intended rationalization of the chemical industry clearly required plant closures and an as yet undetermined reduction in the labour force (*Financial Times*, 6 January 1981, p. 4).

THE INDUSTRIAL RECONSTRUCTION AND RECONVERSION ACT AND THE PROBLEMS OF SUBSIDIZED CREDIT

The Law no. 675, the Industrial Reconstruction and Reconversion Act of 1977, was the most ambitious effort of the 1970s to develop a comprehensive and coherent industrial policy in order to facilitate the adaptation of Italian industry to new cost structures and market conditions. Although it failed to achieve its objectives, it deserves to be treated at some length, for it highlights some of the conditions and constraints of economic policy-making in Italy. The main objectives of the law were, first, the renovation of Italy's productive structure through a variety of measures such as aid for the reconversion of big industry, an improvement in the mobility of the labour force, subsidies to applied research and the promotion of handicraft industry; and second, the rationalization of subsidized credit. A clearing of the 'incentive jungle' that had been created by successive interest-rebating laws appeared all the more urgent as 'soft' loans had often been used to finance investments that were chosen 'on the basis of expected political, rather than economic, returns' (Luciani and Sacco, 1980, p. 203).

The origins of the Law no. 675 go back to the summer of 1975, when economic policy-makers drew the lesson from the oil price shock and the recession that state action was necessary to facilitate structural adjustment in Italian industry. Moreover, the financial plight of many large companies created a sense of urgency. In December 1975 the Moro–La Malfa Cabinet passed a draft law that provided for an increase in the endowment funds of the state companies and authorized L.2000 billion for subsidized credit. The projects that were to be financed were to be selected by the special credit institutes and not, as had been customary, by bureaucratic bodies. The bill included also measures to enhance the mobility of workers. The project came to naught because of a coalition crisis that was staged by the Socialists and led to early elections. The Christian Democrat minority government that was formed after the 1976 elections was supported by a broad parliamentary coalition including the Italian Communist Party (PCI). Consequently, the government had to take into account the positions of the PCI with respect to economic and industrial policy when it framed legislation. The PCI advocated a revival of the policy of national economic planning. Industrial policy was to be conducted through sectoral plans. These plans were to indicate the priorities and methods of government intervention in key industrial sectors. Another major preoccupation of the PCI was the elimination of clientelistic practices by a limitation of the government's discretionary authority in decisions on credit subsidies and a strengthening of democratic control. The expansion of public action that was apparent in the proposals of the Andreotti government as compared with those of the Moro–La Malfa government, and the resistance that was offered by the representatives of vested interests made for a slow and laborious legislative process. Only in August 1977 was the Law no. 675 promulgated. Although the law was intended to be comprehensive, there was a lack of coordination with Law no. 183 of May 1976: the latter had been passed in order to reorganize the incentive system for the development of southern Italy (Marchini, 1981, esp. pp. 9–19).

The major institutional innovation of Law no. 675 was the creation of the Inter-ministerial Committee for the Coordination of Industrial Policy (CIPI), a subcommittee of the Committee for Economic Planning (CIPE). The new committee was composed of the Ministers of the Budget, Treasury, Industry, State Holdings, Labour and the South and was chaired by the President of the Council of Ministers or, in his absence, by the Minister of the Budget. The main functions of CIPI were defined as:

(1) establishment of the guidelines for industrial policy;
(2) annual examination of the situation of industry on the basis of a report that was to be submitted by the Minister of Industry;
(3) designation of sectors in which interventions and processes of restructuring and reconversion were necessary;
(4) determination of the financial requirements and the priorities of public aid programmes; and
(5) approval of the 'finalized programmes' (sectoral plans) proposed by the Minister of Industry for individual industrial sectors.

The law established a 'fund for the reconstruction and reconversion of industry'. It was to provide interest rate subsidies for firms that realized projects of restructuring or reconversion in conformity with the sectoral plans that had been approved by CIPI. The total amount available for this fund was L.2630 billion over a period of four years. At least 40 per cent was to be spent on projects located in the South. Applications for 'soft' loans were to be submitted to a medium-term credit institute which would then pass them on — through the Ministry of Industry — to a technical committee for decision. However, final approval belonged to CIPI. The law obliged the Ministry of State Holdings to submit a medium-term investment programme of the state companies and determined that the projected increases in the endowment funds were to be used only to finance new investments or to enlarge or modernize existing plants. To strengthen parliamentary control a mixed Senate/Chamber of Deputies commission was created. Its task was to examine *ex ante* the programmes of the state holdings and the programmes to be financed through the fund (*Business International*, 1978, pp. 67–9); Luciani and Sacco, 1980, p. 203).

Applied research, which had been something of a stepchild of industrial policy, was to be encouraged by grants of up to 40 (under certain conditions 60) per cent of total cost for projects of 'particular technological relevance and high industrial risk' (*Business Inter-*

national, 1978, p. 69); Banca d'Italia, 1981, pp. 167-8). The movement of redundant workers was to be facilitated by a complicated mobility procedure whose rationale was to ensure that redundant workers would be able to move to firms that were willing to hire them without an interruption of employment. With its heavily bureaucratic character, the mechanism was ill equipped to achieve its purpose. In fact, the Industrial Reconstruction Act did little more than modify the rules under which workers of crisis-ridden firms were entitled to payments from the Cassa Integrazione Guadagni, the wage compensation fund. This institution, which is administered by the social security agency INPS and largely financed by the state, guarantees in most cases 92 per cent of net salary (with almost no time limit) to workers made partially or totally redundant (Regini and Esping-Andersen, 1980, p. 117); Dell'Aringa, 1981, pp. 39-49; Nava, 1981, pp. 42-8). It has contributed to a high level of job security. Mass redundancies can be avoided once CIPI has declared a state of occupational (sectoral) or enterprise crisis.

After the promulgation of Law no. 675 it took almost three years until the first applications for 'soft' loans could be processed. In part because the fund for the reconstruction of industry became operative only about a year before it was supposed to expire, its life was extended. The delays in the implementation of the law were caused by problems of interpretation that had to be clarified by the highest administrative courts; by difficulties of reaching agreement among the operative agencies (Ministry of Industry, Treasury, special credit institutes); and probably by some bureaucratic obstructionism (Marchini, 1981, pp. 16-17). Because of these delays, Law no. 675 may have slowed down rather than promoted structural change. Apparently, many firms that expected to benefit from the aid schemes postponed programmes for restructuring while they waited to become eligible for public funds.

Even though it may be too early to evaluate the results of a law that became operational in the second half of 1980, the Industrial Reconstruction Act was widely considered a failure. Its major weaknesses have been pointed out by a number of Italian economists. The advocates of the law had unrealistic expectations about the employment effects of industrial restructuring. They overestimated also the potential of sectoral planning. What the PCI and the unions expected from the plans was very different from their real function. For example, the unions had demanded that the sectoral plans should become the instrument for the expansion of industrial employment in the South and should set binding objectives that were to be respected by firms. In reality, however, the plans, which were worked out by three or four experts within four months, could hardly do more than provide an analytical description of the problems of the particular sector. The critics of the actual programmes argued that the plans were largely descriptions or reflected decisions already taken by the firms. The decision to pursue the sectoral approach had partly been inspired by the intention to narrow the scope for discretionary decisions dictated by criteria of clientelism. In fact, the sector concept was too broad for a useful discrimination between those firms that deserved to be redeemed and those that deserved to be sacrificed. The lack of selectivity of the sectoral approach became most evident when CIPI approved a growing number of programmes that almost covered the entire industrial sector. The legal requirement, that projects presented by companies should be verified for their conformity with the relevant sectoral programme, was turned into a purely formal act. Official attention focused on the question of whether the initiatives to be subsidized entered into one of the sectors for which a programme had been approved. The large number of sectors opened up, once again, enough room for the exercise of discretion on the basis of clientelistic distribution of public funds (Luciani and Sacco, 1980, p. 204).

The inglorious fate of Law no. 675 stimulated a reappraisal of the functions and forms of subsidized credit. According to the critics of this system of incentives, both the efficiency of industrial policy and the efficiency of the banking system required a reform of subsidized credit. It was argued that subsidized credit had ensured the survival of unproductive firms. In some branches, especially in the chemical industry, it had contributed to excessive borrowing. In institutional terms, the manner in which subsidized credit was distributed had encroached upon the responsibility of special credit institutes (Cantaro, 1980, pp. 1291–1318; Marzano, 1980, pp. 305–23). The annual report of the Bank of Italy for 1979 stressed the difference between credit and subsidy. Public subsidies had to be administered according to the criteria of public administration and in conformity with clearly defined procedures of evaluation and selection. This administrative evaluation was not to be confused with the entrepreneurial judgement of the credit institutes. In place of the system that bound together the administration of incentives and the management of credit, Governor Ciampi recommended that incentives should be given directly to subsidize investment or the employment of labour specifically. The concession of incentives according to some automatic method was to be preferred to discretionary distribution (Banca d'Italia, 1979, pp. 387–8). In January 1982 the Spadolini government introduced a bill to reform the system of subsidized credit. In the future, banks were to provide loans at market rates. Subsidies were to be distributed in the form of capital grants. If adopted by Parliament, this legislation would establish the separation of credit and incentives that had been advocated by the central bank.

CONCLUSION

Italian industrial policy has been unable to meet successfully the major challenge of the 1970s — the need to create favourable conditions for structural adaptation in Italian industry. There was certainly no lack of initiatives, programmes and interventions: nor was there a dearth of public funds for industry. The missing ingredients were a coherent strategy, the readiness to make hard choices, and the capacity to implement policy. The dominant pattern of industrial policy has been short-term crisis management, *ad hoc* interventions that were aimed at safeguarding employment and ensuring the financial survival of floundering companies. Such a pattern does not satisfy a demanding definition of industrial policy. Industrial crisis management all too often disregarded the criteria of economic efficiency and long-term competitiveness, criteria that might have required drastic measures of reorganization painful for both labour and management. In other words, the principal objective of industrial policy, as of economic policy in general, was 'to reduce social tensions over the short term and not to stabilise and develop the economic system over the medium or long term' (Cassone, 1981, p. 77). It is, therefore, not surprising that Italian industrial policy was most inventive with regard to the diversification of rescue instruments. Institutions like GEPI, the consortium of credit institutes or the commissarial administration of large companies were created as alternatives to the traditional form of rescue, the takeover of ailing firms by the state sector. The changes that have been introduced in GEPI's mandate in recent years, as well as the weak attractive power of the consortium model, have revealed clearly the limits of these alternatives. The Industrial Reconstruction and Reconversion Act was an attempt to move beyond the status quo approach to crisis management and to develop a modernization strategy for the promotion of structural change. However, this effort was marred by conceptual flaws and frustrated by the resistance of vested interests and the inefficiency of public administration.

In the absence of a well-defined and effective strategy, the following measures provided some breathing space for industry:

(1)   the devaluation of the lira (until floating was ended by Italy's entry into the European Monetary System), which enabled Italian companies to regain competitiveness in foreign markets;
(2)   the partial budgetization of social security contributions, which reduced the wage costs of industrial companies;
(3)   the transfers from the state budget to private and public industry in the form of credit subsidies, endowment fund increases, capital grants, tax holidays and so on, which in 1978 added up to 2.2 per cent of GDP (Artoni and Termini, 1980, p. 7).

The public financing of industry compensated partially for the 'crowding out' of companies on the capital market by the very heavy borrowing of the state. On the other hand, economists feared that the channelling of funds towards loss-making sectors and firms had reduced the efficiency of resource allocation within the economy.

The poor performance of Italian industrial policy, and its bias towards short-term crisis management primarily aimed at job protection, can be explained partly by structural characteristics of the political system. Italy lacks a stable policy network that facilitates elite interaction and provides a communication infrastructure for the formulation and implementation of industrial policies comparable to the state–industry nexus based on the *grands corps* in France or the symbiotic relationship between banks and industry in Germany. On the contrary, there is a constellation of factors that is highly detrimental to any coherent medium-term economic policy: the archaic ways and the inefficiency of a bureaucracy that is regarded with disdain by the business community; the fragmentation of economic policy-making; the pervasiveness of party and of factional politics, which often subjects economic policy decisions to the logic of clientelism; the short life of governments; the acuteness of distributional conflict; and the veto power of trade unions. These conditions do, however, permit the building of coalitions in the defence of employment as industrial crises arise. The potential for intervention of the most powerful instrument at the disposal of the Italian state, the state holding companies, has been greatly reduced. Industrial crises have been concentrated in their domains, and this concentration is due in part to the subordination of state industry to the peculiar rules of the Italian political game. It may not be unfair to assume that a state that manages its own industry, its budget or the postal service in such a manner will also prove incapable of steering the private sector towards higher levels of economic efficiency and international competitiveness.

In many cases, private companies have adapted themselves successfully to new cost structures and market conditions. Large firms like Pirelli and Olivetti made remarkable recoveries by pursuit of rationalization. Medium-sized and small companies have displayed an extraordinary dynamism. Often the strategy of adaptation followed by private companies has relied heavily on the decentralization of production: the farming out of manufacturing to small suppliers has allowed for a more flexible use of the workforce.

The same function is served by the increasing recourse to the wage compensation fund as a functional equivalent to redundancy. However, the continuing vitality of private industry has not been sufficient to improve the specialization profile of Italy's foreign trade, as the stagnant share of high-technology products in Italian exports indicates (Banca d'Italia, 1981, p. 401; Forcellini, 1978). Unless industry and government rise to the challenge of technological innovation, the weaknesses of the productive structure are likely to undermine Italy's position in world markets.

NOTES

1 According to La Palombara (1964, p. 262), 'the *clientela* relationship exists when an interest group, for whatever reasons, succeeds in becoming, in the eyes of a given administrative agency, the natural expression and representative of a given social sector which, in turn, constitutes the natural target or reference point for the activity of the administrative agency.'

2 According to Grassini (1981, p. 79), 'All the textile and clothing companies ENI has acquired over the last eight years have been "lame ducks", purchased at the government's request. In terms of labour, 36% of ENI's clothing industry and 22% of ENI's textile industry are made up of workers from politically acquired companies. According to my calculations, these lame duck companies generated a loss in the range of 30 billion lira in 1977. However, losses in the entire chemical industry for ENI in 1977 were 250 billion lira, and in the textile industry 100 billion; thus politically acquired companies bear only part of the blame for ENI's poor performance.'

3 Between April 1979 and June 1982, 133 firms with 33,500 employees had been placed under commissarial administration.

REFERENCES

Allen, K. and Stevenson, A. (1974), *An Introduction to the Italian Economy*, London, Martin Robertson.
Artoni, R. and Termini, V. (1980), 'I trasferimenti dello stato all'industria', *L'Industria*, January–March 1980, pp. 7–38.
Banca d'Italia (1979, 1981, 1982), *Relazione del Governatore sull'Esercizio*, Rome, Banca d'Italia.
Bognetti, G. (1981), 'Il sistema delle partecipazioni statali negli anni 1970', in E. Gerelli and G. Bognetti (eds), *La Crisi delle partecipazioni statali: motivi e prospettive*, Milan, Franco Angeli.
Business International (1978), *Italy: How International Companies View It Today*, Geneva and New York, Business International.
Cantaro, A. (1980), 'Credito speciale e credito agevolato', *Rivista trimestrale di diritto pubblico*, no. 4, 1307–18.
Carabba, M. (1977), *Un Ventennio di programmazione 1954–74*, Rome, Laterza.
Cassone, A. (1981), 'The Industrial Policy Role of Public Owned Companies in Italy', *Industrie und Strukturpolitik in der Europäischen Gemeinschaft*, Baden-Baden, Nomos.
Cesarini, F. (1981), 'La situazione finanziaria', in E. Gerelli and G. Bognetti (eds), *La Crisi delle partecipazioni statali: motivi e prospettive*, Milan, Franco Angeli.
Dell'Aringa, C. (1981), *L'agenzia per la mobilita della manodopera*, Milan, Vita e Pensiero.
De Michelis, G. (1981), 'Rapporto di sintesi: le linee di una politica delle partecipazioni statali', in *Rapporto sulle partecipazioni statali*, Milan, Franco Angeli, pp. 1–283.
Diebold, W. (1980), *Industrial Policy as an International Issue*, New York, McGraw-Hill.
Economist (1981), 'Facing the Facts. A Survey of the Italian Economy', *The Economist*, 23 May 1981, pp. 33–4.
Financial Times, 19 November 1979, 6 January 1981, 11 June 1982.
Forcellini, P. (1978), *Rapporto sull'industria italiana*, Rome, Editori Riuniti.
Fraenkel, G. (1975), 'Italian Industrial Policy in the Framework of Economic Planning', in J. Hayward and M. Watson (eds), *Planning, Politics and Public Policy*, London, Cambridge University Press.
Gatti, B. (1981), 'La politica industriale', in E. Gerelli and G. Bognetti (eds), *La Crisi delle partecipazioni statali: motivi e pròspettive*, Milan, Franco Angeli.
Grassini, F. (1981), 'The Italian Enterprises: The Political Constraints', in R. Vernon and Y. Aharoni (eds), *State-owned Enterprise in the Western Economies*, London, Croom Helm.
Holland, S. (ed.) (1972), *The State as Entrepreneur*, London, Weidenfeld and Nicolson.

La Palombara, J. (1964), *Interest Groups in Italian Politics*, Princeton, New Jersey, Princeton University Press.

Lubitz, R. (1978), 'The Italian Economic Crises of the 1970s', *International Finance Discussion Papers*, no. 120, June 1978.

Luciani, G. and Sacco, G. (1980), 'The PCI and the International Economic Crisis', in S. Serfaty and L. Gray (eds), *The Italian Communist Party: Yesterday, Today and Tomorrow*, Westport Connecticut, Greenwood Press, pp. 191-210.

Marchini, L. (1981), *Nel labirinto della politica industriale*, Bologna, Il Mulino.

Martinelli, A. (1981), 'The Italian Experience: A Historical Perspective', in R. Vernon and Y. Aharoni (eds), *State-owned Enterprise in the Western Economies*, London, Croom Helm.

Marzano, A. (1980), 'Credit Subsidies and Efficiency', *Review of Economic Conditions in Italy*, June, 305-23.

Mediobanca (1979), *Dati cumulativi di 856 societa italiane (1968-78)*, Milan, Mediobanca.

Ministero dell'Industria, del Commercio e dell'Artigianato (1979), *Relazione sullo stato dell'industria*, Rome.

Mondo Economico, 26 August 1981, 4 November 1981, 27 January 1982, 19 May 1982.

Nava, G. (1981), 'I salvataggi industriali nella esperienza italiana', *Politica ed Economia*, March, 42-8.

Pasquino, G. and Pecchini, U. (1975), 'Italy', in J. Hayward and M. Watson (eds), *Planning, Politics and Public Policy*, London, Cambridge University Press.

Prodi, R. (1974), 'Italy', in R. Vernon (ed.), *Big Business and the State in Western Europe*, Cambridge Massachusetts, Harvard University Press.

Ragazzi, G. (1981), 'La componente finanziaria nella crisi e nel risanamento delle partecipazioni statali', in *Rapporto sulle partecipazioni statali*, Milan, Franco Angeli.

Regini, M. and Esping-Andersen, G. (1980), 'Trade Union Strategies and Social Policy in Italy and Sweden', in J. Hayward (ed.), *Trade Unions and Politics in Western Europe*, London, Frank Cass.

Romeo, R. (1972), *Breve storia della grande industria in Italia* (4th edn), Bologna, Capelli.

Savona, P. (1980), 'Real and Financial Capital in Italian Economic Development: Some Remarks', *Review of Economic Conditions in Italy*, June, 279-303.

Schioppa, P. (1980), 'State, Market, Bank, Firm: Objects and Instruments of Public Intervention', *Review of Economic Conditions in Italy*, June, 243-303.

Scognamiglio, C. (1979), *Crisi e risanamento dell'industria italiana*, Milan, Giuffre.

Solustri, A. (1975), 'Italian Industrial Policy in Economic Programming in 1966-70', *Rivista di Politica Economica*, December, 143-83.

Templeman, D. (1981), *The Italian Economy*, New York, Praeger.

8

Welfare State and Employment Policy: Sweden

Kjell Lundmark

During the 1960s Sweden established a reputation as a distinctive, social democratic model. In particular, its imaginative combination of counter-cyclical economic policy with labour market policy was seen as the basis for the reconciliation of high economic growth, full employment and a generous welfare policy. Sweden's so-called 'middle way' appeared to combine economic modernization with social justice and to exemplify a policy style that united political consensus with policy innovation. This model excited the attention of foreign observers, for it seemed an ideal means of coping with the economic and social stresses that confronted most other advanced industrial societies (Anton, 1980; Hancock, 1972; Childs, 1980). Despite the political dominance of Social Democratic governments since 1932, the economy remained committed to liberal principles. Tariffs and quotas were minimal. Government found little reason to interfere with market forces, in large part because of rising industrial output and low unemployment. The Social Democrats were able to rely on a sophisticated private banking system, centred on the Wallenberg family, to provide a financial infrastructure for growth; and on the high quality of management and technology in a country where engineering and science have long enjoyed a high social status.

The most important contribution of the Social Democrats in the 1930s was the introduction of a pre-Keynesian counter-cyclical economic policy in the form advocated by Wicksell and the Stockholm School of Economics and pressed by the Swedish Trade Union Federation (LO). Another major example of the imaginative, positive response of Swedish social democracy to economic problems was the 'active' labour market policy of the 1960s. This policy emphasized a socially conscious modernization and was also the brain-child of the Trade Union Federation. A spirit of innovation and of consensus rather than of conflict characterized industrial politics − indeed, many policy sectors — during these years. The need for structural modernization of industry was accepted by the major political parties and associational groups. In practice, as well as in theory, they were prepared to pay the price of structural adjustment, including increased emigration from the poorer regions and a decline of traditional craft industries and agriculture. Such costs were justified by reference both to the rising standard of living, the consequences of which were visible and presumed to benefit all, and to a generous labour market policy, the implementation of which involved the collaboration of the 'social partners' (employer organizations and trade unions).

Like many other countries, Sweden used much of its economic growth for public expenditure. Public education, health insurance and old age pensions were seen as integral parts of a comprehensive social security network. Both the Social Democrats, who had been in office since 1932, and the 'bourgeois' opposition gave priority to the goal of economic growth on the basis of the 'mixed economy'. In particular, top priority was accorded to the welfare objective of full employment. Fundamental ideological issues were ignored in favour of technical debates about small issues in a spirit of collaboration and objectivity. In short, the basis of the Swedish model was a combination of, on the one hand, an unyielding faith in the market economy and, on the other, a simultaneous expansion of the welfare state with a 'cradle-to-grave' social security programme and an active and increasingly costly labour market policy that facilitated mobility in the interests of adaptation of the economic structure. All in all, the late 1950s and the 1960s were the golden age of the 'Swedish (Scandinavian) model'.

This 'welfare-oriented' model of a modernization policy involved an economic policy strategy that combined general and selective measures. Among the traditional general measures were monetary policies such as interest rate adjustments and open market operations as well as such aspects of the labour market policy as matching jobs and unemployment and support for industrial mobility. Other aspects of the labour market policy, such as public works and location aid to industry, were used selectively and on an increasing scale. Tax and credit policy were other selective measures that were employed. The labour market policy was, however, a key element of the Swedish model. It was designed to solve three different problems. First, unemployment and jobs had to be matched to each other by encouragement of regional and sectoral mobility. Second, the policy was supposed to serve as an overall anti-inflationary economic policy by reducing wage pressures in expanding sectors and regions through the mobilization of a plentiful supply of skilled labour. Third, the policy was a political precondition for a unified wage policy that was intended gradually to close down inefficient and obsolete firms and industries (Meidner and Niklasson, 1970; Meidner, 1981). The workforce was to be squeezed out of sectors with low profits and, correspondingly, depressed wage-levels, and to be encouraged into growth sectors by such measures as retraining, financial incentives and new housing stock.

The pivotal role of the labour market policy brings into focus yet another peculiar aspect of the Swedish model. Successive Social Democratic governments concentrated on the redistributive role of the Swedish state and the development of social policies. Industrial policies have displayed a preference for regulation rather than for an involvement of the state in the details of structural modernization through, for instance, public ownership. Public ownership has been much less important in Sweden than in Britain, France or Italy. The combination of expansive social policies and high public expenditure with private ownership of industry placed considerable responsibility on government's effective use of macroeconomic policy. Government's discharge of this responsibility was, however, seen to be dependent on conditions in the labour market. While wage negotiations were left to the employer and trade union organizations, their concern for conditions in the labour market was encouraged by their 'official' co-optation into the administration of the National Labour Market Board, the government agency responsible for labour market policy.

The cornerstone of Swedish trade union ideology was the concept of a unified wage policy, a concept that was based on the principle of solidarity and that aimed at equalization. The main objective of the unified wage policy was to ensure for the workers a fair share of the gross national income and to reduce the wage differentials among different groups within the labour market. In effect, this wage policy implied a uniform increase of wage rates regardless of turnover and surplus within different sectors of the economy and individual companies. Implementation of such a wage policy called also for a rather centralized trade union movement. The Trade Union Federation (LO) had to 'control' the wage bargaining process and, in particular, to ensure a restrictive use of selective strikes as a bargaining weapon. Hence, a centralized system of collective bargaining emerged. This solution functioned smoothly for many years without much government intervention and with comparatively few industrial disputes

(Lund, 1981).

Swedish economy policy rested on a recognition of the country's openness to world markets and consequent vulnerability if its industry were not capable of flexible response to changes in the international economy. Roughly one-half of Sweden's industrial output is exported; in the technologically advanced sectors the proportion is close to two-thirds. On the criterion of scale of productive operations abroad in relation to the size of the domestic economy, Sweden has the most multinational industrial development in the world. In per capita terms, only the Netherlands and Switzerland are more engaged in international business operations. Such firms as SKF, Volvo, Saab, ASEA, Electrolux and Eriksson symbolize the technical proficiency of Sweden in international markets.

The Swedish model was viewed variously — as a welfare policy, as a strategy for economic modernization, or as a 'responsible' collective bargaining system. Whatever its essential character, it appeared to function well during the 1960s and was exempt from political attacks in the early 1970s. The necessary prerequisites for consensus about the model were present: economic growth, widely shared material prosperity, and stable government. The Social Democratic Party controlled the executive alone after the coalition with the Agrarian Party broke down in 1958. Governments enjoyed stability, and ideological consensus prevailed more than ever before. However, political and economic developments during the late 1970s undermined the effective functioning of, and appeal of, the Swedish model. Oil dependence was the highest in the world, oil accounting for some 70 per cent of fuel imports. As a consequence of the election of 1976, the Social Democrats lost office for the first time since the Second World War. The imbalance in the economy was reflected in a combination of high tax rates and large budget deficit that was unique among OECD countries, while the deterioration in the climate of industrial relations was apparent in the general strike of 1980. The Swedish model had, according to many observers, lost its rationale and relevance. Political consensus had vanished; industry was in crisis; stabilization policy was a failure; and industrial policy became more and more a patchwork of selective measures.

The next two sections discuss the development of industrial policy in Sweden, its institutional context and instruments. Particular attention is given to the management of industrial crises by industrial policy-makers. A further section considers two important cases of industrial rescue, and the final section draws conclusions.

INDUSTRIAL POLICY: THE BACKGROUND

Many of the ideas behind the Social Democratic industrial policy of the 1960s derived from a report that was presented to the Congress of the Trade Union Federation in 1961. The central theme of this report, 'Coordinated Industrial Policy', was a firm belief in the efficiency of the market economy (Lewin, 1967; Bröms, 1977; Elander, 1978). Emphasis was placed on measures to remove barriers that prevented firms and industries from operating according to the principles of liberal economic theory. An open, competitive credit market was to make finance more easily available to expanding industries and to exert constraints on inefficient companies. Government was expected to pursue a liberal economic policy of free trade abroad and to take strong measures against unfair methods of competition at home (Lewin, 1967). The report did not conclude that government must undertake large-scale direct interventions in industry. Indeed evidence of doubts about the wisdom of government intervention was to be found in the report. Government could cause harm as well as be of help to the economy.

> General measures have to be complemented by more selective ones. The latter must be coordinated with general measures and used with care to avoid unforeseen and uncontrollable developments. Above all, interventions have to be designed not to subsidize economically weak, and in the long run dying, firms and industries thereby conserving an obsolete industrial structure. [Samordnad Näringspolitik, 1961, p. 168]

Labour market policy and industrial location policy were the key features of the report's proposals. The labour market policy was not just a theoretical blueprint; it had already been implemented and tested during the temporary recession in 1958. Although the regional development policy drew on a different ideological background from that of the labour market policy, they were both to form part of the same overall programme. The report emphasized that regional policy was not designed primarily to slow down urbanization and to distribute industrial sectors and companies evenly across the whole country. Regional policy could not, and should not, guarantee prosperity and development to all regions. Instead, government had to concentrate its efforts on expanding and viable areas (Lewin, 1967). The Trade Union Federation was, in other words, advocating an 'active' industrial strategy of 'picking winners'. An official regional development policy programme was introduced in 1964 when the government introduced a bill into Parliament (Riksdag). Although the immediate background was a Royal Commission report, the intellectual and political inspiration came from the trade union report, 'Coordinated Industrial Policy' (Lewin, 1967; Elander, 1978).

The losses of the Social Democratic Party in the 1966 municipal elections were in part blamed on a conservative reliance on traditional labour market instruments and the limited experiment in regional development policy. These electoral losses led the Social Democrats to adopt the term 'offensive industrial policy'. This policy was to encompass all possible economic and political measures that could have an impact on the restructuring of the economy (*Tiden*, 1967, p. 580). Emphasis continued to be placed on promotion of a structural modernization of the economy. Four major areas were singled out as primary targets for an 'offensive' or 'active' Social Democratic industrial policy: assurance of sufficient capital flow to industrial enterprises; improvement and strengthening of society's resources for economic planning; encouragement of technological research and development; and extension of public enterprise. Even in the early 1970s — in the aftermath of the prosperous 1960s — the economy was growing and the number of unemployed was comparatively low. However, in the background were indications that large parts of Swedish industry were confronting growing structural problems. The staple industries of timber and iron ore were facing increased international competition. Sweden's economy was very exposed because of the high proportion of foreign trade in gross national product and because of a heavy reliance on imports of oil. The unified wage policy appeared to be generating inflationary pressures rather than structural adjustment. Compared with some other advanced countries, industrial investment and productivity had been declining since 1965. Sweden was hard hit after 1973 by the international recession and energy crisis. Shipbuilding and the steel industry were left with idle capacity. The iron ore mines, which had traditional ties to West European steelworks, were facing similar difficulties. The expansion of the wood-processing industry came to a halt owing to unanticipated constraints on the supply side. The textile industry was doing even worse than before: its output was not even sufficient to cover domestic demand (Carlsson *et al.*, 1981).

The political response to the oil shock was an expansive economic policy that was approved by a large parliamentary majority in 1974. As Parliament was divided into a socialist and a non-socialist bloc, each of which controlled 175 seats, the Social Democratic government was in a weak position. Such a closely balanced political situation encouraged political parties to avoid association with recession, austerity and unemployment. The government faced particular difficulties because the Social Democratic Party's share of the vote had been declining since the 1968 election. Consequently, during the 1973–76 legislative period the Social Democrats attempted to create as broad majorities as possible for their legislation. The Constitution of Sweden prescribes that, in the case of propositions and bills that receive an equal number of votes, decisions are to be taken by way of a lottery. The government was therefore naturally eager to avoid roll-calls that could lead to resort to a 'lottery-ticket' procedure of legislative decision. The expansive economic policy stimulated private consumption in 1975, and in 1976 a bundle of other programmes to support production and employment was added. In terms of job creation, the result may be described as successful. The question was. however, whether this policy response resolved or exacerbated the fundamental problems of the economy. The expansive economic policy was an attempt to stall the effects of the international recession until, as in the past, the larger economies recovered. It was sometimes argued that this economic policy was to be blamed for the wage explosion that resulted from the 1975–76 wage round. Inflationary pressures could also be ascribed to the huge industrial profits that were the product of rising export prices for timber and metalware products (Åberg, 1981). Prices and costs rose much faster in Sweden than among her overseas competitors. At the same time, Sweden's traditional staple industries faced a sharp reduction of demand in the international market. Consequently, Sweden was unable to take advantage of the limited international recovery after 1975.

The non-socialist government that came into office after the 1976 election responded to these challenges by devaluation. The devaluation promised to strengthen Sweden's ability to compete on the international market. However, the new three-party government was not able to implement a coherent long-term economic policy. The budget deficit grew drastically, even when the international business cycle recovered. Structural crises in industry were tackled by large commitments of public expenditure in the form of industrial and labour market programmes. Industrial crises took place in a new political context of a three-party government after more than 40 years of Social Democratic rule. The concern of each of the three parties of government to have its own reforms enacted made the budget deficit worse than before and generated chaos in public policy. Further, the major nightmare for this government was unemployment. As the Agrarian Party had committed itself during the election campaign to the creation of 400,000 new jobs, the government could not start dismantling labour market programmes. Of the governing parties, the Agrarians were the most eager for selective policies. Although the Conservative Party and the Liberal Party emphasized macroeconomic policies, especially the ideology of the market economy, they were unable to dissociate the government's policy from the particular influence of the Agrarians or from the general influence of a political climate that was formed by social democratic values.

INDUSTRIAL POLICY – INSTITUTIONS AND INSTRUMENTS

The growth of industrial policy in the 1960s was encouraged by the decline in the competitiveness of Sweden's raw materials (iron ore, timber) and of the traditional industries that were based on these raw materials. The response to Sweden's loss of world markets was complex. From 1965, direct subsidies were given to individual firms as locational aid within the framework of regional policy. Previously public aid had come from the credit market, in which a few credit institutions that were funded by public money had been in operation since the 1930s. The locational aid was first offered to firms in a special support area in the north. Local firms or firms that were contemplating location there could receive direct subsidies as well as loans for investments in equipment and premises. In addition to a growing concern with regional policy and rapid expansion of labour market policy, important new institutions were established in the late 1960s. The Swedish Investment Bank was founded in 1967 to finance projects that might be profitable but that had limited prospects in the existing credit market. It was designed to channel the huge and rapidly growing pension funds into medium- and long-term investment projects. Special emphasis was placed on projects that would encourage structural modernization. The Investment Bank's ability to buy shares in individual firms involved a new form of public intervention – mixed ownership as well as risk-taking. In 1968 the National Board for Technical Development was established to promote industrial research and technological change. In addition to a consultancy service, the board could support industry by direct subsidy. In 1968 a Department of Industry was finally created. The so-called 'active industrial policy' that was introduced in the late

1960s found its expression in other institutions as well. Examples are the Swedish National Development Company and the Swedish Industrial Establishment Company. In 1970 the Swedish State Holding Company was formed as a consequence of the industrial policy programme that had been accepted by the Social Democratic government. Three years later the establishment of the National Industrial Board was an indication of an industrial policy that was more in accordance with the forms of the traditional Swedish administrative system. Programmes are 'traditionally' administered through the characteristically Swedish device of autonomous boards organized at national, regional and sometimes local levels. At present, more than 40 of these national boards or agencies are engaged in the management of economic support to firms within industry, agriculture and services. Some ten national boards deal primarily with industrial support, the most important being the Labour Market Board, the National Industrial Board and the National Board for Technical Development. Although every ministry is involved, support for industry is mainly the responsibility of the Ministries of Industry, Trade and Agriculture. The small size of these ministries, however, reflects their traditional functions of policy planning and legislative preparation.

The 1970s witnessed a major 'takeoff' of industrial support in terms of public expenditure as well as of the number of programmes and institutions that were created to help particular regions, sectors and firms. Most industrial policy instruments were still aspects of regional and labour market policies, although the first signs of special aid to industrial sectors were becoming visible. Sectoral aid was introduced for the textile and glass industries in 1970 and then for the timber and foundry industries. In 1974 the shipyards, the metalware and fur industries became recipients of public aid. Within regional policy and labour market policy new programmes included employment promotion, transport aid, allowances to municipalities to support industry with premises, special governmental grants to encourage production for stock, and special allowances to firms for education and temporary employment as well as to make them avoid lay-offs. Up to the mid-1970s such temporary programmes were in fact often prolonged, supplemented by more sophisticated and detailed policy instruments, and allocated more money. Even so, the programmes were quite marginal in scope and numbers compared with what was to follow.

From 1976 a dramatic change occurred in Swedish industrial policy and suggested a completely new departure. The figures for 'non-permanent industrial support' rose very rapidly (see table 8.1).

Table 8.1 *Industrial support in Sweden, 1970–80*
Amounts disbursed in 1980s prices (milliards of krona)

	1970/ 1971	1971/ 1972	1972/ 1973	1973/ 1974	1974/ 1975	1975/ 1976	1976/ 1977	1977/ 1978	1978/ 1979	1979/ 1980	Sum	%
Industrial location aid and transportation grant	0.8	1.1	0.8	1.2	1.5	1.1	1.1	1.1	0.8	1.1	10.5	10
Small firms' contributions (mainly loans from the Industrial Credit Bank, The Swedish Business Credit Association Ltd, the Development Foundations)	1.6	1.6	1.5	2.0	1.8	2.0	2.4	2.5	3.1	2.7	21.1	20
Firm and branch contributions through the Investment Bank and the National Industrial Board	1.4	1.4	1.1	1.0	1.5	1.9	1.4	2.6	1.5	1.3	15.0	14
R and D contributions through the National Board for Technical Development and the Nordic Industrial Foundation, R and D deductions at company taxation and contributions to energy research and energy savings	0.4	0.4	0.5	0.5	1.2	1.2	1.3	1.4	1.4	2.1	10.3	10
Export credit financing through the Swedish Export Credit Corporation and the Investment Bank Ltd	1.0	1.4	2.3	1.2	1.9	2.1	2.2	2.2	1.1	1.6	16.9	16
Non-permanent industrial grant	0.3	0.9	0.5	0.5	0.9	1.9	5.1	5.0	8.8	8.1	31.9	30
Sum of grants	5.5	6.8	6.8	6.3	8.7	10.2	13.4	14.8	16.6	16.9	105.8	100

Note. Recalculation GNP-deflator. The figures include grants in the form of contributions, capital contributions, stock purchase, loans, redeemed guarantees and so on, but not published guarantees.
Sources: SOU (1981, p. 72) Royal Commission Report, *Att avveckla en kortsiktig stödpolitik.*

These measures were introduced outside the framework of the older
programmes for industrial development. They required Parliament's
approval for every single intervention. The traditional procedure of
implementing programmes through various kinds of administrative
boards continued. The sharply rising figures for 'non-permanent
industrial support' was, however, complemented by a change in the
way industrial policy was implemented during the late 1970s. More
striking than the establishment of new agencies and institutions since
the late 1960s has been the fact that ever more resources are allocated directly by the government and Parliament to enterprises. This
development has reduced the importance of the operations of the
autonomous agencies and boards both at national and regional levels
(see figure 8.1). These institutions no longer played a decisive role in
policy implementation.

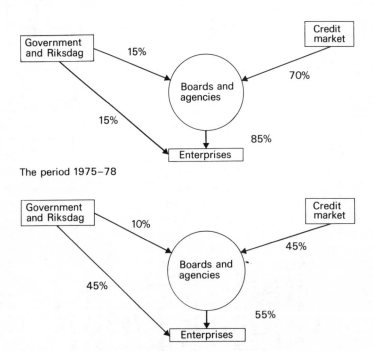

Figure 8.1   The Intermediaries in Allowances and Loans to Enterprise
under Swedish Industrial Policy Programmes, 1970–74
and 1975–78.
(*Source: Att avveckla en korsiktig stödpolitik,* 1981)

Although the measures under the heading 'Non-permanent industrial support' are not categorized as 'emergency rescue operations', most of them perform this function. No less than 90 per cent of the fundings under this heading were accounted for by seven cases of industrial crisis. These rescue operations were undertaken between 1974 and 1980 (SOU, 1981, p. 72). The shipbuilding and the steel industries were the major recipients; they took 46 and 35 per cent respectively of the 23 billion krona ($3.8 billion) distributed. The LKAB Mining Company's share was 9 per cent, and two wood-processing firms, the Cellulose Company of the Norrland Forest Owners and the South Swedish Forest Owners' Association, got 7 per cent together. The remaining 3 per cent was divided among three enterprises within data electronics (Data SAAB), television and radio electronics (Luxor Industry Ltd) and the foundry industry (Hälleforsnäs Ltd).

MANAGING INDUSTRIAL CRISES:
THE CASES OF SHIPBUILDING AND ELECTRONICS

Three of the industrial rescues could be characterized as part of the international structural crisis: shipbuilding, steel and the iron ore industry. The remaining four involved individual firms that faced particular troubles of their own. Although structural difficulties were present in the latter cases, internal managerial problems played a key role in their crises. In this section two cases, one from each group, will be considered. A simple analytical approach (model) is used in order to illuminate the way crises were managed. Problem definition is the first stage of this analysis. What is the nature of the problem, and who is defining it and in what terms? The next stage is resource identification. What resources are available and appropriate to solve the problem, and who is suggesting what strategy? What strategy is chosen? Finally, resource mobilization is analysed. What procedures are actually used to deliver the earmarked resources to the industry or enterprise in crisis?

Shipbuilding

For a long time Sweden has been one of the biggest shipbuilders in the world. Some of her biggest shipyards, in many cases owned by shipping companies, have a long history. At the beginning of the 1960s shipbuilding accounted for 3 per cent of total employment in

Swedish industry. The shipyards have enjoyed public aid of various kinds since the late 1950s. Till 1973 this aid amounted to no more than a few hundred million krona, mainly in the form of credit guarantees. In one case a special rescue operation ended in nationalization. In a bill of 1970 a word of warning was given about further expansion of shipbuilding. The government was not prepared to encourage an expansion of capacity. The shipyards were under financial strains because of low earnings and weak investment. Industrial policy was to concentrate on vital and expanding lines of business. In case of emergency, government was to opt for selective intervention rather than relying on general support (SOU, 1981, p. 72). The shipyards recovered, however, during the early 1970s without more intensive public support. The biggest shipyards tried even to cooperate through a committee in which the government was represented.

In 1974 government's resolve to avoid an expansion of capacity within the shipbuilding industry was weakened. A special investigation by the Ministry of Industry had been influenced by the optimism of the industry and by the expansive investment plans that were produced by the shipyards themselves. Although government was aware of the risk of future idle capacity, it declared its willingness to help preserve the industry's competitiveness even if that meant expansion. Parliament voted for public credit guarantees on a five-year basis, and a special committee was appointed to investigate the use of these guarantees. A policy for expansion replaced the old search for consolidation (DS I 1981:8).

In the following years the industry's problems were put on the political agenda by the shipyards themselves. They faced crises at an accelerating rate. In 1975 one of the shipyards in Gothenburg faced bankruptcy, and the government had to take it into public ownership. In the next year this shipyard was merged with another shipyard in Gothenburg. An agreement resulted in state ownership of more than 50 per cent. Demands were now raised for temporary public loan guarantees in order to finance production for stock. The late 1970s were marked by apparently endless problems for shipyards. The new public-owned shipyards incurred losses every year. The only remaining large private-owned shipyard (in Malmö) sought public aid from 1977 and finally submitted to public ownership in 1979 (DS I 1981:8). Although the government had seen the general signs of forthcoming structural problems, each individual crisis was unanticipated. Problem definition was in the hands of the shipyards. The government had to rely on reports and data from the shipyards themselves: and in most cases the problems were presented as a matter of 'life or death'.

The Social Democratic government responded to the crisis of 1975 by the device of public ownership. According to the government's bill, there was no alternative. Closure of the Gothenburg yard was unacceptable from the point of view of the labour market, while the owner (a shipping company) was not regarded as economically viable enough to shoulder a reconstruction. In addition, sharp criticism from the trade unions against the owner and the management increased political pressures on the government for public ownership. It proved impossible to find interested buyers. The government's bill was the work of special working groups *within* the Ministry of Industry. In place of the Swedish tradition of reliance on the royal commission, a special governmental commission was appointed. This Ministry of Industry commission was composed of managing directors from two other shipyards, a lawyer from the metal workers union, an under-secretary of state for Industry, and the Chairman of the Royal Commission on Shipbuilding Credits. It took one year to prepare a long-term solution to the difficulties in Gothenburg. Negotiations with the owners of one of the other shipyards in Gothenburg led eventually to an agreement to merge the two companies. The state owned a majority of the shares in the new enterprise (DS I 1981:8). The Royal Commission on Shipbuilding Credits meanwhile proposed a system of public credit guarantees for stock production. Its work was conducted in the usual 'institutionalized' way, in other words, through careful research, lengthy deliberation and consultation among all interested parties (Anton, 1980). Parliament accepted the proposed bill and voted for a policy of stock production on the explicit condition that shipbuilding capacity had to be reduced by 30 per cent by 1979 (SOU, 1981, p. 72).

During its last few days in office, the Social Democratic government appointed yet another royal commission, which was asked to come up with recommendations for a public group of shipyards. However, the new non-socialist Minister of Industry was not satisfied with this approach when he took up office in the autumn of 1976. Instead he appointed a working team of his own. This team was composed in part of some members of the royal commission and in part of new representatives from the metalworkers union and the Ministry. It was asked to produce a long-term plan for a public group of shipyards. Scope and organization as well as capital requirements were to be considered. The proposals that emanated from the royal commission and the working team favoured the establishment of a group of public shipyards. However, one of the members of the Minister's working team dissented from this solution: he was the representative from the Swedish State Holding Company. He opposed also the suggestion of financial support for shipyard-owners and pleaded for a 'radical' solution of closure of shipyards. Even if the government was tempted to adopt such a tough attitude towards the shipyards, labour market considerations made it impossible to propose anything that might worsen the already strained situation in the Gothenburg area (Åsling, 1979; Ericson, 1979).

The organization, particularly the character of the board of directors of the new publicly owned Swedyard Ltd, was the next problem to be solved. The trade unions were opposed to the proposals of the Swedish State Holding Company, which they did not trust in matters of employment. The metalworkers' union suggested a troika principle for the management of Swedyards and wanted to reduce the strong local interest that seemed likely to be built into the company. Eventually, Swedyard was organized as a set of dispersed, independent units in different regions. As the metalworkers' union had anticipated, the consequence was encouragement of an intense 'localism' that meant strong 'grass-roots' political pressures in future crises (Ericson, 1979).

In 1978 the government had to ask Parliament for further aid. Swedyard was facing bankruptcy. The government responded by forming a series of teams headed by under-secretaries of state from five ministries. The teams were to investigate the future of the shipbuilding industry in Sweden and to make recommendations. At the same time, the metalworkers' union and the negotiation cartel for salaried employees in the private business sector were analysing the industry's problems independently (Åsling, 1979; Ericson, 1979). The management of Swedyard was asked by the government to analyse the situation from the strictly commercial perspective of market viability. Its response was that such a perspective implied that the government would have to consider a total closure of the shipbuilding industry in Sweden. As a 'second-best' solution they proposed a time scale for closure of three of the biggest shipyards. The trade unions reacted vehemently, both in the mass media and in meetings with the minister. Their counter-proposals included restructuring with job protection; investment to diversify production; refinance; widening of the economic support to the shipyard owners by more contracts; and incorporation of the shipyard in Malmö into Swedyard (Ericson, 1979). Swedyard received more public money. The Social Democrats pleaded for even more public money for diversification of production as well as for a postponement of decisions on future levels of employment. The unions tried lobbying before the Standing Committee on Economic Affairs of Parliament.

The Ministry's team presented to the government a new and drastic scheme involving closure of two shipyards. The final result was a compromise within the government. This compromise involved a reduction of capacity that varied for different shipyards. The government's bill was, however, never presented to Parliament because of a governmental crisis on energy policy. The new minority government of the Liberal Party agreed on a modified bill with the Social Democrats. Once again the employment issue was central. An even smaller reduction of capacity was planned, and every worker affected was to be re-employed within each company (Åsling, 1979; Ericson, 1979; SOU, 1981, p. 72).

At the end of 1978 an agreement was made between the government and the last big shipyard outside Swedyard. Kockums in Malmö was taken over for the very low price of 20 million krona. The government was already involved in the company through public subsidies to avoid its bankruptcy. At the same time a large demonstration in Malmö indicated the strength of local support for public intervention. In addition to the traditional anxiety about jobs, the government had to consider Sweden's creditworthiness abroad. The shipyard had billions of krona in the form of foreign loans that had been supported by government guarantees (Ericson, 1979; SOU, 1981, p. 72).

The situation of crisis continued into 1979. A new structural plan of Swedyard proposed once again closure of two shipyards. The new three-party, non-socialist government in office after the 1979 elections tried to implement this proposed plan. However, a majority of only one in Parliament meant that the government had little chance of success. The combination of rebellion by two Liberal MPs from one of the threatened areas with the votes of the Social Democratic opposition meant a postponement of closure.

The main actors in crisis management for the shipbuilding industry were the enterprises themselves and the government. Although other interests advocated various measures, the final decisions have always involved financial reconstructions based on public funds. These decisions have never included agreement with the creditors. In the face of bankruptcy, negotiations about issues like the partial repayment of loans did not enter the political agenda. The process of resource identification has been influenced by government's ambition to contribute to a structural modernization of the shipbuilding industry.

These ambitions have been notably supported by the trade unions. In particular, the necessary scale of resources for structural modernization could be found only in government. The reconstructions, through a mix of subsidies, loans and public ownership, were always outside the framework of ordinary industrial policy programmes. In other words, Parliament was the final arbiter of each individual crisis intervention. Once resources had been identified and strategy determined, resource mobilization was not just a formal procedure. Negotiations with interested parties were the task of the Ministry of Industry. After an agreement had been reached within the industrial policy community, it had to be considered by the government. This second round of negotiations involved other ministries, including the Ministry of Budget and the Ministry of Labour.

Response to crisis is, therefore, hampered by a time-consuming process of intra-governmental negotiation. These negotiations are also strained by the facts that ministries are small (on average around 100 people each), and that they are used to general policy-making rather than to the processing of complex, detailed cases of industrial crisis. There is only a limited pool of persons who can devote time to crisis management. Moreover, when they take part in such operations, they have to engage in operational issues of daily management with which they are unfamiliar. The ministries, therefore, are not really prepared to cope with the management of industrial crises. A third stage of negotiation commences when the issues that are posed by an industrial crisis are tackled in a bill and are subjected to parliamentary proceedings. The situation of party political balance in Parliament, with two almost equally large and competing blocs, has often resulted in amendments to government's bills. Consequently, in crisis management for the shipyards the solutions that resulted from negotiations between government and interested parties and within government were only preliminaries to the negotiations and votes in Parliament.

Creditors, especially the banks, were indemnified in the rescue operations for the shipyards. The owners were not always so fortunate. The first rescue operation of 1975 assumed that the owners of the shipyards would contribute to reconstruction. The next rescue operation represented a rather successful outcome for the shipyard owners. The Malmö nationalization involved compensation of 20 million krona for the owners. Although the sum appeared small, the owner was faced by a worse alternative — bankruptcy. During the years of shipyard crises the trade unions were represented in the royal commissions and also in one of the special commissions that were established within the Ministry of Industry. The metalworkers' union monitored the crises very closely. Moreover, the unions could observe developments through their statutory representation in the boards of directors of the enterprises. Nevertheless, they complained that crisis measures were *fait accompli*. At the local level there was continuous and very strong political pressure for preservation of jobs.

Television and Radio Electronics

Luxor Industries Ltd was established in the 1920s and was a family business enterprise until a reconstruction by public intervention in 1979. After a period of steady growth and prosperity, a turning point was reached in the mid-1970s. Market stagnation resulted in over-production, and technical change within the production process proved both rapid and costly. In addition, one of their plants was completely destroyed by fire. Luxor suffered as a consequence from the mounting 'war' for market share in Sweden. Its strategy to meet these challenges involved expansion and export. The strategy proved unsuccessful, and during 1978 signs of an impending crisis appeared. The banks' reaction included a demand for posts in the board of directors of Luxor. Problems were accumulating, and early in 1979 the managing director was dismissed. Luxor was very close to bankruptcy (DS I, 1981:9; SOU, 1981, p. 72).

The problem that was presented to government was primarily financial. Luxor approached the Swedish Investment Bank with a request for a loan of 100 million krona. The Ministry of Industry was also asked for a loan guarantee, which Luxor had already sought unsuccessfully from the National Industrial Board. The Investment Bank was briefed by one of its directors. After a visit to the company and discussions there, he recommended that the bank refuse a loan. Luxor asked for a meeting with the Ministry of Industry. This meeting took place at the beginning of February 1979 and was the start of a hectic week that ended up with a reconstruction that was drafted in the ministry. The problem to which the government had to respond was defined by the enterprise: without public money, financial collapse would occur in a few days.

During the first meeting with representatives from Luxor the officials from the Ministry of Industry were not mandated to arrive at any undertakings. They suggested that the company should inform the Minister of Industry and the Minister of Labour. The team within the Ministry of Industry, which was now deeply involved in the problems of Luxor, also contacted the Swedish Investment Bank and the company's own bank. Together with officials from the Investment Bank, the Ministry attempted to find a solution. The Investment Bank pleaded initially for bankruptcy as the only way to solve the crisis. The Ministry of Industry called attention to the labour market situation in the area and could not see bankruptcy as a way of maintaining employment. In a few days there was a meeting at the Ministry of Labour that was attended by numerous prominent personalities. Besides the Ministers for Labour and Industry, there were key representatives from the Investment Bank and the Industrial Board. The meeting faced three possible strategies: public money to contribute to working capital, reconstruction after agreements with creditors, or bankruptcy. Bankruptcy was seen as a 'non-viable' option; the government believed that it had to intervene for political reasons, notably for labour market considerations. The trade unions played a very important part by moulding public opinion at the local level. As the metalworkers' union is very strong in Motala, where Luxor had its plant, it followed the crisis closely even at the central level. A contribution to working capital could worsen the future burden for Luxor. Hence it was decided that Luxor's crisis would be managed by a reconstruction for which resources would be provided by the government. The form of reconstruction was an agreement with Luxor and its creditors. The Swedish Investment Bank provided one of its directors as acting managing director for the period of reconstruction.

The agreement with creditors ensured that the government would share the losses with other interested parties; also, it favoured smaller creditors who were regarded as safe and as blameless. The big creditors, banks and multinational corporations were forced to accept this solution, although they could hardly argue that the government had to cover their losses. The rescue package also involved the owners, who had to accept a transfer of shares for a nominal payment. The reconstruction was rapidly designed and promptly implemented. On the basis of a verbal promise from the Minister of Industry that a Bill would later provide the necessary money, the Swedish Investment Bank was able to make up the deficit (DS I 1981:9; SOU, 1981, p. 72).

The management of the Luxor crisis is an example of resource mobilization that was broadened beyond the top political level — Ministry of Industry — to encompass the Swedish Investment Bank and to some extent the Industrial Board. Together they could form a potent group for the design of a rescue package. The Ministry of Industry could, therefore, draw on resources not found within the

Ministry itself, in this case 'know-how' in management as well as in financial reconstruction.

CONCLUSION

Until the mid-1970s, direct public subsidy to industry was based on long-term considerations of regional development and an efficiently functioning labour market or was aimed at the modernization of industrial sectors. As we have seen, from the mid-1970s onward a growing proportion of public intervention in industry was accounted for by short-term measures to rescue sectors or enterprises in crisis. These rescue operations involved huge expenditures that no one could really have foreseen. The causes of this sudden shift in the pattern of expenditure on industrial policy are, of course, complex and include a wide variety of economic and political factors. Sweden has had the fortune to be spared much of the economic dislocation and reconstruction problems that faced the rest of Europe following the Second World War. By the 1970s, however, she had to face the same problems as many other West European states and to compete on more equal terms.

An examination of the management of industrial crises in Sweden cannot overlook two important factors. First, despite the existence of non-socialist governments from 1976 to 1982, 40 years of Social Democratic rule had shaped the political climate of Sweden. Indeed, traditions of paternalism are even more deeply rooted in Swedish politics, and helped to make it possible for social democracy to emerge as the 'natural' and dominant element in political culture. The political alternative to the embrace of this social democratic hegemony was the adoption of an aggressive, assertive political style by the new governments. They were, however, unwilling to do violence to the consensual mores of Swedish politics.

Second, a radical change took place in the parliamentary arena. The effectiveness of parliamentary government was gradually eroded during the 1970s. Although the Social Democratic Party continued to hold office from 1973 to 1976, the socialist bloc (Social Democrats and Communists) in Parliament consisted of only just half the members. During the 1976–79 legislative period a three-party, non-socialist government held office for the first two years and was then replaced by a small minority government formed by the Liberal Party. After 1979 there was once again a three-party, non-socialist government; the non-socialist bloc in Parliament had a majority of only one seat. A Cabinet crisis in the spring of 1981 led to a new minority government that was formed by the Liberal party and the Centre Party (Agrarians) and excluded the Conservatives. This shifting parliamentary balance and the difficulty of sustaining government coalitions made it difficult for government to appear as a resolute actor with a firm commitment to priorities.

What were the characteristics of industrial crisis management from the mid-1970s? The explosion of 'non-permanent support to industry' is to be explained both by the traditional attachment to the 'welfare' objective of full employment and by the new parliamentary situation. Although some industrial crises emerged during the Social Democratic government from 1973 to 1976, the major 'fire-brigade operations' began after the three-party, non-socialist government took office. As newcomers, they accused the former Social Democratic government of bequeathing to them a country in crisis. At the same time they were very keen to achieve a good record themselves: unemployment was perceived to be central to any assessment of that record. When the government was suddenly faced by a number of crises that affected whole sectors as well as individual firms, it dare not risk the higher unemployment that would have resulted if the market had been left to its own devices. Hence the government was predisposed towards crisis interventions by a mixture of structural and electoral factors. At the same time, management of these industrial crises posed questions about institutional arrangements that proved ill suited to an active and constructive role.

The 'older' industrial policy programmes were implemented within the framework of the traditional government process, which emphasized participation and collaboration of all affected interests (for instance, by co-option in the management of the National Labour Board and by reliance on investigation by 'representative' royal commissions as a preliminary to legislation). Even in exceptional cases, when government had the capacity to intervene selectively, stress was placed on a process of consultation that ensured that all ministries, boards and organized interests were informed and/or committed. From 1970, however, there were more direct, face-to-face confrontations between firms and government (witness the case of Luxor). Indeed, in 1970 the processing of location aid was altered to permit firms to apply directly to the government when they planned investments of great significance to sectoral or regional development. Direct, face-to-face confrontations became the norm as firms began to face structural crises as well as internal managerial crises of their own. Management of industrial crises was politicised in the sense that every case came to involve the Ministry of Industry. Although other central ministries and boards were occasionally involved, the Ministry of Industry was the focal point of action. The regional and local levels were, by contrast, hardly ever involved.

The Ministry of Industry was, however, not really prepared to cope with industrial crisis management. It proved unable to develop or sustain an anticipatory policy style in the absence of a traditional network that facilitated close personal communications with industry. Although the Ministry of Industry had sufficient information about the enterprises to identify signs of mounting crisis situations before crises broke, no real possibilities were available for it to act before the crisis was a reality. Officials felt that it would be too risky to draw the public's attention to mounting industrial problems, especially when the interests concerned denied them. Identification of the difficulties that faced particular regions or individual towns was likely to mobilize local opinion and create additional political problems. Hence, for political reasons government was ill-prepared for each crisis. There was, in particular, no explicit policy and no adequate administrative apparatus within the Ministry of Industry to cope with industrial crises. To a very large extent government had to rely on information and a definition of problems that derived from the 'crisis-ridden' firms themselves. When the Ministry of Industry and the government became involved, they had to take action on a very tight time schedule with few options and little expertise of their own. The firms in crisis were nearly always on the verge of financial collapse. In other words, government's management of industrial crises was entirely reactive.

The processing within the Ministry involved bargaining primarily with firms. As rescues often included financial reconstructions, creditors were involved at this stage. Other interested parties, such as trade unions, customers and regional and local authorities, were seldom drawn into the more formal negotiations. Because the rescue operations were always finally dependent on parliamentary approval, the unions and the local interests had opportunities to influence the final outcome through lobbying. Parliament could, however, do no more than alter the government's Bill. When the recommendations involved agreements with owners and creditors, Parliament found it difficult to force these actors to accept deviations from preliminary agreements. The negotiation of an acceptable solution by ministry officials was sometimes hampered by political statements that announced government support before an agreement was finalized. When the processing within the ministry and the government was completed, and a rescue strategy and package presented, the problems were always described as structural or as the product of economic recession. Although the rationale for government intervention was described in public as a contribution to structural modernization, the underlying motive remained employment. Conditions were seldom attached to public aid for structural modernization.

The most striking feature of Swedish crisis management was that six of the seven major rescue operations involved public ownership. The government sought structural solutions that involved mergers of a lot of firms into new nationalized enterprises like Swedyard and Swedish Steel. However, the ambition to solve structural problems was frustrated by the political difficulties that governments had to face, notably the political importance of such towns as Gothenburg and Malmö. All the new nationalized enterprises have been more or less reduced in capacity. One special factor that encouraged the government to opt for public ownership was fear of reactions if foreign creditors were to be faced by a loss because of bankruptcy. Since the nineteenth century, Swedish governments have recognized the importance of foreign credit to industrial development and have tailored their economic policies to its expansion. In most cases all creditors were indemnified. The willingness to intervene in cases of industrial crisis did not require the commercial banks to take an active role in reconstruction. In any case, the number and the scale of crises went far beyond the resources of Swedish banks.

The form of management of industrial crises in Sweden meant that the 'public sector' crisis that had been attributed to decades of Social Democratic ascendancy was not tackled by the 'bourgeois' governments. Thus, in 1982 the OECD criticized Sweden for having one of the highest budget deficits among the 24 OECD countries (5.3 per cent of GDP in 1981 compared with 2.4 per cent in Britain). Alongside Britain and Norway it was one of three OECD countries with a lower manufacturing output in 1982 than in 1973/74. Since 1970 Sweden had forfeited almost a quarter of its share of world trade. She remained the most heavily taxed country in the world. Tax receipts as a proportion of GDP came to 49.9 per cent in 1980, compared with an OECD average of 36.6 per cent and a British figure of 35.9 per cent. Despite protracted criticism of Sweden's 'public sector' crisis at home and abroad, unemployment remained low and stable at 3 per cent.

After the emergency of a Social Democratic majority in October 1982 the new government of Olof Palme sought to break the impasse in economic policy and to reverse the reactive style that had crept into industrial policy by a bold strategy of 'the third way'. The objectives of economic recovery and high employment were to be achieved by a mix of policy measures, some expansionary to maintain employment and some deflationary to prevent higher inflation and deterioration of the balance of payments deficit. The central element of the expansionary measures was the massive 16 per cent devaluation of the krona in October 1982; the central element of the deflationary package was a strategy of moderate wage settlements to reduce real income and thereby to contain the inflationary pressures that were released by devaluation and to preserve the competitive advantage in world markets that followed immediately from devaluation. Other economic measures were geared to maintain the loyalty of the trade unions. Companies had to pay 20 per cent of their profits in 1983 into an account carrying no interest at the Riksbank (central bank); these funds could be withdrawn over the following two years for capital investments that had been approved by the local trade unions. For 1983 companies were also to pay into the state pension fund a charge equal to 20 per cent of the dividend paid to shareholders. This step towards profit-sharing was complemented by the promise to introduce a plan for wage-earner investment funds before the end of the legislative period.

As far as industrial policy was concerned, the essential and distinctive feature of the new Social Democratic government was the emphasis on making Swedish industry less reliant on government. Subsidies to sectors and firms were to be reduced, particularly to the shipyards. Palme was convinced of the need for drastic restructuring. Between 1980 and 1982 output had dropped by about 2.5 per cent a year, industrial investment by 11.5 per cent a year. It was forecast that the state would have to pump some 10 billion krona into the state mining, shipbuilding and paper-making companies in 1983. Nevertheless, despite the succession of industrial crises and mounting state subsidy, Sweden had managed to maintain a very efficient core of manufacturing industry.

Symptomatic of the extent of restructuring was the remarkable progress in the introduction of advanced production technology (notably computer-aided manufacturing and computer-aided design). ASEA, the Swedish electrical engineering group, emerged as a major international producer of industrial robots. It took over the robot operation of Electrolux and doubled its sales every year following its commencement of robot manufacture in 1974. In 1981 Sweden had installed more industrial robots relative to the size of its population than any other country. Companies continued to display a high level

244   K. Lundmark

of confidence in their technical ability (especially for short-series
production, as for example in the success of Volvo and Saab) and
continued to receive the support of the big industrial unions for
structural modernization. The problems of restructuring that faced
some shipyards, special steels and the forest products industry in
1983 had to be seen against the background of a continuing commitment to structural modernization.

REFERENCES

Åberg, C. J. (1981), *Keynes på 80-talet. Kan sysselsättningen räddas?*, Stock-
    holm, Tidens förlag.
Anton T. J. (1980), *Administered Politics Elite Political Culture in Sweden*,
    Boston, Martin Nijhoff.
Åsling, N. G. (1979), *Industrins kris och förnyelse*, Stockholm, LT:s förlag.
Bröms, J. (1977), *Den selektiva politiken i Social Välfärd genom Marknads-
    ekonomi*, SAF, Kugel Tryckeri AB.
Carlsson, B., Bergholm, F. and Lindberg, T. (1981), *Industristödspolitiken
    och dess inverkan på samhällsekonomin*, Industrins Utredningsinstitut,
    Stockholm, Gotab.
Childs, M. (1980), *Sweden: The Middle Way on Trial*, New Haven and London:
    Yale University Press.
DS JU (1979:1), *Report from the Special Delegation on Industrial Policy: 'Vagar
    till Ökad Välfärd'*, Stockholm, Gotab.
DS I (1981:8), *Två samhällsekonomiska utvärderingar av icke-permanent indus-
    tristöd*, Special Report to SOU 1981:72.
DS I (1981:9), *Icke permanent stöd till tre industriföretag*, Special Report to
    SOU 1981:72.
Elander, I. (1978), *Det nödvändiga och det önskvärda*, Arkiv avhandlingsserie,
    Kristianstad, GL-tryck.
Ericson, B. (1979), *Huggsexan: Spelet kring det dukade bordet*, Stockholm,
    LT:s förlag.
Hancock, D. M. (1972), *Sweden: The Politics of Post-Industrial Change*, Hinsdale,
    Illinois, Dryden Press.
Lewin, L. (1967), *Planhushållningsdebatten*, Stockholm, Almqvist & Wiksell.
Lund, R. (1981), 'Scandinavia', in A. Blum, *International Handbook of Indus-
    trial Relations*, London, Aldwych Press.
Meidner, R. (1981), Anförande vid Metalls kongress den 9 Juni 1981, 'Har den
    svenska modellen någon framtid?' (stencil).
Meidner, R. and Niklasson, H. (1970), *Arbetsmarknad och arbetsmarknadspoli-
    tik*, Malmö, Studentlitteratur.
Samordnan Näringspolitik (1961), *LO Strukturutredningen*, Stockholm, Tiden.
SOU (1981) Royal Commission Report, *Att avveckla en kortsiktig stödpolitik*,
    Stockholm, Liber förlag.
Tiden (1967) no. 9, November, årgång 59.

9

Conclusions

Kenneth Dyson and Stephen Wilks

A major hazard of a book about a topical policy issue is the tendency for analysis and, more embarrassingly, for conclusions to be overtaken by events. Thus, judgements in 1981 about the effectiveness of 'private sector' management of industrial crises in West Germany were shown to be over-optimistic when AEG-Telefunken was forced to ward off bankruptcy in the autumn of 1982. Because management of industrial crises is shaped by a complex of economic and political factors, judgements about the effectiveness of particular institutional arrangements must be tentative and provisional.

More importantly, the framework within which debate about industrial policies is conducted may be transformed. During the early 1980s it became clear that the international recession was qualitatively more severe and prolonged than any other since 1945. As recovery was delayed, and the expectation was established that any recovery would be small and unstable, parallels were increasingly drawn with the 1930s, and the parameters within which industrial crises were analysed and managed began to alter. The 'growth' mentality that had been fostered by 30 years of unparalleled postwar economic advance began to dissipate. As far as management of industrial crises was concerned, the expectation of resumed growth had led in the 1970s to an emphasis on 'stop-gap' expediency and minor amelioration in order to 'buy time' until economic recovery took place. The temptation to avoid fundamental restructuring and painful adaptation was understandably great. There was a tendency to stress what Kreile in chapter 7 above calls the 'financial', as opposed to the 'real', components of industrial crises (p. 197), in the hope that financial reorganization could substitute for reorganization of management, products and technology.

By the early 1980s industrial crises appeared as part of a long-term structural development involving protracted high unemployment, emergence of industrial wastelands, the dangerous 'over-extension' of bank lending, in part as a consequence of industrial rescues, and a chronic problem of financing the high public expenditure that is induced by recession and by its impact on social and industrial policies. The character of this long-term structural development remained more problematic. Explanation by reference to Kondratieff's long-term waves emphasized the importance of exhaustion of the economic possibilities of earlier technical developments and the need to give priority to new technical innovations that could provide the basis for future growth (Ray, 1980). By contrast, explanation by reference to the emergence of a 'post-industrial' society suggested a new qualitative transformation of social relations as the relevance of traditional conceptions of work was challenged. Such explanations were highly general and problematic and did not yield clear policy prescriptions. In France the government of Mitterand sought to combine priority to indigenous technical development with a recognition of the emergence of a new type of society by policies to encourage decentralized 'self-management' and reduction of the length of the working week.

The protracted recession affected management of industrial crises in two important ways. First, it became increasingly difficult to sustain collaborative norms in interest politics, even in those societies like Sweden and West Germany where neo-corporatism has a long history. Interest associations became characterized by shorter-term, more defensive, postures and by a loss of autonomy of action for their leaders. In particular, management of industrial crises revealed a greater asymmetry in the relations between capital and labour. On the one hand, the role of trade associations was strengthened as particular industries sought to reduce the impact of competition through collusion with government in the interests of protection, subsidy and negotiated rationalization. On the other hand, the capacity for defensive collective action by the trade unions declined as they lost members and revenue and began to calculate the use of the strike weapon with greater caution. Management of industrial crises has involved a subordinate and declining role of the trade unions.

Second, protracted recession, new international competition and industrial crises also brought a resurgence of bilateral trade pacts and protectionism. The EEC sought to combine protection with structural adjustment for its steel industry, while within the EEC divergences of economic strength and trade balances among members led to a proliferation of exotic non-tariff barriers to trade and a growing volume of complaints to the European Community about infringements of its rules. More generally, the GATT principle of multilateral trade seemed in danger of becoming a hollow phrase as governments sought to 'manage' trade. Protectionist measures for managing industrial crises could no longer be seen as just short-term and relatively insignificant exceptions to the general regime of free trade in accordance with the 'safeguard' rules of GATT, whereby a country can shelter an industry temporarily from an import challenge. They were cogs on the ratchet of steadily increasing limitations on world trade and threatened the ability of world trade to function as a source of recovery.

FROM INDUSTRIAL TO FINANCIAL CRISES?

As the problem of managing industrial crises has grown in severity since 1974, analysis must increasingly focus on crisis mis-management and its impact on the Western economic system as a whole. By 1982 the black cloud on the horizon of the Western economic system was the ability of the banks to cope simultaneously with over-extended loans to sovereign borrowers and to corporations in crisis. While the problem of repayments by sovereign borrowers excited dire predictions, corporate crises involved the banks in substantial immediate losses and threatened a dangerous collapse of financial confidence unless the banks were able to balance their obligations.

The spectre of crisis for banks and the banking system has been implicit for some time in the high level of lending to Comecon countries, the vulnerability of which was revealed by the Polish and Romanian debt rescheduling early in 1982. The level of lending to 'non-oil' developing countries has posed a larger and even more obvious threat. Between 1973 and 1981 official long-term external debt of these countries to 'official' (governmental) creditors increased by 367 per cent and to private creditors by a staggering 508 per cent. Although the recycling of the OPEC surpluses performed a useful function, it was a fundamentally unstable process. The 'debt service' ratio (debt repayments as a percentage of exports of goods and services) of 'non-oil' developing countries rose from 14 to 21 per cent (Llewellyn, 1982, p. 32). The exposure of individual banks was revealed by a deterioration of their equity-lending gearing and prompted Moody's credit rating agency to downgrade nine of the ten top American banks from a triple-A to a double-A rating on 9 March 1982. This move seemed to signal the onset of what could become an international banking crisis.

The financial crisis was given fresh urgency in August 1982 by the freezing of Mexican debt repayments and the subsequent acute shock to the international banking community. Some of the biggest American banks held huge lines of Mexican credit: for instance, Manufacturer Hanover, the fourth biggest American bank, had as much as 70 per cent of equity committed in Mexican loans. Consequently, the IMF meeting in Toronto in September 1982 was conducted in an atmosphere of foreboding about world liquidity. In October 1982 the world's largest clearing banks agreed to establish an international institute as an 'information exchange' about sovereign borrowers. The problem of the 'over-extension' of bank lending was clearly soluble, given good will and good sense. Nevertheless, the complex and unpredictable rationality of international banking was summed up in Arthur Burns's observation that 'the banks have been very foolish. We must now pray that they will go on being foolish'.

In an atmosphere of frightened and unstable financial markets, industrial crises take on a new dimension. Their size and cumulation threatens unpredictable macroeconomic consequences. Confidence is the life-blood of banking, and the troubles that arise from the involvement of individual banks in corporate crises could snowball uncontrollably. Even the biggest banks have suffered setbacks. Among the British 'big four', the Midland's profits for the first half of 1982 were reduced by 10 per cent as a consequence of a doubling of the bad debt provision. Among the German 'big three', Commerzbank's profits in 1981 dropped by 77 per cent. The worst rumours were encountered in the USA, where banks appeared to be confronted by more serious problems. The Chicago-based Continental Illinois, the sixth-largest American bank by assets and the leading corporate lender, was in serious trouble over its credits to International Harvester and losses from the failure of the smaller Penn Square Bank. In Canada the Canadian Imperial Bank of Commerce had huge lines of credit to Massey Ferguson and Dome Petroleum, both of which renegotiated loans as part of rescue packages backed by the federal government.

In these circumstances, managing industrial crises becomes a rather different issue. Governments must add to the customary calculus a concern for the exposure of the banking system and the impact on confidence in volatile financial markets. It may seem a perverse and sad irony that the importance of the intangible value of financial confidence may weigh more heavily than the tangible impact of lost jobs and closed factories in a government's decision to intervene in corporate crises. The assessment of success in managing industrial crises may also need to be revised. As the following discussion of economic adaptation shows, the most successful country in managing industrial crises in the 1970s seemed to be West Germany. This success was explained largely by structural inheritance and the 'virtuous circle' of economic success. Nevertheless, the role of the 'universal' banks and their close involvement with industry was also important. Such close involvement may, however, begin to appear a serious economic liability rather than an asset if corporate crises like those of AEG and Korf Industries threaten to drag the banks down with them. Then, as in the 1930s, Britain's clearing banks could begin to argue that conservative lending policies and an 'arm's-length' approach to industry insulated the financial sector from the deep industrial malaise and avoided a catastrophic 'knock-on' effect from corporate crises. At the same time, this argument appears as too convenient a rationalization for the traditional insularity from domestic industry and international outlook of the financial community. Ironically, it should be remembered that it was in London that the threat of financial collapse came closest, in the banking crisis of 1974. The secondary banking crisis and the Bank of England's 'life-boat' provided a cautionary warning and reminder of the danger of exposure by the banks. In 1974 the National Westminster Bank took the extraordinary step of announcing that it was *not* in trouble. The domestic difficulties that faced British and American banks in 1974 and 1975, including in the latter case the threat of bankruptcy for New York City, gave way in the early 1980s to the problems of sovereign borrowers.

Lessons were learnt from the banking crises of 1974. In addition to the tightening of national banking regulations, international co-operation was increased. The Basel Agreement of 1974 provided for greater central bank support for their national banks at home and abroad. It provided also for meetings every four months between the main bank supervisors (mainly central banks) of the 11 largest OECD countries. While the Basel Agreement supplied a useful increase of 'prudential control', there was no guarantee that sovereign or corporate defaults would be better anticipated and even less certainty that effective remedial action would be taken. As Sampson (1981, p. 212) notes, 'while they can anticipate a rational crisis, they can never be sure that a country, or even a bank, would not behave irrationally.' The international financial system remained vulnerable, and, for industrial and economic policy-makers, this made it increasingly important that industrial crises should not escalate into a collapse of financial confidence.

THE CONCEPT OF 'GOOD' CRISIS MANAGEMENT

The fundamental question about the characteristics of 'good' crisis management appears both complex and intractable. For three reasons, any answer is likely to be contentious and tentative. If it is argued that 'good' crisis management must facilitate economic adaptation to changes in the international economy, the basic technical problem of how to define and measure successful adaptation remains difficult to resolve. Attempts to anticipate and forecast the development of demand, relative costs and technology are riddled with imprecision. The process of 'picking winners' is intrinsically difficult for both banks and governments and requires a mix of careful research and good fortune. What might appear in 1983 to be a successful, adaptive crisis intervention might appear in later years to be a serious commercial misjudgement, as with earlier decisions about aluminium, computers and civil aeronautics in Britain.

Second, the content of 'good' crisis management is a normative question whose answer will be shaped by the viewpoint of the observer or participant. For a government, 'good' crisis management may consist of postponing difficult problems of industrial adjustment till after the next election; for trade unions, it will be bound up with preservation of employment and incomes; and for domestic and foreign competitors of a corporation in crisis, it may be defined as bankruptcy and closure. The quality of crisis management is defined subjectively by reference to the distributional impact of the costs and benefits of different crisis measures. The criterion of 'national interest' may of course lead to an altruistic tendency not to examine the individual beneficiaries of a rescue. On the other hand, American rescues and the case of Arbed Saarstahl in 1982 reveal in perhaps the clearest terms an effort to ensure that employees are made to 'suffer' along with creditors as a condition of governmental rescue.

Third, judgements about 'good' crisis management will be shaped by the value that is placed on retaining the existing economic system. Crisis management in the interests of effective economic adaptation performs a function of 'system maintenance'. Correspondingly, radicals might view 'ineffective' crisis management as a spur to major policy change, institutional reform or societal transformation. Hence, neo-Marxists have emphasized the fragile character of the capitalist state. Offe (1972) speaks of the threat of a general 'crisis of crisis management' as the claims of the state to rational action are exposed as a fraud. The capitalist state is pictured as being caught between the rival requirements of maintaining the conditions for capital accumulation (by avoiding heavy entanglement in industrial rescues) and of correcting and compensating the effects of the functioning of the capitalist system on individual capital interests and workers (by assuming responsibility for managing industrial crises). This dilemma can be seen as the source of an erratic pattern of responses by states to the phenomenon of industrial crises. The decision to manage industrial crises can also be seen as a contribution to the emerging 'fiscal crisis' and ultimately the 'legitimation crisis' of the capitalist state (Habermas, 1973). In more general terms, 'crisis becomes a term descriptive of a chronic pathological state if the notion of transition/transformation be removed' (Fraser, 1981, p. 1). It is, therefore, difficult to abstract judgements about the quality of crisis management from judgements about their wider societal context and the desirable direction of social change.

For the moment we shall ignore these problems of evaluating 'good' crisis management by concentrating on those features of crisis management that are conducive to achieving the conventional goals of industrial policy — namely, higher productivity, higher investment and 'positive' structural adjustment. In terms of these more limited and apparently technical criteria, 'good' crisis management would seem to consist of four features. First, crisis management should involve close inter-organizational collaboration between firms and 'rescuing' institutions with market power, so that a learning process can develop and successive crises be managed more effectively. Of course, mismanagement of a particular industrial crisis will not denote complete failure of collective action if it prompts major policy initiatives that improve this learning capacity (like the creation of the inter-ministerial committees in France, the proposals for 'worker funds' in Sweden or the embryonic moves towards investment banking in Britain). Second, crisis management should seek the retention of productive resources in the form of knowledge, plant and workforce. The objective of policy should be to avoid the waste of assets. Third, crisis management should sustain or enhance the efficiency of the prevailing system of resource allocation in the form of the market or, less probably, the plan. The objective of policy should be coherence with economic ideology. Fourth, crisis management should achieve an equitable distribution of the costs of industrial adjustment. At this point crisis management becomes entangled in debates about social justice and the problem of consent, a hornets' nest of ideological problems that cannot ultimately be resolved into a technical formula. As far as policy-makers are concerned, the operational objective of policy is likely to be consent of the trade unions and/or of the works councils. Clearly, even on this limited definition of 'good' crisis management the criteria of success are difficult to reconcile in individual cases, where difficult 'trade-offs' have to be made, and tend to make broad judgements about the quality of crisis management in different societies tentative, provisional and hazardous.

As a general point, it is difficult to abstract judgements about crisis management from judgements about the success of industrial policy in any one state. A useful starting point, therefore, is to ask to what extent crisis management has been consistent with the prevailing ordering of priorities about the types of industry to be assisted and the methods of that assistance. Crisis management is successful to the extent that there is an industrial strategy that integrates discrete policies for industry around common principles and to the extent to which crisis management is integrated into that strategy. By reference to this criterion, the USA and West Germany have exhibited greatest consistency between crisis management and industrial strategy (at the federal level). The principles of industrial policy, the 'free market' in the USA and the 'social market' in West Germany, are clearly evident and operate as guides for crisis management. The least consistency is shown by Sweden and Italy. Both experienced difficulties in evolving a coherent industrial strategy, and both allowed powerful interests, notably labour interests, to determine the parameters of action. Despite oscillations of industrial strategy in Britain (Grant, 1982), consistency has at least been seriously attempted. However, particularly when, as after 1979, liberal principles were ascendant, the pressures for crisis intervention have made consistency very difficult to achieve and have produced a serious 'performance gap'. In France crisis management has been guided to a greater extent by a continuity of strategic ambitions, although, as Green argues in chapter 6 above, these ambitions have not ruled out irrational or opportunist rescues. Industrial crises have perhaps been 'overmanaged' as a consequence both of a French inclination towards protection and insularity and of the French state's ambitious tendency to equate will with ability.

There will be no general agreement that industrial crises have been 'well-managed' in the USA and West Germany. Nevertheless, these states have coherent industrial strategies that are based on widely and deeply held principles and that have served to guide crisis interventions. As Edmonds points out in chapter 3, attachment to the 'free market' remains second nature in the USA; only the argument of national security is seen as a legitimate basis for political recognition of an industrial crisis. Crisis interventions are regarded as special cases. Esser, Fach and Dyson (chapter 4) show that West German industrial strategy is equally clear and more sophisticated. The Principles of Sectoral Policy that were spelt out by Karl Schiller authorize government support for 'private-sector-led' adjustment. Subsequent crisis interventions reveal a remarkable consistency with that strategy. Lack of continuity of industrial strategy has meant that crisis interventions have been based on less secure foundations in Britain. Frequent inconsistency of crisis management and industrial strategy has, however, been accompanied by a consistency of approach that is rooted in an administrative style of 'arm's-length' intervention, which induces reactive problem-solving. A greater consistency of crisis management in France has been facilitated by a continuity of industrial strategy and by an assertive administrative style that has supported that strategy. Swedish crisis management displayed little continuity with established industrial strategy. Originally labour market policy had been based on a commitment to a 'socially conscious' modernization, to a 'positive' industrial adjustment that would ease the burdens on workers. The crisis interventions of the 1970s gave priority to the social objective of employment over the economic objective of productivity and led to growing criticism of the lack of economic logic of crisis interventions. In Italy consistency of crisis management with industrial strategy was made even more difficult to achieve by the factionalism and *immobilisme* of the ruling Christian Democratic Party, by the patronage system and by the administrative inefficiency that was generated by clientelism. In both Sweden and Italy the context of coalition politics made governments vulnerable to demands for employment protection, especially in relation to the presence of the Centre Party and a 'socially conscious' Liberal Party within the 'bourgeois' bloc in Sweden, and the strength of the Communist Party and of pressures for alliance to the Left within the Christian Democratic Party in Italy.

PROCESSES AND INSTRUMENTS OF INDUSTRIAL CRISIS MANAGEMENT

The earlier chapters emphasize the central role of industrial managers, bankers and public officials and the character of the links among them. They would seem to suggest that political parties are not the decisive actors in industrial crisis management. Nevertheless, political parties can be important in influencing the climate of opinion within which crises are managed. Even when excluded from governmental power, the Christian Democrats in West Germany and the Social Democrats in Sweden were able to exercise an indirect influence by means of the ideological consensus that they had forged during earlier periods of government. Ideological disposition to intervene facilitates decisions to rescue, and this disposition is not confined to parties that are normally classified as left-wing. Thus, the influence of the Catholic doctrine of reconciliation on the Italian Christian Democratic Party has fuelled the willingness of governments to intervene in industrial crisis. Irrespective of the 'high politics' of economic welfare and social justice, the pressures of 'low politics', of party political expediency, mean that all governments, whether of Right or Left, are forced on occasion to intervene in industrial crises. Thus the Conservative government in Britain decided in 1982 to maintain the five bulk steel plants of British Steel despite its industrial strategy of the sovereign market. Considerations of partisan electoral advantage and interest group support weigh heavily on party policy-makers. It is, of course, always easy to rationalize decisions that are motivated by politicking by reference to a 'high politics' of concern for the social fabric of an industrial area. Ironically and importantly, governments of the Centre and Right have been obliged by the 'low politics' of recession to be more interventionist than their social democratic predecessors that had not been faced by the same scale of industrial crises. The Conservative government in Britain after 1979 and the 'bourgeois' governments in Sweden between 1976 and 1982 increased subsidies to important sectors of industry; in 1983 the new Social Democratic government in Sweden unveiled an economic strategy that involved a reduction of these subsidies.

The criteria for effective crisis management that facilitates conventional objectives of industrial policy, as outlined above (pp. 251–2), direct attention towards three important aspects of the policy process: disposition towards, and ability to organize, industrial adjustment; level of politicization; and extent of the socialization of the costs of adjustment. A disposition towards 'positive' industrial adjustment requires institutional mechanisms to anticipate industrial crises and organize rescues, as well as clear criteria of adaptation. Clear criteria and mechanisms for anticipation make possible a process of crisis management that can combine structural adjustment with retention of productive resources. The spectrum extends from Britain and the USA, both of which have limited institutional mechanisms for anticipatory crisis management, to France and West Germany.

In Britain anticipatory crisis management is impeded by relative institutional isolation, so that information flow is limited, and by a liberal presumption against public action ahead of a protracted process of bargaining with interests (Dyson, 1980). Both banks and governments have an 'arms'-length' relationship to industry. The liberal constraints on public action are even more marked in the USA. Lack of institutional development for crisis management has proved less important for industrial adjustment in the American case. The different character of the American economy derives from its sheer size and internal variety and a powerful belief in its economic abundance. The consequence is greater optimism about industry's problems, less questioning of the industrial strategy of the 'free market', and a greater coherence of strategy and structure than in Britain. In addition, a long experience of 'managerial capitalism' has led to greater reliance on 'internalized' crisis management by large conglomerates and their professional consultants. As Edmonds (p. 71 above) points out, collective forms of action to avert industrial crises by price-fixing, market sharing and similar collusion are actively prohibited by tough anti-trust legislation. West Germany shares America's 'private sector' adaptability, although in the form of a capitalist 'self-organization', which draws more heavily on the big banks and trade associations. France's anticipatory capabilities are based on a more formal statement of sectoral priorities, development of a set of interlocked inter-ministerial committees and an intimate elite network that is based on the public service. Hence the state is comparatively well informed about industrial problems and is prepared to act to forestall crisis if a firm is an important actor in a 'strategic' sector.

The Italian and Swedish cases are more difficult to classify with respect to disposition towards, and ability to organize, industrial adjustment. In Italy industrial crises have been concentrated mainly in the large state sector. The problems are well understood and are theoretically susceptible to public action. At the same time, crisis management reveals a pattern of short-term amelioration rather than long-term 'positive' adjustment. The consequence has been a 'crisis mentality' in state industry, where the requirements of immediate survival have been stressed. Crises are managed as an expression of the clientelism of state patronage and reflect a 'low politics' of partisan advantage. The case of Sweden appears more surprising. The 'coordinated industrial policy' initiative of the trade union federation in 1961 consolidated the principle of solidaristic wage bargaining, identified adjustment to the international market as a fundamental objective of that policy, and until the mid-1970s appeared to be as effective a basis for political consensus and consistency of policy as the principles of sectoral policy in West Germany. However, in the face of serious structural crises in shipbuilding, which were aggravated by the geographical concentration of employment, the capacity of the trade unions to maintain a strategy of centralized wage bargaining in the interests of self-restraint was undermined. In place of refashioning industrial strategy, the 'bourgeois' coalition traded job protection for votes and began an open-ended process of subsidy and nationalization. Italy and Sweden are cases of successful systems of industrial adjustment that broke down under the impact of proliferating industrial crises. The speed of emergence of structural problems was not, and perhaps could not be, compensated by institutional development.

The second important aspect of the process of crisis management concerns the level of politicization. How controversial is the presence of crisis management on the political agenda? Is industrial crisis managed technocratically by reference to criteria like productivity, competitiveness and market share? Those who support the existing system of resource allocation will tend to fear politicization of crisis management, whether in the sense that the principle of managing crises is challenged in an *étatiste* economy or in the sense that the very principle of managing crises is advocated in a 'free market' economy. A 'de-politicized' process of crisis management that is uncontroversial, consensual and marked by substantial agreement about technical criteria will tend to reinforce and stabilize the system of resource allocation. By contrast, 'politicized' crisis management will tend to call that system into question, threaten confidence and undermine the credibility of government.

It might be expected that the strength of the principle of competition would make crisis interventions in Britain and the USA relatively controversial; that the strength of social democracy in Sweden and of Catholic social ideas in Italy would generate greater sympathy for *étatisme* and acceptance of crisis interventions; and that the tradition of *dirigisme* in France would lead to an expectation of crisis interventions. Reality is less simple. Each economy justifies departure from the rule of market forces in particular spheres. While the USA is most wedded to the ideal of perfect competition, crisis interventions have been justified for decades by reference to defence imperatives. Several troubled American corporations have benefited from the close, privileged contacts to government that their big defence contracts and membership of the 'military industry complex' have brought them. This complex has established an ideological priority and a neo-corporatist avenue of influence that encourages positive governmental response to corporate crisis. In Britain the weight of inherited structural problems and more class-related social and political institutions have produced greater dissent about the appropriate system of resource allocation. Politicization of the process of crisis management reaches a high point in Britain. West German governments have displayed a willingness to refine the formula of the social market economy to accommodate elaborate programmes of regional and sectoral support. The rapid expansion of the federal Research and Technology Ministry between 1972 and 1982 under Social Democratic ministers reflected a belief in an active technology policy that could lead the market. The combination of this gradual growth of governmental action on the basis of consensus, a tradition of neo-corporatism in interest politics and the organized structure of German capitalism ensured a relatively smooth and 'de-politicized' process of crisis management. In Italy regional policy, and in Sweden labour market policy, provide important examples of areas where a national consensus exists that the market is inadequate. Nevertheless, in contrast to West Germany, it proved difficult in both countries to establish a 'de-politicized' process of crisis management. Defensive crisis interventions could not be made consistent with established strategies — with the orientation to the world market of the private oligopoly sector in Italy and with a traditional commitment to modernization and competitiveness in Sweden. The relatively wide societal acceptance of crisis intervention in these two countries was to be explained in Sweden by the established priority to employment, and by the shift of the trade unions to a short-term defensive posture, and in Italy by a fatalism about the importance of patronage to the political system and a consequent resignation about continuing fragmented subsidy to state industry.

France and West Germany are the closest approximation to a model of 'technocratic' crisis management. 'Closed' public sector management occurs in France on the basis of the *grands corps* and of the coordinating role of the Trésor; 'closed' private sector management is facilitated in West Germany by the industrial role of the banks. Of course, crisis management becomes a political process of contest in all states once the 'closed' mechanisms fail to contain conflict. The entry of a 'low politics' of partisan interest is encouraged when a political system offers multiple points of access (as in the USA) or when parliamentary majorities are low or non-existent and unstable (as in Sweden after 1976). The importance that party political electoral calculation can play in crisis management was illustrated by the hectic activity of the Chrysler congressional lobby in the USA, by the Chrysler rescue and the decision to maintain the Ravenscraig steel plant in Britain, by the concern with state elections in West Germany (as in the programme of aid to the shipbuilding industry), and by the employment subsidies that were an outcome of Swedish coalition politics in the late 1970s. Nevertheless, as the cases of France and West Germany indicate, institutional structures and policy networks play an important role in shaping the influence of politicking on crisis management.

The third aspect of the process of crisis management concerns the extent of socializing the costs of industrial adjustment. Workers and organized labour are more likely to be inclined to accept adaptive, productivity-oriented crisis management if society compensates individuals and areas. In particular, maintenance of neo-corporatist mechanisms of crisis management depends on the socialization of costs of adjustment. Although the case for socializing costs of adjustment has been supported by 'enlightened' oligopoly capital in all societies, it is accepted to a greater extent in Sweden and West Germany than in Britain and the USA. Such socialization requires a close working relationship between industry and the state and, in particular, a cooperative approach by organized labour. Perhaps the best example of the principle of cooperative socialization of costs of adjustment is Sweden's labour market policy. In Sweden, manpower planning remains the primary economic and industrial policy despite the fact that, since the late 1960s, the trade unions have begun to emphasize direction of capital: the State Investment Bank was an early, if feeble, product of this discussion. At the hub of the complex and costly system of labour market policy stands the Labour Market Board, which is dominated by union and employer representatives and has control over investment aid as well as elaborate programmes to encourage labour mobility. The adaptive capacity of this collective system of adjustment was tested by the heavy load of industrial crises that emerged after 1974. A combination of escalating costs of support with increasing union militancy and defensiveness indicated a collapse of Sweden's distinctive socially conscious modernization and led to a new initiative to socialize costs of adjustment. As in the case of the labour market policy earlier, the Social Democratic Party's policy initiative was the product of trade union economists. The 'Meidner plan' sought to increase productive investment and to socialize investment decisions by proposing 'collective wage-earner funds'. They would receive 1 per cent of companies' wage bills and a proportion of 'excess' profits and would be controlled by employees through regional boards. This proposal for uniting economic modernization with worker self-determination formed a highly controversial element in the 1982 election that returned the Social Democrats to power.

Although the West German social–liberal coalition spoke of an 'active' labour market policy after 1969, and a cooperative labour market policy had been gradually extended since the 1950s, West German labour market policy was never as politically prominent as that of Sweden. The German Trade Union Federation (DGB) was not as politically powerful, ideologically confident or organizationally centralized as Sweden's LO. On the other hand, cooperative social planning involving detailed negotiations with works councils was a systematic feature of crisis management and was often, as in the cases of the Saar steel industry and of Volkswagen, complemented by special regional plans to ease the process of adjustment. In the 1970s France attempted to give greater attention to the social management of industrial crises, with memories of the political crisis of 1968 fresh in the mind of policy-makers. Procedures for social planning by firms that were faced by crisis were toughened, and an attempt was made to look at industrial crisis in regional terms (notably in the Vosges Plan, which incorporated special measures of support for a frontier region that had been badly affected by the crisis in textiles). In Britain, measures of social support for crisis management were haphazard. On occasion *ad hoc* programmes of generous redundancy assistance were offered, for instance by British Steel in the 1976–78 period. There was little provision for coordination of social policy programmes with crisis management.

The case of Italy was atypical. In some respects crisis intervention in the shape of subsidy is social support in Italy. Italian trade unions have preferred job security to a policy of labour mobility on the Swedish model, which, they argue, leads to unemployment. For private firms the Cassa Integrazione Guadagni (CIG) guarantees salaries (currently 80 per cent) to all workers in industry, construction or agriculture made partially or wholly redundant. For public enterprises, increases in equity finance or the support from GEPI for employment of workers in 'substitutive activities' has maintained 'uneconomic' jobs. By contrast, the Mitterand government in France sought to combine modernization with labour market considerations in its proposal for 'contracts of solidarity' with firms in industries that were experiencing structural problems. Such firms, for instance in the textiles industry, received aid for new investment and technical innovations if they replaced workers over the age of 55 with younger men and women. Generous provision for early retirement proved very costly, particularly when firms could benefit also from a cut of up to 12 per cent in social charges for each employee.

A broad comparative analysis of processes of managing industrial crises suggests that West Germany has approximated most closely to the characteristics of disposition towards industrial adaptation, depoliticization of crisis management and socialization of costs of adjustment. France combines a resolute pursuit of modernization, especially for 'industries of the future', with a tradition of protection and subsidy, while the tradition of weak relations between state and unions and the fragmentation of the unions has not encouraged as high a degree of socialization of costs of adjustment as in Sweden and West Germany. Britain is at the other end of the spectrum. Mechanisms for economic adaptation are weak; the process of crisis management is highly politicized in the sense of being public and confrontational; and the burden of adjustment bears harshly on individuals and areas.

Such broad judgements do, of course, invite detailed qualification. Perhaps the most ominous case was that of Sweden. Management of industrial crises in Sweden indicated the vulnerability of even the most sophisticated systems of 'socially conscious' modernization to radical changes in the structure of international competition. In the late 1970s crisis management revealed a syndrome of party politicking, defensive subsidy and a vacuum of strategic leadership. The election of a Social Democratic majority in 1982 that was committed to adapting 'Model Sweden' was likely to show whether the period 1976–82 had been exceptional or a turning point in Sweden's fortunes. Similarly, deepening recession in West Germany in late 1982 cast a shadow over the new conservative–liberal coalition of Kohl and raised questions about the vulnerability of the traditional system of 'closed' consensual crisis management.

It might be expected that comparison of management of industrial crises could yield some simple lessons for policy-makers about the policy instruments that are available and that might be borrowed when management of industrial crises is clearly weak. Thus, reformers and policy-makers in Britain are likely to be attracted by the concept and practice of the inter-ministerial committee in France and by the German model of industrial banking, by French 'contracts of solidarity' and by German 'crisis cartels'. At the same time, sensible comparison must acknowledge the differences of inherited industrial structure, industrial culture, political arrangements and concepts of public authority that make the borrowing of policy instruments a far from simple panacea. Nevertheless, comparison offers to policy-makers interesting insights on which to base institutional and programmatic reforms. It is important to identify the role of different policy instruments, just as it is important to understand that their mode of functioning reflects a particular social, economic and political context.

American and British policy-makers suffer from a relative dearth of policy instruments for crisis management. Since the Industry Act of 1972, British policy-makers have had ample legislative authority to engage in programmes of industrial support and restructuring. However, the instruments for putting that authority into effect have been limited. The NEB was pressed very reluctantly into involvement with several crises, notably British Leyland, Ferranti, Herbert and Rolls Royce: it was not in fact designed for such a role. Otherwise, crises in private or nationalized industries have been handled in a haphazard, bilateral fashion between firms and a central government department, while the Treasury — unlike its French counterpart — brooded unsympathetically in the background. The USA has, surprisingly, an interesting, if limited, range of policy instruments. In addition to measures at the state level, the federal government has employed defence contracts, restructuring under the auspices of the Department of Defense, reorganization under a federal agency like the Interstate Commerce Commission, and the *ad hoc* Loan Guarantee Boards. According to Edmonds (chapter 3), the Boards appeared relatively successful and offered an interesting response to the difficult problem of devising rescue packages. The Loan Guarantee Boards might be particularly appealing to reformers in other countries who favoured a 'free market' approach.

France and Italy devised important new policy instruments for crisis management to supplement a battery of traditional institutions and programmes of industrial policy. In France the major development was the inter-ministerial committees, while regional programmes and the Socialists' programme of nationalization of key banks and firms were also seen as instruments of crisis management. Other French policy instruments developed greater maturity and potential for crisis management. Thus the system of contracts, as in the *programme d'action concertée*, provided a flexible means for a negotiated management of particular industrial crises. Italy too established an inter-ministerial committee in 1977. Italian initiatives included a state holding company, EGAM (1971–76) and a financial institution, GEPI (founded in 1971), both of which operated specifically to manage corporate crises. Attempts were also made to encourage involvement of the banks in restructuring by forming 'rescue consortia' which would convert debt into equity and organize and monitor crisis interventions. As Kreile explains in chapter 7 above, only GEPI had any degree of success, and was indeed proving less adequate by the late 1970s.

In West Germany prime emphasis was placed on bank-led rescues. When such rescues broke down or were not a viable proposition, reliance was placed on informal 'crisis cartels', which appealed to the theory and practice of social partnership and rested on loan guarantees by government and on special regional programmes.

The country studies reveal three important types of policy instrument: the role of the banks (notably in West Germany); mechanisms of coordination of government action (notably in France); and special purpose rescue agencies (notably in Italy). The banks and financial intermediaries provide perhaps the most important issue in the comparative analysis of crisis management. There is wide variation in the main instruments of lending to industry. In Italy the state-owned Instituto Mobiliare Italiano (IMI) is a special credit institute that provides the bulk of industrial lending. In Britain and the USA industrial lending comes from the big private deposit banks — mainly from the 'big four' clearing banks in Britain and from a much more fragmented system of big banks in the USA (such as Chase Manhattan and Citicorp). France's system of industrial lending is complex, and until the wave of nationalizations by the Socialists included various public and private banks as well as important public credit funds. Even prior to their nationalization after 1981, the *banques d'affairs* like Suez and Paribas were large bank holding companies, managed by public officials — inspectors of finance — and responsive to state priorities (Bayliss and Butt Philip, 1980, p. 140). In West Germany the big three commercial banks are supplemented by other private banks as well as by the public savings and giro banks that became increasingly involved in industrial lending during the 1970s and began to act as 'house banks' and 'universal banks'.

Banks can adopt three main roles in crisis management: as channels of communication within and among industries; as sources of investment advice and advice on executive recruitment; and as flexible tools of rescue. The interesting cases for comparison are Britain, France and West Germany. In Germany the importance of the universal banks can be overstated. They are, nevertheless, the lubricant of the German system of 'organized capitalism' and perform all three roles in crisis management. The 'house bank' can, and is usually willing to, mobilize credit, enlist federal or state (*Land*) support, find industrial partners, reassure trading partners, and if necessary change management and recruit new executives. Apologists for the British clearing banks have argued that the levels of industrial support, maturity of lending and gearing requirements of British and German banks have converged (Vittas and Brown, 1982). They cannot, however, claim that British banks match the close practical involvement of the German 'house bank' in its firms. The commitment of a German bank to a firm is reinforced by regular contact, usually through a seat (often as chairman) on the supervisory board, and by 'the strength of the bank's research and experience of industrial problems in each sector' (Bayliss and Butt Philip, 1980, p. 188). The German universal bank combines the activities of the clearing bank and the merchant bank in Britain. Bayliss and Butt Philip (1980, p. 189) conclude that 'there is clearly a different approach to banking in West Germany from which the British banks could learn much if they are to be of value to British industry in assisting it to invest during a period of slow growth or recession.'

After 1973 the British clearing banks entered into a more public discussion about problems of industrial lending, in large part in response to political disquiet and suspicion; the Bank of England attempted to instil a more committed attitude to industrial customers; and the new loan guarantee programme for small businesses of the Thatcher government indicated a closer relationship between banks and government in industrial policy. The establishment of 'intensive care units' for corporate crisis management suggested an awareness of the drawbacks of the traditional 'arm's-length' relationship. Nevertheless, the British clearing banks remained a long way from the sense of duty to manage corporate crisis, the technical expertise and the mechanisms for 'early warning' of the German universal bank.

The character of the role of French banks in crisis management differs from that of both British and German banks. On the one hand, like German banks and unlike British banks, they display a devotion to their industrial customers. In the absence of a vigorous stock market, they are often 'locked in' to shareholdings from which it is difficult to disengage during a crisis. On the other hand, unlike the German banks, the French banks are often drawn into crisis management by the state. Indeed, a central motive behind nationalization of the major remaining private banks by the Socialist government was the desire to involve them even more closely in crisis management. The Trésor has further consolidated its grip on crisis management. Consequently, the process of crisis management by the banks is influenced by the strategic ambitions of the French state and its predilection for protection and subsidy. The German banks are much more market-oriented.

A second important policy instrument has been the attempt to coordinate the activities of public agencies. The scale of the problem of crisis management represented a test of this capacity for coordination. The capacity for intra-governmental coordination in turn depended on whether the political environment gave the executive a potential for autonomy of action, and on the presence of political will and imagination. These conditions were most closely approximated in France, where the political arrangements of the Fifth Republic had focused power on the President. By contrast, the checks and balances of American politics combine with congressional localism and the weakness of national party loyalties to encourage a 'riotous pluralism' of public agencies and a fluid legislative politics. In Italy the functioning of mechanisms of coordination is undermined by a factional politics of clientelism as different party factions cultivate their relations with industry, public and private, large and small, northern and southern. Despite these important variations of political conditions, the technical complexity of issues and requirements of confidentiality tend to produce pressures for internalization of crisis management within the executive in all countries. At the same time, the variety of 'industry-related' ministries and agencies and the involvement of non-industrial policy priorities (like defence) exacerbate problems of coordination in all countries.

Institutional mechanisms for coordination of crisis management have been most developed in France and Italy. In both cases inter-ministerial committees have been established with overarching authority and independent budgets for crisis management. The French inter-ministerial committees are the most systematic and powerful innovation because they are located in the *direction du Trésor* section of the Ministry of Finance, and because the CODIS committee is chaired by the Prime Minister. The prestige, contacts and control over the financial system of the Trésor make the French machinery for managing industrial crises the most centralized and authoritative as well as the best financed of all those studied above. Even in the 'executive-centred' and formally coordinated system of crisis management in France, however, electoral politics and local political pressures have had an important impact, especially after Giscard d'Estaing's narrow victory in the presidential election of

1974. Bayliss and Butt Philip (1980, p. 92) refer to 'a politics of the pork barrel' at the level of deputies, and a clear understanding of 'the necessity of maintaining politically selected government largesse' in the Paris ministries and the prefectures.

The Italian inter-ministerial committee experiment of 1977 introduced a framework similar to that of France. The objectives were to increase coordination in order to hasten industrial adaptation, to increase the rationality of governmental action, and to develop economic planning by a programme of sectoral intervention (in order to meet the requirement of participation of the Communist Party in the voting majority of the Andreotti government of 1976). Kreile (chapter 7) argues that this ambitious initiative was largely a failure. The problem of coordination of agencies for crisis management in Italy was one of political will and administrative efficiency rather than of diagnosis. Intellectual insight could not be matched by capability for integrated institutional action.

Strong, centralized executive coordination is alien to the American pattern of pluralistic policy-making and to the Swedish pattern of collegiate and egalitarian policy-making. In Sweden as in West Germany, a traditional reliance on private sector management of industrial crises has deflected attention from the development of policy instruments for the coordination of public agencies for the purpose of crisis management. Swedish policy-makers were exposed and confused once the capacity of private sector mechanisms to deal with problems of industrial adjustment was overwhelmed. In Britain governments oscillated between faith in private sector solutions and reliance on the traditional *ad hoc* arrangement of the Cabinet sub-committee. The potential strength that such subcommittees acquired from the convention of collective ministerial responsibility for cabinet decisions and from the cult of official secrecy in Whitehall was not realized because of the absence of a strong centralized administrative leadership that was committed to industrial priorities. The Cabinet Office, which services Cabinet committees, lacks relevant technical expertise and contacts to industry and finance, while the Treasury is noted for its aloofness from industry. This vacuum of assertive administrative leadership has prevented a strategic management of industrial crises and encouraged the influence of departmentalism and short-term political considerations on crisis management.

A third policy instrument has been the special purpose agency for crisis management. Their rationale is typically to encourage concentration on the issue by experts who can introduce economic objectivity into decisions. In practice, special purpose agencies have tended to adopt a 'low-key' role and to resist pressures for involvement. Thus Sweden's Statsföretag, a state holding company, resisted pressure for continuing disbursement of subsidy to corporations in crisis. France's IDI also adopted a modest and independent approach. It avoided involvement with the troubled Lip watchmaking company when it was called in to provide expert advice. The involvement of Britain's NEB in big crisis interventions like British Leyland and Ferranti was always regarded as exceptional and was separately financed. In the absence of other methods of organizing rescue, the NEB's role was probably beneficial. Nevertheless, this role was eliminated by the new guidelines of the Conservative government in 1979.

The experience of these special agencies, especially the decreasing success of GEPI, demonstrates the difficulty of introducing economic objectivity into an essentially political process of crisis management. Their appeal grows once political pressures seem to make crisis interventions unavoidable, the burden of decision for governments increases sharply, and government appears incapable of a strategic management of crises. The promise of economic logic combines with the advantage of de-politicization. As in the case of the Reconstruction Finance Corporation during the American depression of the 1930s, they can provide a useful safety net for industry and banking. However, evaluations of their role will in the end be shaped by the ambitions and expectations of the state. These ambitions and expectations were always lower in the USA than in Italy or France. In the USA a special rescue agency like RFC was a controversial highpoint in the development of policy instruments for crisis management; in France and Italy such agencies tended to be seen as subsidiary and corrective instruments of crisis management.

A CRISIS OF CRISIS MANAGEMENT?

By the early 1980s it had become clear that industrial crises were posing central problems of political economy for Western societies. In particular, industrial crises began to reveal the limitations of existing models of political economy and suggested the possibility that reformers might be left with no practical, 'country-specific' models of political economy for inspiration. Inspiration could be found only by reference to highly abstract models of monetarism and ecology, which seemed remote from the practical problems of economic management that were posed by industrial crises. Model Sweden was tested by Sweden's industrial crises of the 1970s and increasingly questioned; Model Germany was tested by West Germany's mounting industrial crises of the 1980s and also lost some credibility. The threat to Model Sweden appeared mainly economic; loss of market shares, falling rates of profit and the 'crowding out' of industrial investment by a high public sector borrowing requirement were taken as evidence of the decline of the economic conditions that had supported it. The threat to Model Germany seemed at first to be political rather than economic; the emergence of the 'Green' movement, the blockage of the nuclear power programme and the debate within the SPD about the political problem of Aussteiger and their integration were all taken as evidence of the decline of the political conditions that had supported it. Model Germany and Model Sweden were, of course, different. The former emphasized the central importance of the international market and the need for an active modernization policy to ensure efficient adaptation to that market; the latter also emphasized the central importance of the international market, but focused more on the need for social policies that would encourage efficient adaptation. Despite different priorities, both models rejected the idea of an active role for the state in industrial decision-making. Both models were, therefore, vulnerable to claims of incoherence and mere expediency once their well-organized capitalist economies failed to contain industrial crises and the state was drawn inexorably into difficult and detailed decisions about corporations like Arbed Saarstahl and AEG or Luxor. They lacked the policy instruments with which to manage industrial crises directly, and they were left without a shared strategy that could guide the development of such instruments. By contrast, the French state had a tradition of *dirigisme* in industrial affairs that facilitated the development of policy instruments enabling government to respond to industrial crises in a more flexible, coherent and bold manner. The French state was less committed to the notion of the dictates of the international market and was convinced of the need for the state to guarantee a national presence in strategic sectors.

From the perspective of political economy, industrial crisis cannot be seen just as a problem of economic adjustment. Such a narrow definition of the problem suggests a danger of technocratic solutions that generate new and unanticipated social and political problems. An increase in the scale and intensity of industrial crises has begun to produce new social problems and an important issue of social justice. Once the concept of economic adjustment to the international market defines the parameters of the management of industrial crises, there is a threat that policy-makers will either ignore the social distribution of the costs and benefits of adjustment or be content just to 'contain' the political effects of that distribution. Policies and institutional arrangements will be evaluated also by reference to their contribution to a 'fair' distribution of the social costs associated with industrial crisis. At a general level, the 'distributional' impact of industrial crises will be assessed in terms of two models of fairness. The market model of fairness will favour individual achievement and emphasize the importance of reward for the productive workers and managers in crisis management. The sanction of exit from a sector of a firm or from the workforce of employees is essential for the maintenance of incentive for achievement. The communitarian model of fairness will favour the value of solidarity and the importance of the criterion of need in crisis management. The welfare of a sector and the physical and psychological wellbeing of the workforce is essential for the maintenance of community.

Market and communitarian models of fairness take various forms and are combined in various ways. A general survey of Western economies indicates the pervasive power of the market model. At the same time, countries vary in the weight that they attach to the two models. In France, for instance, general economic policy measures of a defensive character (such as insulation from the international economy) and of an offensive character (like the Vosges plan) have reflected a concern for communitarian values. Sweden also has sought to combine offensive labour market policies that attempt to socialize the costs of adjustment with defensive subsidies to firms in the interest of job preservation.

Management of industrial crises has been politically important because it has forced governments to reveal their concepts of social justice. They must define 'whose crisis' in each individual case – a crisis for the majority party or parties, for creditors, for shareholders, for management, or for workers. Their answers are rarely simple; at the same time, they reveal priorities. In the West German case, for example, communitarian values have been reflected in a preference for neo-corporatist forms of industrial crisis management; these involve collaborative rescues in which the major interests are seen to share power and to play a part in the implementation of rescues. Nevertheless, management of industrial crises in West Germany was 'tough-minded' even with the social–liberal coalition in the sense that it involved the subordination of communitarian values to market values and a consequent willingness to abandon those social interests that were seen as marginal to the requirements of economic adjustment — foreign workers, female workers, unskilled workers in general and the handicapped. Esser and Fach (1981) characterize the Saar steel crisis as an example of 'selective' corporatism. Social partnership as an instrument of crisis management has isolated the trade union leadership from the unskilled workers and has threatened to create a two-tier society of skilled, well-paid workers on the one hand, and of unskilled, unemployed workers on the other. In their view, corporatism has become a technocratic instrument in the service of stable economic development rather than an instrument of redistribution in the interests of social justice. Of course, many observers would question their concept of social justice and, in particular, its relevance to modern industrial society; they would also see stable economic development as no mean achievement.

The two introductory chapters underlined the numerous and complex changes that OECD countries are experiencing, as well as the differing backgrounds of ideas, institutions and cultures within which they confronted these changes. In the context of turbulence within industrial structures, it proved difficult for policy-makers or their advisers to identify accurately the future direction of change. Governments fell easy prey to new, fashionable and easily digestible notions. Thus, the concept of 'de-industrialization' drew attention to the problem of decline of the manufacturing base rather than to the opportunities that were offered by the service industries. Such a concept helped to keep the focus of industrial policies on manufacturing rather than on services. Similarly, the concept of the 'life-cycle' led to a simple distinction between 'mature' or 'sunset' industries and 'sunrise' industries or 'industries of the future'. The consequence was a tendency to fail to identify the possibilities for industrial renaissance within mature sectors like steel and automobiles. Such industries could exploit new market segments that were not mature and benefit from the determined exploitation of technological opportunities (Abernathy, Clark and Kantrow, 1983).

A conventional view of industrial crises is that they have a positive function of forcing overdue change on recalcitrant managers and workers. Thus, the crisis of Krupp in 1966 suggests that it is inherent in the growth of firms that they cannot adjust to change continuously and must on occasion reach some critical level of vulnerability before response is forthcoming. Such a view is more easily justified when industrial crises occur during a boom or a short-lived recession, when expectations of an upswing of the business cycle are high. At such times the option of diversification is simpler to manage in financial and political terms. Industrial crises are anyway discrete 'one-off' events. Crises that occur against an economic background that combines protracted recession with structural transformation in the international economy pose more serious managerial problems. An accumulation of industrial crises generates dilemmas for rescuing agencies. Banks are caught between loyalty to the interests of their shareholders and depositors and loyalty to industrial customers; governments are caught between the desire to avoid the emergence of industrial wastelands by a 'generous' policy approach and the desire to reduce the tax burden and to avoid a 'crowding out' of industrial investment by a 'restrictive' policy approach. These strategic dilemmas form the context for managing industrial crises.

More significantly, the mounting scale of industrial crises and a growing failure to manage them effectively by reference to conventional criteria of 'positive' industrial adjustment,' de-politicization and socialization of the costs of adjustment created collective unease and a new uncertainty about how industrial societies should and might develop. As factory closures and corporate collapse created industrial wastelands, Western societies faced the danger of a growth of social *anomie* — racial riots, youth riots, unemployment demonstrations and general disillusionment, disaffection and cynicism. Political indifference did not in fact lead inexorably towards political explosion. Some compensation was provided by the emergence of a 'black' or 'hidden' economy of part-time irregular work that escaped official recognition. This phenomenon was identified as a central element of the Italian economy and a growing factor in other Western economies. The flexibility of the 'black' economy combined with the bureaucratic shelter of the welfare state. Political indifference did, however, undermine the appeal of any political idealism that transcended national boundaries. The idealism of European integration seemed increasingly remote from the practical difficulties of work and 'non-work'. In particular, the aid that began to be distributed by the EEC in the 1980s under the non-quota section of the regional development fund to areas that were affected by sectoral crisis (notably in textiles and steel) proved modest and invisible in relation to the problems of adjustment of these areas. It was even more difficult to alter the terms of political debate about industrial crises by shifting the level of spatial analysis from the advanced, industrialized societies of the West to a global perspective that emphasized the need for a redistribution of resources and economic activity from North to South. In so far as industrial crises reflected a structural transformation in the international economy, they could be seen simply as evidence of the geographical expansion of the industrial system to incorporate a new category of countries. In this sense, the vital motor of industrial growth seems to be shifting from its traditional centres, just as earlier it shifted away from Britain.

The social and political impact of escalating industrial crises proved difficult for politicians to assess, and their assessments were of course influenced by the nature of their traditional electoral clientele and ideology. For instance, the French Socialist Party and the German Social Democratic Party were more affected by, and more divided by, the debate about 'the new politics' than were the Gaullists and Independent Republicans or the Christian Democrats. In particular, the electoral successes of the Green Party in West German local and state elections combined with survey evidence of greater uncertainty about political priorities among the electorate to suggest to some observers the possibility of a qualitative transformation in German politics. In various countries new political groups questioned 'the old politics', in which the central issue had been the distribution of the surplus that had been generated by continuous economic growth. 'The new politics' emphasized the values of 'non-work', job-sharing, cooperative self-management, small-scale social and economic organization and decentralized initiative. In the short run the established parties were attracted by 'the new politics' to the extent of its electoral success. In the longer run they might be attracted to it by collective bad conscience at the failure to manage industrial crises effectively by reference to the conventional criteria. It might prove easier to deal with such failure by a redefinition of the criteria of 'good' crisis management to incorporate the priorities of 'the new politics'. This adaptation to 'the new politics' would be speeded if collective unease and a sense of guilt and pessimism spread to industrial management itself and undermined confidence in the vitality and resilience of the conventional values of industrial society.

REFERENCES

Abernathy, W., Clark, K. and Kantrow, A. (1983), *Industrial Renaissance*, New York, Basic Books.
Bayliss, B. and Butt Philip, A. (1980), *Capital Markets and Industrial Investment in Germany and France*, Farnborough, Hampshire, Saxon House.
Dyson, K. (1980), *The State Tradition in Western Europe*, Oxford, Martin Robertson.

Esser, J. and Fach, W. (1981), 'Korporatistische Krisenregulierung im Modell Deutschland', in U. von Alemann (ed.), *Neokorporatismus*, Frankfurt.

Fraser, J. (1981), *Italy: Society in Crisis, Society in Transformation*, London, Routledge and Kegan Paul.

Grant, W. (1982), *The Political Economy of Industrial Policy*, London, Butterworth.

Habermas, J. (1973), *Legitimationsprobleme im Spätkapitalismus*, Frankfurt, Suhrkamp.

Llewellyn, D. (1982), 'Avoiding an International Banking Crisis', *National Westminster Bank Review*, August.

Offe, C. (1972), *Strukturprobleme des Kapitalistischen Staates*, Frankfurt, Suhrkamp.

Ray, G. (1980), 'Innovation in the Long Cycle', *Lloyds Bank Review*, January, 14–28.

Sampson, A. (1981), *The Moneylenders*, London, Hodder and Stoughton.

Vittas, D. and Brown, R. (1982), *Bank Lending and Industrial Investment: A Response to Recent Criticisms*, London, Banking Information Service.

Author Index

273

Subject Index

275